From Schnitzel to Nockerln and Everything That Happened In Between

JOY WINKIE VIOLA

DORRANCE
PUBLISHING CO
EST. 1920
PITTSBURGH, PENNSYLVANIA 15238

Dorrance Publishing Co
585 Alpha Drive
Pittsburgh, PA 15238
Visit our website at *www.dorrancebookstore.com*

ISBN: 978-1-6386-7157-2
eISBN: 978-1-6386-7690-4

PROLOGUE

ON SEPTEMBER 1, 1939, Hitler marched into Poland. On that same date, the children of London began to be evacuated into the countryside in anticipation of a Nazi invasion. War was declared September 3rd.

He had arrived in England from Vienna via the Kindertransport, a British undertaking that, during the course of World War II, transferred 10,000 Jewish children from Austria and Germany to safe haven on England's shores. His father had put him on the train as a nine-year old, alone with other children, none of whom knew if they would ever see their parents again. After a placement in Leeds with a family that took him only for the stipend they received, he was whisked away by the police, his school teacher having alerted them to a problem. Alfred had little money for food and he was covered in bed bug bites. He was sent to London, but soon thereafter, he was evacuated with all the other children in the city. Buses took the children to various towns south of London. Alfred ended up in Broad Oak where he soon found no one wanted him.

After what seemed an eternity to the child, a young woman dashed into the village Town Hall, sorry she was late to pick up a child. Alfred was the only one left. "Well then, I'll take him," she said. She took him to a farm where she and her father cared for him. Indeed, they spoiled him and he loved them dearly. Six months later, March 1940, he set sail for the United States with his mother who had managed to get to England on another British program that offered employment to Jewish refugees as domestic servants. His father, an official at the Bank of Vienna, managed to obtain an affidavit of support though a bank client in Chicago. Alfred and his parents were reunited in New York City. But not all of the family were there. His older brother fled to Palestine, and his beloved grandmother died in a Nazi concentration camp.

That frightened little boy went from tragedy to triumph becoming a professor of organic chemistry, a wildlife photographer, a conservationist, and animal rescue advocate.

I met Alfred in 1962 having moved from Minnesota to Boston in pursuit of my own career as a writer. We married, had our individual careers at Northeastern University in Boston, MA, and shared 56 years together traveling the world birding, leading tours, and doing nature photography. When he was taken down by COVID-19, I decided to write this book detailing some of our many travel adventures as well as the myriad of activities that filled our days when we were not "on the road." The first meal I served Alfred was schnitzel and the last was Viennese nockerln . This is the story of what happened in between.

Joy Winkie Viola.

CHAPTER 1

I Thought He was Italian, but I Served Him Schnitzel Anyway.

"THE NAME'S VIOLA, Alfred Viola," he said with his teasingly James Bond-style introduction.

He stood as he introduced himself, bowing his head slightly in a European manner. He was tall, good looking, had wavy black hair, and a very gentlemanly demeanor. He spoke with a slight accent, but it was the twinkling hazel eyes that got me. At that moment, there were no bells or cymbals crashing in my head, but I was young, single, and intrigued. "Who is this man?" I thought. Little did I know that we would marry within the year and spend the next half-century traveling the world doing wildlife photography, birding, leading safaris, and sharing all manner of adventures, both at home and abroad.

There were three new bachelors on the Northeastern University Chemistry faculty in 1962, and Efthalia, a woman chemistry professor, was Greek but still something of a Jewish matchmaker. One day, in the Faculty Lounge, she introduced me to everyone, but when she didn't introduce Alfred, he stood up and introduced himself. "Oh," she said, "I thought you knew one another." I'd never before laid eyes on him, although it seems we had been working in the same building for years.

It was early December 1962 when Alfred and I met. I saw him occasionally with other faculty over lunch or coffee and we chatted casually. He had driven cross-country to the West Coast and visited several national parks along the way. I had traveled to Europe and taken a tour to the Soviet Union, but I'd never seen Yellowstone or the Grand Canyon. I entertained international visitors to Boston, but I told Alfred I had no photos to show them the beauty of the United States. He had photos which, he said, he'd be happy to share. We made a casual date to get together after Christmas break. We'd not yet done anything but chat in small groups, but he went home and told people "I've met someone." As he was 34 and had never mentioned a girlfriend, that was big news to those back in Maryland.

We had our first date the weekend after Christmas break. Alfred brought slides of his trips to the western national parks and I cooked dinner. Every woman has her "company dishes"—the meals you prepare when you have guests and you want everything to come out well. Being of German origin from Minnesota, I had two company menus, one of which was wiener schnitzel and red cabbage. I thought, with the name Viola, he was Italian, but I served him schnitzel anyway. Then I found out, not only was he Austrian, he was born in Vienna. It was a Viennese accent I had been trying to identify. And by now I was seeing the full force of the Viennese charm that went with those twinkling eyes.

The next weekend he took me to a hockey game—the Boston Bruins in Boston Garden. This European charmer turned out to be a major hockey fan. I soon learned this was not just any hockey game—this was the big, bad Boston Bruins playing at the Boston "Gahden." I knew nothing about hockey, but I was growing more and more interested in Alfred, so I suddenly developed an interest in the game. And when the Bruins were out of town, he took me to Northeastern hockey games! Soon thereafter, the Bruins added a young skater from Parry Sound, Ontario named Bobby Orr, who, with greats like Johnny Bucyk, Derek Sanderson, Phil Esposito, Pie McKenzie, and Gerry Cheevers, went on to win the Stanley Cup in

1970, and Bobby Orr scored one of the most famous goals in the history of hockey. I became a hockey addict!

One night, on our third date, after a hockey game of course, we sat in the Howard Johnson's restaurant on Huntington Avenue in Boston, and he told me his story. He was born in Vienna of Jewish parents, and when Hitler marched into Austria with his anti-Semitic views, Vienna was no longer safe for his family. His mother got out on a British program for domestic servants needed in England. Alfred was put on a train at age 9 and sent with other children to England on what was known as the Kindertransport. His brother, being older, did not qualify for the Kindertransport and he fled to what was then Palestine. His father eventually got a Chicago-based client of his at the Creditanstalt in Vienna to agree to be his American sponsor. I went home and cried that night, though I didn't know why. I'd never known anyone who had gone through such horror, but something was telling me his life story was important to me. What an amazing life this skinny little frightened nine-year-old kid, who didn't speak a word of English, had made for himself, I thought.

I finally asked if we could do something different, and just at the time the Metropolitan Opera came on tour to Boston. I'd been to but one live opera before—Wagner's *Die Meistersinger von Nurnberg*—and I slept through the entire third act. I wasn't keen to try opera again, but Alfred was smart; he started me on *Carmen* and gave me the libretto beforehand so I'd understand what was going on. I loved it!

Three weeks after our first date he said, "How long do I have to wait?" Three weeks! I was stunned, and by the fourth week, I thought, yes, I think this is the one. And by Valentine's Day, when he sent me a bouquet of violets, I knew he was indeed the man I wanted to marry.

We were cut from different swaths of cloth. Alfred was fine wool. I was basic cotton. He was reserved, almost shy, brought up in European and Southern traditions. And he was Jewish. I was a bubbly

Minnesota Protestant girl for whom hospitality was my middle name. His family was torn apart by war; my clan gathered for holidays and on July 4th, ate fried chicken, corn on the cob, potato salad, fruit Jell-o, and jokingly said "Ja, Ja betcha". He loved Strauss and opera; I loved Beethoven, pop music, and Dixieland. He drank old fashions. My drink of choice was A&W root beer.

As a teenager, he lived with his parents in Baltimore, Maryland.While a doctoral student at the University of Maryland, he lived with Professor Fletcher Veitch and family, a family who traced their roots to the Civil War. He became like a third son.Doc Veitch taught Alfred the fine art of the pre-prandial hour with old fashions and salted nuts. Marion Veitch took Alfred shopping for "interview" clothes. My mother took me to tap dancing and piano lessons.

Alfred spent a research year at Boston University after receiving his doctoral degree. Then, there was an opening across town at Northeastern University. He applied and he took a teaching position as a one-year replacement for a man who took leave of absence. Like the "Man Who Came to Dinner", he stayed for 41 years. He found he loved teaching and the interactions with students. He began research and founded the chemistry doctoral program at Northeastern. He would often bring exams over in the evening to grade them while I busied myself with one of my myriad projects. Around 10 p.m. I'd make grilled cheese sandwiches.

I came to Boston with a bachelor's and master's degree in journalism and political science from the University of Minnesota. My goal was to become a reporter for *The Christian Science Monitor* based in Boston. I'd met the Paris Bureau Chief while on a postgraduate trip to Europe and he assured me there would most likely be a place for me on the *Monitor.* The then managing editor had a different idea. When I showed up for an interview, he said, "I don't like to hire women. We get them trained, they get married, start a family, and we lose the time invested in them." Well, that was 1958.

Now what, I thought. My father had died and my mother had

moved with me to Boston. I needed to find a job. I walked two blocks down the street to Northeastern University, walked into the Press Bureau with my scrapbook of *Minnesota Daily* clippings, and said I'd like to apply for a job.

The Press Bureau Director said, "Well, I'd like to talk to you, but we have 800 people coming for President Ell's retirement dinner tonight, so today I'm a little busy. Can you come back tomorrow?" I agreed I would do so only to be told the next day that he wasn't budgeted for a new position, but he'd very much like to explore the possibility of adding me to the staff. As I wasn't flooded with job offers, I made one of my own. "I'll work for you free of charge for a week," I said, "and if you like my work, perhaps you can speak persuasively to the president." I got the job—$3,600 a year. I saved my money, and three years later I took a Soviet sponsored tour of "Soviet Industry and Agriculture" in the wake of which I wrote my first travel diary. I also began writing political freelance articles for *The Christian Science Monitor.*

By spring, we both felt a commitment, and on July 8th, 1963, his 35th birthday, Alfred got down on one knee and proposed marriage. My father having passed away, I wanted to have an uncle from Minnesota give me away. He had had a heart attack, however, so we had to wait until October for our wedding.

We were married at Boston's historic Old South Church. The church administrator had asked if we wanted them to hire police to direct traffic. We assured him that wouldn't be necessary as most people attending were from Northeastern University and they knew their way to Copley Square. When Alfred arrived at the church that October morning there were police everywhere! 'What has Joy done?' he thought. Joy hadn't done anything, but President John F. Kennedy was about to speak at the Copley Plaza Hotel across the street and there were security men on every corner!

We spent a honeymoon week in a small cottage in the Pocono Mountains. A lovely couple prepared beautiful dinners for us each evening, and the husband took us "deer spotting" with his search light at night. It was the beginning of our joint efforts at wildlife photography.

The following spring, when heavy mountain snows had New Hampshire's rivers and waterfalls rushing with snow melt, Conrad and Gerry, our best man and matron of honor, asked if we'd like to go on a camping weekend.We had no camping equipment, but they had enough to loan us air mattresses and sleeping bags and we slept in the back of our station wagon.

I was the small one in this quartet as Alfred, Conrad, and Gerry were all over 6 feet tall. I was a mere 5'8" so I had to stretch my legs to keep up with their long strides as we hiked along the mountain trails. The waterfalls and streams were indeed spectacular, but everything that could go wrong that weekend went wrong. The car wasn't parked on an exact level so Alfred kept rolling over on me. The air mattresses leaked and we had to get out and pump them up at midnight and again at 4 a.m. It was raining! The next morning, we were famished only to find Gerry hadn't brought nearly enough food for the four of us, and as it was early in the season, there were no food stores or cafes open. I became ill and couldn't wait to get home. That's when the transmission went out on our brand-new car! We limped from the Kancamagus Highway in New Hampshire's White Mountains some 200 miles all the way back to Boston in first gear.

The way I saw it, camping couldn't possibly be any worse than what I had just experienced and survived, so the next weekend we went shopping and came home with a tent, air mattresses, sleeping bags, cooking utensils, a Coleman lamp, and a Coleman ice chest I'm still using 57 years later!

That summer we took our first of many camping trips out West. And I wrote the first of 46 diaries that I would subsequently write as we traveled to all seven continents during the following fifty years. From seven safaris to Africa to the glaciers of Antarctica to the shores of Canada's Hudson Bay where we photographed polar bears and slept in tundra buggies—we did it all. And every trip produced a diary.

When Alfred was in the nursing home at the end of his life, I began reading those diaries to him at his bedside, and when COVID-19 no longer permitted me to visit him, I read them over the phone, two hours each day.

How we laughed as I read about $2 steak dinners, $8 motel rooms, and $1.80 to fill the gas tank. And we well remembered the first night we set up camp at Lake Mary Campground near the Grand Canyon. Dark clouds appeared and thunder rumbled over the not-too-distant hillsides. That tent went up in record time, although we'd had but one practice session in our backyard at home.

The year 1965 was plagued by the ongoing Vietnam War and the shock of the Watts Riots in Los Angeles. People turned to the entertainment world for distractions. *Bonanza* was the number one TV show of the year, *A Charlie BrownChristmas* premiered and became the first of the Peanuts TV specials, and Sonny and Cher got their first number one hit, "I Got You Babe."

We drove west again in 1966, this time camping in the Canadian Rockies, but in 1967 we tried something new, a guest ranch in Wyoming in the shadows of Grand Teton National Park. And for the first time in his life, Alfred faced the challenge of mounting a horse, a very large horse with the ridiculous name of Peanuts! Peanuts had to have been a cousin of the Anheuser-Busch Clydesdales. He was huge. When Alfred expressed doubt that he could get his foot in the stirrup and swing up that high, the ranch manager said, "Well we have a crane we use to lift the hay into the loft. We could put you in that and swing you up like the knights of old." Alfred decided he would not be humiliated by a horse and somehow he'd make it onto the back of that animal—and he did!

I had a horse when I was in grade school, but it had been years since I had ridden. My biggest problem was that my horse wanted to head for the barn the minute we ended our ride and started back to the ranch. "Whoa, whoa" did not appear to be in his vocabulary as he took me under low tree branches and brushed my legs against tree trunks hurrying down the trail. I yelled for our guide to "slow up" as my glasses flew off when a branch hit me in the face. But the horse was headed for the barn and intent on getting there as quickly as possible. It was a rocky introduction to horseback trail riding, and during the rest of our visit we elected to leave the horses in the barn and hike!

In 1968, we moved into our first house in Wayland, Massachusetts, a home that would remain ours for the rest of our lives. We had seen the house advertised for sale by the owners, and when we saw the woodland setting and a Scarlet Tanager flew across the driveway, I knew this was going to be it. We moved in on a beautiful June day. And as the truck was unloading our furniture, a Wayland Police car blocked the driveway. Alfred walked down to speak to the policeman and the officer said, "I'm just checking to see if it is going in or going out." That was our invitation to what a wonderful community we had found. Our home was the last house on a series of four dead-end streets, each only one block long. Neighbors welcomed us with a casserole, a plate of cookies, and friendly waves as we drove by. But as Alfred was scheduled to teach the second half of the summer, it meant we had to leave the boxes unpacked and immediately head west on our vacation.

This year our driving was interrupted by stops at national wildlife refuges as I had introduced Alfred to birding and we were both getting into nature photography.Slade National Wildlife Refuge in North Dakota and Bowdoin Refuge in Montana provided opportunities to see pronghorn antelope, burrowing owls, and many bird species. There were "pwarie dogs" there too—as Alfred called them with his still pronounced Viennese accent.

Then it was on to the Canadian Rockies and all the way further west to the Olympic Peninsula in Washington State. Driving so many miles to get to specific destinations can get boring, so what do you do? You eat! And having lived a few years in Seattle as a child, I was well aware of and eager to find some Pacific Northwest specialties—huckleberries, boysenberries, and loganberries. Unfortunately, one usually found these in pies, and I never let a berry pie on the menu pass me by. Then there was a 3,000-mile drive home. Upon returning to work, my boss took one look at me and said, "Well, you sure packed it on!" I had indeed gained weight and it took far longer to get it off than it had to put it on.

Back home we began the unpacking process, but one of the first priority projects was the installation of bird feeders and a birdbath. Word got out to the avian community, and many different species started arriving in our yard. So too did the deer, raccoons, skunks, rabbits, possum, foxes, and chipmunks, including a very special little fellow, an all-white chipmunk which I named Whichi.

Many years later when I became a columnist for our local paper, the Weston/Wayland *Town Crier*, I wrote an article "Of Black Squirrels and a White Chipmunk."(Reprinted courtesy of the Weston/Wayland Town Crier)

The black squirrel appeared beneath our bird feeder just before the Memorial Day weekend.I had heard of Wayland's black squirrels and a neighbor told me a pair had been living in his big pine tree for a couple of years. And then there was Whichi. He was a white chipmunk, hence his name, but he was not a true albino as he had dark eyes and cream tinted stripes across his otherwise white back. But other than that, he was snow white with pink ears and a pink nose.

My first summer with Whichi was spent slowly getting acquainted. Our initial meetings were very formal as Whichi was hesitant to accept my friendship. Eventually the woodpile became our meeting ground. Whichi loved sunflower seeds and I began to leave a few at the entrance to his burrow. In time, Whichi learned that there were also small piles of seeds for him on the woodpile.

When fall came and the maple leaves began to turn red and the Red-winged Blackbirds gathered to fly south, our lunches on the woodpile became more frequent. The woodpile had become Whichi's territory and he would chase all intruders from it. In time, Whichi's storehouse was filled and with the first snowfall, he tucked himself into his burrow for a long sleep.

Spring came, the skunk cabbage and marsh marigolds and musk plant appeared along the stream, the Scarlet Tanager returned to nest and Whichi emerged from his burrow. He was far less formal now and in time he would sit at my feet eating sunflower seeds while we shared a silent companionship. I knew I'd been accepted when at one point, still hungry, he put his tiny foot on my knee looking for yet a few more seeds.

This was Whichi's third summer with us (the previous owners had told us about him when we bought the house). And it proved to be his last. When he went into hibernation that next winter, it was a permanent sleep. About two years later I looked into the yard one day and there to my astonishment was a cream-colored chipmunk. The albinism was in the gene pool and I had no doubt this was a descendant of Whichi.

In 1969 we continued our pattern of taking camping trips to the western states each summer, but this year we tried something new. We drove to Denver and then rented a tent trailer. That little Star-Craft trailer was wonderful. It had a table that made into a bed, and a small kitchen with a refrigerator. Our meals got quite sumptuous as I no longer needed to cook over a camp stove, and Alfred loved it when I turned a ready-made graham cracker pie crust, a box of instant pudding, a banana, and milk into a banana cream pie – topped with Redi-Whip!(I could make chocolate and coconut cream pies too!) Alfred didn't care what I fixed for dinner, as long as I produced a fine dessert! Well, he was Viennese!

From Denver we headed to Salt Lake City and the nearby Bear River National Wildlife Refuge, clearly the most spectacular of any of the refuges we had visited thus far. By this time, Alfred had really gotten into birding at my prodding. I had been a birder since I was eight years old, and I still have my Minneapolis Audubon Society checklist from 1946! Alfred tackled this new birding world with great enthusiasm. He was the only person I ever knew who took *Peterson's Guide to North American Birds* into the bathroom with him to study bird identification while on the throne. Not only were we adding to our birders' life lists, we were getting some great photos and seeing some wonderful sights—like a Western Grebe carrying her young on her back. You don't see that in Wayland, Massachusetts.

(That Peterson's Guide was important to us and we almost lost it. The previous summer we signed up for a shore bird identification short-course on Cape Cod under the direction of Wayne Petersen of the Massachusetts Audubon Society. The first morning we stopped at the Cape Cod Museum of Natural History to use their restroom facilities before heading to the beach. Alfred came back with an embarrassed look on his face and said "I dropped the field guide into the toilet." Stunned I replied "Well, get it back, it's got our Life List in it!" As they had opened up just for our group, no one had used the chemical toilet since it was cleaned the night before, the museum staff member took Alfred to the small trap door, opened it and he was able to reach inside and remove our bird book from the dry cedar shavings. Wayne Petersen told that story to many and one day, when birding in New Hampshire, I mentioned the story to a group of birders and one said, "Oh *you're* the ones!" We were infamous!)

Continuing on our trip to Utah, we drove to Logan Utah to Utah State University where Alfred conferred with chemistry colleagues on research matters and I searched out faculty in the College of Natural Resources. One of them offered to take us along on a Canada goose banding expedition in two days. As we were to meet him at 5:30 a.m. at a distant lake, we headed for a nearby campground in

Cache National Forest some 70 miles away. About ten miles out of the little town of Woodruff, it started to rain. Five miles later, it began to snow. We were climbing up to a higher elevation, and before long we were in a full-scale blizzard, towing our little tent trailer behind us. Due to a construction detour, we were now on a dirt road. There were deep ruts of mud and snow, and the car and trailer couldn't handle it. We were skidding badly so Alfred decided to unhook the trailer, turn around, and try to make it back to the Woodruff Ranger station. Once he got turned around, he directed me to get blankets, sleeping bags, and some food from the trailer. If we couldn't make it back down, we'd at least be warm and have some food. We slowly started back, and after about a mile two men in a jeep from the Utah Sheriff's Search and Rescue team appeared out of the blinding snow. They advised us to turn around yet again and follow them in their tracks down to Ogden. After much slipping and skidding, we got turned around but we could go no further. "Where are your chains," they asked. Chains? In July? Of course, we had no chains with us. One doesn't need chains in July, we had thought.

The men put a chain on our car and towed it over the summit then went back to get our little trailer. They pulled our trailer, so it wouldn't jackknife on us, and we followed in their tracks. They called their office and told them to call the man we were to meet.Clearly, we wouldn't be joining him for any bird banding the next morning! When we stopped by the sheriff's office the next morning to thank his crew, we found these men were from a volunteer organization that worked with the sheriff's office. Volunteers maybe, but angels to us.

Well we missed the Canada geese, but not the endangered prairie dogs.

A contact at the Springville Fish and Game Farm told us of his study of endangered Uinta Prairie Dogs. He offered to escort us out to the Awapa Plateau where we could set up camp if we would promise to send him photos. After a nearly two-hour drive, we arrived at the site—in the middle of nowhere. There was nothing around but open spaces and a prairie dog settlement. Having shopped with foresight, we had fried shrimp and coconut cream pie for dinner that night with nothing but a full moon across the prairie to accompany us. The prairie was soundless—no insects, no birds, just silence. And no humans for miles. So, feeling very smug about my advanced planning, I pulled out a small portable toilet, which looked something like a metal chair with a cut out and a bag beneath. I was taking care of my morning business, alone on the prairie, when suddenly I heard an airplane. I panicked. I was sure all those people were looking out the window at me sitting on my metal throne. Alfred laughed assuring me the plane was too high up for any passengers to see me, but I was certain they were all looking down, pointing and laughing! Well I heard about that for the rest of the trip!

We circled around through Utah and Colorado making our last camping spot adjacent to the Maroon Lake Wilderness area near Aspen, Colorado. That Monday, July 20, while we were on the edge of an earth-based wilderness, Neil Armstrong tackled a planetary wilderness and became the first man to set foot on the moon!"The Eagle has landed," he reported to Houston Command Center.Apollo 11 with Neil Armstrong and Buzz Aldrin had accomplished an unbelievable feat.

The year 1969 turned out to be one of several diverse occurrences. The Woodstock Festival drew 350,000 folk/rock fans to concerts in a field in New York, Dwight Eisenhower died, and Richard Nixon was elected President of the United States. *The Saturday Evening Post* had its demise after 147 years of publishing, and a television show called *Rowan and Martin's Laugh In* chased *Bonanza* and *Gunstock* out of first and second place in TV ratings.

That December, we began our own special event back home in Wayland. We initiated a "Viennese Night" for which I baked four different Viennese pastries. For three days I mixed chocolate, ground hazelnuts, flour, sugar, cream, poppy seeds, flavorings, and whipped cream into four beautiful creations—Vienna's famous Sacher Torte, Haselnuss (hazelnut) Torte, Moen (poppyseed) Torte, and the pièce de résistance, Rigo Janci, an incredibly rich combination consisting of a thin layer of flourless cake, topped with two inches of chocolate and rum flavored whipped cream, and another layer of cake.A dark chocolate glaze was then poured over the entire creation. Making Rigo Janci was an all-day affair.And, of course, it was served with Viennese coffee, meaning coffee "mit schlage obis" (whipped cream) topped with shaved chocolate! Our Viennese Nights became an annual event for many years, and our friends vied for an invitation. As our home could not accommodate all who wanted to attend, we began offering invitations for 2-4 p.m., 3-5 p.m., and 4-6 p.m. The problem was some people came early and stayed late, meaning at one point we had 60 people spread out in our small split-level ranch home!

In 1971, Alfred had ridden horseback but once, but I convinced him to undertake a two-day horseback journey into the wilds of British Columbia to reach Assiniboine Lodge at the base of Mount Assiniboine.Mount Assiniboine is often called the Matterhorn of North America. It has a pyramidal shape that rises to an elevation of 11,800 feet. Assiniboine Lodge nestles in a valley at 7,200 feet. A small lake separates it from the base of the mountain. The lodge was accessible only by horseback or hiking from Cranmore, near Banff, several miles away.

But I need to begin the Assiniboine story by telling the story of Erling Strom, who ran the lodge and enabled our journey to this mountainous Shangri-La. Erling was 73, a rather crusty old Norwegian, when he led us by horseback for two days through the woods, streams, snowfields, and up a shale mountainside.

Erling was born in 1897 in the mountains of Norway where he was given his first pair of skis at age two. He gained a reputation for himself in competitive skiing in Norway and the United States. He was invited to Lake Placid in 1927 and spent eleven years there as a ski instructor teaching the likes of renowned broadcaster Lowell Thomas, and C. Minot "Minnie" Dole, "Father of the American Ski Patrol." Erling participated in many notable long-distance wilderness ski expeditions including a 250-mile trek across the Canadian Rockies. He even climbed Mount McKinley on skis! It was no wonder he was elected to the United States National Ski Hall of Fame in 1972. The following year he undertook a winter expedition with his friend and ski pal, the Marquis degli Albizzi, an Italian nobleman, into the Mount Assiniboine wilderness.

It took them several days to reach Assiniboine Pass, but when they did, Erling is reported to have said, "Before us lay the most beautiful little valley one could imagine as well adapted to skiing as any we could hope to find." After spending seventeen days skiing in the region, Erling said, "This is going to be the place where I could spend most of my life if I can swing it." The Marquis convinced the Canadian Pacific Railway, which was promoting tourism to the region, to build a log lodge complex at Assiniboine "for fancy clientele." Assiniboine Lodge became the first backcountry ski lodge in the Canadian Rockies, and Erling spent the next 50 years there.

In 1971, Alfred and I weren't "fancy clientele", just a couple who enjoyed out-of-the-way adventure. And adventure we got!

We were driven ten miles out of Banff in a jeep and there introduced to Erling where his crew of Swiss cowboys prepared to load up our gear. Our luggage was packed in duffle bags, as instructed, so it could easily go on the back of the pack horse. But then there was the lawn chair. Actually, it was part of a photo blind, but when Erling saw it…

"I'm supposed to pack a lawn chair on the back of a horse?" he asked.

"Well, no, Erling, it's actually part of a photo blind. There's a metal rim that goes across the top and a camouflage canvas with zip-out windows that goes over the frame and lawn chair," said I meekly.

"Well, I once had a lady who wanted to pack in eight rolls of toilet paper, but this takes the cake!" he said, as he shook his head in bewilderment, but then instructed one of the cowboys to put the canvas-webbed lawn chair on a pack horse.

We got underway at 3:30 p.m., and after three hours of riding through woods, across a meadow, a stream, through tall timber, and over a snow field, we came to Halfway House where our caravan was to spend the night.

Erling was a magnificent storyteller. He spoke knowingly of the well-known von Trapp family immortalized in the Broadway show and movie *The Sound of Music,* and he told us many tales about his early ski adventures. Laughingly he spoke of his early experiences with Assiniboine guests including a lady with a portable bathtub and a gent with a case of soda pop. I suppose my lawn chair will become a part of his future stories.

The next day, July 4th, after a breakfast of porridge, bacon, eggs, and toast, the pack horses were loaded and we started out at 11 a.m. The trail took us over a pass and into a valley where we stopped for lunch. An out-going pair of wranglers and pack horses told Erling that Og Pass was still snowed in so we'd have to go across Assiniboine Pass. The latter had had many snow slides and downed trees were everywhere. The horses picked their way around the trees after which Siri, my horse, was eager to trot, and it was all I could do to rein her in.

The trail began to climb a series of switch backs and we were traversing loose shale. Loose shale and a step mountain slope had me terrified.

"I'd like to get down and walk," I called to Erling.

"You sit there!" he replied. "Give the horse her reins. She knows what she's doing even if you don't."

I sat there like a scolded puppy, my head down, as I gave Siri the reins. It made sense. The horse didn't want to fall down the mountainside and she'd done this before.

At the top of the second pass, it began to snow, lightly, and then with more vigor. We headed back down and then began to climb once again. Suddenly, when I looked up the mountain trail before me, I saw Norwegian and Canadian flags flying. We'd made it!

We were each shown to our cabins outfitted with hand-carved bedposts, chairs, and two tables made of logs. We had a wash table with a pitcher and basin, a wood-burning stove, pegs, shelves, and closet for our clothing, and three windows adorned with bright red plaid curtains. The water pipe didn't work so I went to the nearby stream for water, which we heated to wash up and change clothes for dinner. We also had our own individual outhouse! While at dinner, the cabin boy came to light our fire and warm our cabin.

Thus it was while Arthur Fiedler was leading the Boston Pops complete with fireworks in a July 4th concert on the Charles River Esplanade in our hometown of Boston, we were snuggled in our beds in the wilderness of British Columbia gazing up at a star-filled sky and the snow-capped profile of Mount Assiniboine.

There followed ten days of hikes, rides, bridge games during snowstorms, explorations of wildflower-filled meadows, and yes, time in the photo blind which I had set up a discreet distance away from a nest. Unfortunately, the next day I found something had eaten the eggs in the nest.

A herd of twenty elk was ensconced nearby, and one stuck his nose in the outhouse window one day as I was using the facility! I had my own private elk, it seemed. On another day I was photographing an elk at the horse salt lick when it decided it didn't like my presence and jumped the fence into the corral to chase me away. Elk are big animals, but they can move quickly. And so did I! A wolverine visited the garbage dump one day, and chipmunks scampered at my feet, having no fear of man. One of the guests caught a ten-pound trout in the seldom-fished lake at the base of the mountain. There was fresh fish for dinner that night.

On July 14th, a helicopter brought in a distinguished guest. In those days, Erling didn't permit helicopter access to the lodge, but an exception was made for Tenzing Norgay, the renowned Sherpa to Sir Edmund Hillary on his ascent of Mount Everest. Tenzing had heard of the distinctive shape of Mount Assiniboine, often referred to as the Matterhorn of North America, and he wanted to see it during his Canadian lecture tour. Unfortunately, Erling was in Banff that day, but his daughter Siri (yes, she had the same name as my horse) welcomed the famous climber and we all sat down to tea together. Like Erling, Tenzing was a wonderful storyteller and we sat enchanted by his tales. He was a humble, very unassuming man, willing to answer everyone's questions.

Immediately after his visit ended, we packed up and headed back through the meadows and Allenby Pass to the Halfway House. The next day, a three-hour ride brought us back to Banff and civilization. That night Erling joined us for dinner at a local steak house. No longer the crusty Norwegian telling me to "sit there and give the horse her reins!" Erling in jacket and tie cut quite a handsome figure! He entertained us with more of his stories, and subsequently, I wrote my own story about Erling.

The article, written for a Norwegian publication was titled "In the Hall of the Mountain King" (with due acknowledgement to Edvard Grieg). But when translated into Norwegian, the headline read "En mann og hans fjell" (A Man and his Mountain.) Erling was not one to give compliments, so I worried about what he would say when he saw the article. When he wrote to me, I opened the envelope with trepidation. "I have finally gotten hold of *Nordmann's Forbundet* magazine and read your excellent article," he wrote. "The translation is also fine, and I want to thank you for a job well done. Usually one finds something to criticize, something that makes me a little mad, but not this time." That was a compliment I treasure to this day.

For seven summers now, Alfred and I had been seeking refuge from the pressures of the academic world in the solitude of the

American West. We had hiked, camped, and photographed our way from the Patagonian Desert of Arizona to the icefields of the Canadian Rockies. Our life lists, a carefully charted phenomenon maintained by earnest birders, was rich in western species but woefully lacking in many others. Our slide cases were filled with photos of bighorn sheep, western tanager, and Colorado columbine, but we had yet to see any tropical species and we felt the need to look for interesting sites further afield.

A perusal of advertisements in the National Audubon Society's magazine revealed an invitation to visit Trinidad's Asa Wright Nature Centre (British spelling), where "bellbirds, trogons, manakins, motmots, guacharos, honeycreepers, and tanagers are only a few of the exotic species seen daily." I quickly sent off a letter of inquiry, but for weeks I heard nothing in reply. We were learning our first lesson about communications in the tropics. It is often slow and occasionally impossible. Finally, a letter arrived after being two weeks in transit. It looked like it was going to take a month to accomplish an exchange of letters.We were told summer was the rainy season in Trinidad so we had concerns as to whether it might be a bad time for photography. A query about this took another month's exchange and got only a succinct response: "It depends on what you mean by bad." We decided to take the plunge and cabled a reservation. Having been told we should go to Tobago while in the general area, we had a similar pattern of delayed correspondence with a woman to whom we were referred who would occasionally take birders into her home. Getting information about these two remote locations was difficult as few people appeared to have been to either locale. Travel agents could produce an abundant supply of literature about beaches, hotels, car rentals, currency exchanges, and local customs, but there wasn't a one who could give advice on the protocol of sleeping with a motmot. We had to learn about that for ourselves.

CHAPTER 2

Bananaquits in the Lemonade, and a Motmot in the Bedroom

THERE WERE TOADS ON THE FLOOR, geckos on the walls, wood rats in the trees, and the motmot slept in the bedroom!

I have encountered elk in an outhouse, chased bears from our campsite, ridden horseback through snowstorms, but in all of our many outdoor experiences, I had never shooed a bananaquit out of my lemonade or slept with a motmot.

"You're going where?" people would ask. "Where's Trinidad and Tobago?"We were intrigued by an advertisement enticing birders to a faraway spot of which I'd never heard. We had traveled a great deal at this point, but only in the United States, and never to the tropics. We knew we'd be going into a rain forest, near the equator to a site rich in bird life. It proved to be tiring, stimulating, exacerbating, exciting, hot, wet, shocking, and quite marvelous, but unlike anything we have ever undertaken before.

Trinidad isn't exactly on the way home from the office. It is a small island, actually a chip off the old block of Venezuela, which lies just eleven miles off its shores. It is only 50 miles long and 37 miles wide, but that's enough to give it three mini-mountain ranges, one of which is considered an eastern spur of the Andes. It has a fresh-water swamp and a brackish mangrove swamp as well as savannah and rain forests. In between there are sugar cane fields and oil fields. Pitch Lake, often called the eighth wonder of the world, is the largest natural deposit of asphalt in the world. Another local product is Angostura Bitters, which my husband used to make his old fashion cocktail. So, in fact, there's actually a good bit of diversity crammed into this little package. The population is also a potpourri of ethnic origins. In addition to descendants of the African slaves brought to the island, there are also descendants of indentured East Indians and Chinese, who came when slavery was abolished. Hence, there are many Hindus and Moslems in this otherwise predominantly Catholic population.

JULY 28, 1972.

It was raining as the big Pan Am jet revved its engines at Miami International Airport. It was only an afternoon shower, but I wondered if it was an omen of things to come. Most people don't travel to the tropics in the rainy season, but our vacations had to be timed during the summer given our academic careers. The PA system began playing "Put Your Hands in the Hands of the Man from Galilee". Feeling that I had infinitely better communications with the Man from Galilee than the Postmaster in Port of Spain, I settled down to enjoy the flight

We arrived in Port of Spain at 9 p.m. I expected to find a bustling terminal so full of people our contact would have difficulty finding us. Contrary to our expectations, the terminal was tiny, and it seemed there was no one there to meet us. Moreover, they turned the terminal lights out once we were outside.

"Youwantataxi?" said a rain-soaked, but happy, black face smiling at me. All of his words seemed to run together like a babbling brook, but I got the message and smiled back.

"No, we're being met by someone from the Asa Wright Nature Centre," I replied.

A frown covered his face. "I don't see the boy here. I know him, but I have not seen him tonight."

"We'll wait," I replied. "I'm sure he'll be along. We sent a letter..."

I couldn't, I didn't dare consider the possibility, but communication with the Centre had been difficult.

When they began to turn off the lights in the terminal, I began to consider the possibility! If the postmaster had failed us, the Man from Galilee had not. A fellow passenger, a native Trinidadian and a fellow birder, quickly came to our aid. During the next thirty minutes, he kept us in his custodial care, bartering with the taxi drivers and exacting a promise that the driver would indeed deliver us to the door. When we got in the cab, we had no idea where we were going, but we were getting there on the wrong side of the road. We had forgotten that Trinidad had once been a part of the British Commonwealth and certain British traditions remained.

I strained to catch and understand the rhythm of the taxi driver's speech, as he attempted to identify all we were passing, but it was now after 10 p.m., dark and rainy, and one could see very little. When we arrived in the town of Arima, the driver explained that he had to stop for gas before going into the mountains. There were few lights and only a few houses, but scores of people just out walking around.When the gas tank was full, the car wouldn't start. The driver hopped back and forth from the ignition to the uplifted hood but with no apparent success. By now it was 10:30 p.m.; it was still raining—part of the nearly 90 inches received annually—and the night seemed exceptionally dark.I began to feel uneasy when I realized the car was surrounded by black faces looking at us through the windows. At that precise moment, the car started and we were on our way.

"What did those fellows want back there?" I inquired of the driver.

"Oh, they just came over to see what was going on and ask if they could help." Locally, it's called "liming" which translates into "just hanging out."

Lesson # 1—learn to relax, take things as they come, and don't be alarmed when you don't understand the situation.

We were climbing into the mountains now, and what few lights there had been disappeared. The road was narrow—no wider than our driveway at home. Guardrails were few, the road was poorly paved, and curves came upon us suddenly. I began to understand why few of the other taxi drivers wanted to make the trip!

Suddenly the taxi slowed and turned into a rough dirt road.

"I have to go slow now," the driver explained. "The road here is very bad."

I thought the road had been bad all along, but now it was going to get worse?

"How far to the house?" I asked.

"About a mile," he replied, and I began to understand why our birder guardian angel at the airport had been insisting that the driver take us "all the way in." It would have been horrific had we been left at the entrance and forced to haul our luggage a mile through the dark.

From what seemed an eternity, we bounded our way over roots, through large puddles, and around sinister-looking vines. (All vines look sinister in the middle of a dark, rainy, tropical forest night.) Finally we came into a clearing, and a single yellow light bulb proclaimed our arrival at the Asa Wright Nature Centre. It was now after 11 p.m.

Three worried faces came out to meet us.

"Where have you been? We've been looking for you since noon. Major been to town three times today looking for a cable."

It was obvious they had not received our letter informing them of our flight and arrival time. Later we were told when the local postmaster had too much mail on his hands, he simply flushed it down the toilet!

We were led down the steps to our room, which was very large, and I then remembered why. Years before, we'd been told, Mrs. Asa Wright had remodeled the stables into guest rooms. Well, I snickered, if the only room in the inn for the Man from Galilee was a manger, I guess I wouldn't question a converted stable.

The Asa Wright Nature Centre is a former cocoa, coffee, and citrus plantation partially reclaimed by secondary forest, but surrounded by rain forest.It is located at 1,200 feet in the northern range of Trinidad's mountains.

Our first order of business consisted of my insisting that the two beds be pushed together. They were on opposite sides of the room, and in these strange surroundings, I wanted to know where Alfred was when I heard noises in the night. We covered the room together like a pair of spaniels sniffing out our new quarters. Satisfied that however austere the accommodations seemed, there were no bugs, snakes, or scorpions in the room, we fell into bed exhausted.

I hadn't been in bed ten seconds when an eerie feeling came over me. Slowly I moved my foot across the bottom of the bed. Then the same stranger sensation crept up my arm. The sheets were wet! Not damp! Wet!

Well, I thought, it is the tropics, it has been raining all day, and the humidity is high. Alfred had said very little since our arrival. Now I looked at him and shook my head. "What have we gotten into?"

"Correction," he replied, "what have *you* gotten us into!"

In less than an hour, we woke up thinking all hell had broken loose. The noise was catastrophic. As we struggled to gain our senses, we began to realize that the noise was the result of a tropical deluge. I am not a stranger to heavy rainstorms having known New England hurricanes and Midwestern thunderstorms, but this was ridiculous. The power generator was off for the night so Alfred grabbed his flashlight and began to investigate the reason for the chaos.

"Tin roofs," he hollered over the roar. "This place has tin roofs."

My husband's midnight proclamations meant nothing to me being unfamiliar with the acoustical properties of roofing materials, but one thing was certain; I had never heard such noise. The windows were screened, but without glass there was nothing to deafen the noise. Sleep was impossible. It was like trying to doze in the percussion section of the Boston Symphony. Variations on a theme by Mother Nature were played often that night. When daylight afforded us a better view of our surroundings, we saw that the noise was amplified by the fact that each raindrop was being heard three times—once when it hit the corrugated tin roof, once again when it fell in waterfall fashion some ten feet to the overhangs above our windows, and a third time when it cascaded off the overhangs onto a cement run-off on the ground.

When the bird chorus began at 6 a.m., I got out of bed and began inspecting my slippers. A book by Ivan Sanderson, a noted naturalist, advised checking your shoes each morning for scorpions, and I thought it wise to follow his advice. Finding none I began to investigate our accommodations.

Daylight revealed a number of interesting features about our room. The bathroom, for instance, was complete with all modern conveniences, but the walls were covered with a strange assortment of eleven different colored tiles. All were placed in a haphazard fashion. It was almost as if someone had dropped the whole load and every tile had been broken and then each piece carefully cemented in place. In subsequent readings, I learned that Asa Wright had indeed obtained broken tile pieces for her own bathroom, so I assume we had the leftovers.

The closet, I discovered, was open to a neighboring room with only a lattice door dividing the metal rods. When guests in both rooms had their closet door open, conversations could be easily overheard. This was no real problem until the honeymooners moved in next door, and from then on, we had to use discretion when we removed our shoes or sought a change of clothing!

At breakfast we met the resident manager. Major Ives de la Motte, a retired major of the British Army. He was very, very British both in manner and speech. Although a small man, with his white hair, mustache, and goatee, straw hat, khaki shorts, knee-high socks, and walking stick, he was every inch an officer and gentleman of the tropics. But he was not British. He was French. It seems he joined the British army when Hitler invaded France and picked up his British mannerisms and way of speech along the way.

His housekeeper for more than 30 years, Celine Cesaire, met us at breakfast with a colorful scarf tied about her head looking like a French Aunt Jemima. A native of Martinique, she had a delightfully infectious laugh and a warm manner that immediately made you feel at home. All of the staff were shy yet helpful, but it was the bilingual major and Madame Celine that gave the Centre its character. Our relationship with both was a happy one. The Major supplied the Latin names for every botanical species I photographed, and Celine plied Alfred with the culinary arts mastered only by the French.

After breakfast the Major instructed us to read a pamphlet on reptiles, which was mandatory reading for all new arrivals. Yes, we were advised, it was quite safe to walk about the grounds, but no, we should not endeavor to do so after dark.

The Nature Centre guesthouse was an interesting structure built in 1906 of hardwoods on the estate, and tapia, a clay-based building material similar to the adobe of the American southwest. The estate passed through many hands, including the Trinidad Agricultural Bank—twice! No one seemed to make a go of it.After a succession of owners, it was purchased in 1946 by Asa and Newcomb Wright. She was a transplanted Icelander and he an English lawyer, both of whom had visited and fallen in love with Trinidad. The estate and the nearby Simla Research Station had attracted naturalists of various interests for many years, but it was Asa Wright who took it over and began providing lodging for paying guests interested in the birds and plants of the area. At the time of our visit, elegance and austerity seemed to go hand in hand. The library contained some beautiful pieces of fine old furniture, but was adorned by vases of broken crockery. Mrs. Wright had been ill in her later years, and it was obvious that some aspects of a fine old home had fallen into disrepair. Although the Centre has been owned by a private foundation since 1967, funds had not been plentiful due to a low occupancy rate, and redecorating had been a low priority. The library housed an unusual assortment of reading materials and reference books. Copies of the *South Pacific Planter*, a magazine of tropical agriculture, rested alongside 19 volumes of the 1901 edition of *The Ridpath Library of Universal Literature*. The works of Rudyard Kipling, Joseph Conrad, Samuel Peps, and Charles Dickens shared shelves with six volumes of Robert Louis Stevenson.*Golden Iceland* served as a silent reminder of the Icelandic origins of Asa Wright, while Rachel Carson's *Silent Spring* heralded the problems of the current age. And, as expected, there are many volumes of botanical and ornithological reference books. At the time of our visit, there was nothing, however, to inform one of the island's mammalian population, an oversight which caused Alfred great concern.

One night, Alfred was awakened by strange sounds outside our window. He discovered the source of the noise was a small animal with brown fur, tiny eyes, and small erect ears. During the days that followed, he questioned everyone he met as to the identity of the creature. Some suggested a manicou, others an agouti, but neither fit the appearance of our nocturnal visitor, and we left the island not knowing who had paid us a call.

Beyond the library lay the gallery, or veranda as we would call it, the social center of the establishment. From this large, screened-in, second-story porch, one could look out over the 100-150 foot forest canopy and down the Arima Valley. Rain or shine, this was the best vantage point for watching tropical birds without getting warbler neck, an ailment common to birders who spend hours during spring migration tilting their heads and binoculars to the tree tops. In the heat of the afternoon, guests assembled here for tea or rum punch, often with long discussions about a specific bird's identity, as it was almost exclusively birders who came here. It was quite astounding to be able to sit comfortably sipping rum punch while watching cuckoos and toucan, blue-grey tanagers and purple honeycreepers in the treetops and hearing the hammer-like call of the bellbirds echoing through the forest. Meanwhile, several species of hummingbirds came to feed on the sugar-water feeders. In the evening, the gallery became a viewing site for a colony of bats. There are more than sixty species of bats on the island we were told—vampire bats, fruit bats, insectivorous bats, nectar feeding, lizard-eating bats, and fish-eating bats.

Meals were served in the dining room, and attire was informal. However, one could always count on the birders bringing their binoculars to the table—just in case something special flew into view. The food was excellent, and there were frequently local native foods on the menu. Fresh fruit and fruit juices were abundant. Occasionally Celine made mango ice cream, which I found always worthy of a second helping. We were introduced to breadfruit, which grew in abundance on the island, and Celine served it in a variety of ways, no one of which tasted like any other. Fish was ample too, and jarlite (king fish) and crab were especially tasty. She was an excellent cook, and we loved it when she made local dishes such as roti, something of an overgrown pancake filled with chicken or beef, curry, onions and peas, and callaloo, a thick soup of land crab meat and dasheen or eddo, local greens similar to spinach, okra, garlic, butter, and salted pork.

Our days at the Nature Centre were unplanned as life in a tropical rainforest in the rainy season can be unpredictable. One had to be flexible and go with whatever nature handed you. We Americans tend to be weather freaks, always checking to see what it is now and what's coming next. Not so in the tropics. Sun and rain come and go, often in succession throughout the day, and those residing there just go about their business unconcerned.

Humidity, however, was omnipresent as I soon learned on the second day of our visit. I found the light meter on my camera was not functioning. I took my hair dryer to it and the problem was solved. But the next day I made the mistake of placing my camera on a sunny step while I watched a toucan in a nearby tree. When I returned, my camera was covered in water as though it had been placed in a bucket. The hair dryer wasn't going to resolve this.My chemistry professor husband suggested we go to Celine and get her to set the oven on low. After ten minutes, all the condensate was gone. And so it was each morning I "baked" my camera at 250 degrees for ten minutes to get it functional. The camera was unharmed, and I never lost a photo.

The camera got a real test of humidity, however, when the Major took us to Dunston Cave to see the renowned Oilbirds or Guacharo. These birds are exceedingly rare, found only in Trinidad, Venezuela, and Peru. Many people, including Teddy Roosevelt in 1917, come to the Nature Centre just to see the colony residing there. Walking through the rain forest to reach them was nothing like a walk in our deciduous New England woods. The high canopy overhead keeps light from reaching the forest floor so there is little underbrush.Air plants cling to the tree trunks, and loops of vines hang from the canopy, giving one childish thoughts of swinging through the trees like Tarzan.

It was quite a trek to the cave, and at one point we had a cloud burst, whereupon the Major cut three leaves of the tannia plant to use as umbrellas. They worked well as they are three feet wide, four feet long, and shed rainwater easily. After about ten minutes of downpour, we continued on climbing down a ladder, over a pool and into the cave.There were multiple chambers between huge cliffs. We passed through a five-foot opening over a cascading waterfall and pool. Tiny crabs scurried over the rocks, and bats flew out from their perches as we entered. The oilbirds peered out as us, some expressing displeasure with loud screams and screeches, unhappy about our having aroused them from their sleep. Roosting on the high ledges of the cave, they looked like pigeons with owl-like heads, their large dark eyes staring down at us. Their nests are simple mud creations on the cave walls, but they seemed to cradle their young successfully and the same nests are used repeatedly. It's believed the pairs mate for life.Egg laying to the fledging of the young takes nearly six months. The young birds are very inactive, accumulating much fat as they idly sit on their cliff perches, month after month. In years past, locals would collect the young birds and boil them down for lamp and cooking oil.Since 1967 and the establishment of the Nature Centre, the birds have been protected and their numbers have greatly increased. These are the only nocturnal, flying, fruit-eating birds in the world, so it was a remarkable experience to crawl down into the cave and see them.

The next day we met the famous Lawrence Calderon, a taxi driver with 15 children who probably weighed 300 pounds. A giant teddy bear of a man, Lawrence was a magnificent self-taught field ornithologist with the ability to whistle in virtually any species of bird in the area. We had been told, in advance of our trip, to ask that Lawrence be our guide, and we booked him for several days of birding. On our first excursion with Lawrence, we went no further than the winding mountainous way we had initially traveled, the Arima-Blanchisseuse Road, and we saw 57 species that one day. Lawrence had a large appetite, and Celine packed us large lunches, so we shared our sandwiches while Lawrence continued to point out and whistle in new species between bites. He had a wonderful sense of humor, and it wasn't long before he and Alfred were exchanging witticisms.

A few days later, Lawrence took us to Caroni Swamp to see scarlet ibis.We went out in a boat with a local guide, Winston Nahnan, who also whistled various birds into close range. At dusk the birds began to fly into the mango-treed islands of the swamp. First, we saw a flock of 50; then they came in by the thousands until the mango trees looked like Christmas trees festooned with large red balls.

On another day, Lawrence took us to Nariva Swamp where, in addition to birds, we saw a variety of sights—Water Buffalo with Cattle Egrets atop their backs, Brown Pelicans fishing, small wooden houses surrounded by prayer flags, coconut palms along the shores of the Atlantic, countless numbers of stray dogs, women and children walking along the road with baskets balanced on their heads, and a host of smiling faces as we passed by. It was nice to see more of the island than just the birds.

When we returned to the Centre, Celine had cut fresh ginger blossoms, and their fragrance filled every room. But not everything was pleasantly aromatic. One of the guests, son-in-law of an esteemed board member, took great interest in bird anatomy. Having found a dead shearwater during his afternoon ocean boating, he put it in the freezer for further examination without seeking Celine's permission. Celine, always quiet and cheery, had a fit. It was stinking up her meat!

We met many interesting people during our visit, most notably Joseph Copeland, Professor of Botany and President Emeritus of City College of New York. He was chairman of the Nature Centre Board and a delightful conversationalist who had traveled extensively looking for exotic ferns. But could he talk! Incessantly! It's been said "those who knew Joe marveled at the strength of his jaw muscles!" The tales of his adventures filled many an evening's hours. Don Eckelberry, a prominent artist, maintained a cottage nearby and dropped by frequently. Seymour and Jean Auerbach were also delightful"working guests." He was a member of the Centre Board, and she, at least while we were there, seemed to be in charge of seeing to the gardens. A frequent presence at the Nature Center, she appeared with her crew of assistants to cut grass, transplant flowers, weed flower beds, landscape hillsides, and plant flowers that bore pollen, seeds, or fruit favored by the local birds. She was the epitome of an English lady in the garden always managing to look lovely even when her hands were dirty. Somehow when I garden, I come up looking like a ragamuffin with pine needles in my hair, dirt on my chin, and bone meal in my shoes.

After ten days at the Centre, we packed our bags and moved on to visit Tobago where we had arranged to stay at Grafton Estate, a private home owned by a woman who catered to birders. Little did we know what awaited us!

GRAFTON ESTATE, TOBAGO: TOADS, AND ANTS, AND GECKOS, OH MY! OH YES, AND THE MOTMOT SLEEPS IN THE BEDROOM!

We had been told by friends at the Massachusetts Audubon Society that should we travel to Trinidad, we ought also to take in its sister island, Tobago. The island lies 18 miles off the northeast coast of Trinidad. It is only 9 miles wide and 27 miles long, but there's much to see within those small confines. Coast lines, a mountain range with peaks rising to 1,900 feet, abandoned cocoa, coconut, and citrus plantations, palm trees and coral reefs. There are also nearly 300 bird species ranging from the tiny Ruby Topaz Hummingbird to the Frigatebirds with their 7-foot wingspan.

The island was first inhabited by the Ciboney Indians as far back as 800 B.C. They were followed by the peaceful and agriculturally oriented Arawak. Next came the fierce Caribe who conquered the island and then moved on up the chain of islands to Puerto Rico. Tobago was first sighted by Christopher Columbus in 1498, but ignored for the next 100 years. The Spanish established the community of St. Joseph in 1592 and endeavored to grow cocoa and tobacco, which grew very poorly. They then invited French immigrants from Haiti to come and bring sugar cane with them. The sugar cane took hold and became a very successful crop. The island was fought over more than thirty times during three centuries by the Spanish, Dutch, French, and British. Pirates and privateers ruled the area for many years as well. Even the Americans tried their hand at capturing it during the Revolutionary War.Eventually the British won in 1797 and established a settlement with 200 Brits ruling 3,000 black slaves who worked the cane fields. The hurricane of 1837 destroyed the croplands bankrupting the London firm that financed the sugar planters.Many of the plantations were then abandoned, and the slaves took over the lands. After such a tumultuous history, Tobago remained a part of the British Commonwealth until granted independence, together with Trinidad, in 1962.

If we went to Tobago, our Audubon friends told us, we must try to contact Mrs. Eleanor Alefounder whose home, Grafton Estate, was a bird sanctuary. And not just any bird sanctuary. Mrs. Alefounder had all manner of bird feeders in place, and the birds had come to realize they could enjoy her full hospitality most anywhere in the house. The beautiful old plantation home had a unique open-air architecture, meaning no screens or windows, so a flyby through the living room was not uncommon. The house was built in 1933. I'm not sure when Mrs. Alefounder purchased it, but after Hurricane Flora devastated the island in 1963, this kindly English lady began feeding the birds and word got around the avian population that food was to be had here. Over the years, her ever-present trays of food laden with cut up fruit and other scraps, together with hanging feeders and sugar-water feeders brought in ever-increasing numbers of avian diners to the banquet laid out beneath her chinaberry tree.

Mrs. Alefounder was a kind-hearted but somewhat eccentric woman, with white hair twisted into a long single braid down her back, a high-pitched voice, and a pronounced upper crust English accent. She was also a bit scatter-brained.

We arrived to find the entrance to her charming home was via a central set of ten stairs, which then merged into a long double stairway that was totally reminiscent of a 1930s Flo Ziegfeld production set. One could just imagine the chorus girls descending the steps in beautiful gowns with plumes of long feathers in their hair. But there were no chorus girls to greet us, just large cane toads who had the acrobatic ability to hop their way up the stairs. No smooth- stepping Fred Astaire, these guys, but they eventually made their way to the top and it was a ballroom for toads in the evening where the lights attracted insects to their liking.The large living room-dining room, easily 50 feet long, came alive after dinner with an amazing wildlife show, i.e. geckos on the walls darting in and out behind the picture frames, toads hopping about the living room floor, wood rats scampering in the trees, and ants on the large white pillars

We were shown to our bedroom suite with dressing room and bath, noting a mosquito net that was strung over each of the two beds. We also noted white bird droppings on the floor between the beds.

"Oh," explained, Mrs. Alefounder,"you have to share the room with the motmot. He roosts on the light cord overhead!"

Okay, we thought, this is going to be interesting.

That same afternoon a large troop of Girl Scout Brownies came through, a common occurrence; according to Mrs. Alefounder's brother, Bobby Smith.Brownies, school groups, birders, and just tourists looking around the island were likely to come by at any time of the day. They were charged no fee and made to feel welcome. Mrs. Alefounder felt she should feed the little Brownies, however, so Bobby and I were dispatched to find some cookies. We stopped at three roadside sheds, three-sided lean-tos that did indeed lean, before finding any cookies. But one did not take the cookies and run. Custom dictates that one converse a bit with the proprietor— cookies or no cookies—inquiring as to his lumbago, his sister's children, the price of fish in the marketplace today etc. etc. The cookie search took over an hour.

When we retired to our room our first evening, we discovered there was no hot water in the bathroom. This in spite of the fact that the bathroom featured a seven-foot bathtub so high it practically required a step stool to enter.

"Oh," said Mrs. Alefounder, "I'll fetch you a tea kettle."

And that's exactly what she did. She brought us a tea kettle of boiling water to heat the water for our baths. Both of our baths!Not interested in climbing the mountainous bathtub to soak only our feet, we decided a simple sponge bath in the sink would have to suffice with each of us getting one-half kettle of hot water.

Not long after we crawled into bed and pulled the mosquito netting over us, the motmot did indeed arrive and assume his position for the night. As far as I know, he didn't snore, but I was too tired to stay awake and listen.The motmot, specifically the Blue-crowned Motmot, is a beautiful 14-inch bird (larger than a Blue Jay but smaller than a Crow) with two eight-inch-long pendulum tail feathers, which to the non-birder might look like two feathered tennis rackets hanging upside down. His plumage is a riot of color—a black mask, turquoise crown, olive back, and chestnut chest. He seemed to tolerate our presence and we his, every night of our three-night visit.

We were up early the next morning, as birders and photographers are wont to do, but soon learned that Mrs. Alefounder maintained a very casual lifestyle so breakfast might come anytime and lunch might or might not happen at all. Dinner was usually about 9 p.m. (God bless granola bars!)

As mentioned, the birds had free rein of the house including the kitchen where open windows stood directly above the counter top. Mrs. Alefounder prepared their bread scraps and other tidbits on large cookie sheets. She also prepared food for her guests there. One evening she presented us with what appeared to be a tray of bread pudding, but before dishing it up, she looked again, and said, "Oh no, that's the bird food!" and retreated to the kitchen to switch the bird food for our "dessert". She returned with a different tray whichAlfred, preferring pastries to bread pudding, declined to try.

I ate it and survived, but it was unlike any bread pudding I've encountered before or since.

Upon my return home, I wrote to Mrs. Alefounder to inquire just what she had been feeding the birds. "Chicken mash with stale bread and boiled rice to hold it together," she replied, "then mashed with fruits including citrus."

Soon after breakfast on our second day, our feeder watching was interrupted by twenty-two ladies from the Church Ladies' Aide Society with their five drivers followed by a separate party of four birders from Florida. The women's chatter outdid the bird chatter, so Alfred and I retreated to the wooded pathways surrounding the house. Tobago is not at all like the rain forests of Trinidad. As noted, much of the island is former sugarcane, coconut, or coffee plantations, but as Grafton Estate had not been cultivated in years, it was now overgrown by palm trees, bamboo, secondary growth, and semi-deciduous forests. It is this habitat that attracts a wide array of colorful tropical birds, many of which we might not have seen were it not for their feeding patterns at Mrs. Alefounder's bird buffet. Most notable were the large groups of chachalacas—sometimes numbering as many as 100 at a time. The Rufous-vented Chachalaca is a large turkey-sized bird with a lot to say and it says it loudly and continuously. A chorus of chachalacas is a sound to be reckoned with. Antbirds, Barred Antshrikes with their trills, whines, and chattering were also frequent and noisy visitors to the feeders. And those well-named Bellbirds with their metallic calls could be heard for a half-mile distance. It was not an environment in which one could sleep in or attempt an afternoon siesta.

Early on our third and final day, another two cars loaded with tourists arrived, and Mrs. Alefounder took off for town. When, by 2:30, there was no sign of her and I could find nothing she had left in the refrigerator for our lunch, I took it upon myself to make lettuce and tomato sandwiches for a very hungry husband. When Mrs. Alefounder returned, she had a lovely large Red Snapper for our "lunch", but this was only five minutes before our 4 p.m. taxi arrived to take us on to Tobago's lovely Arnos Vale Hotel.

MEET THE BANANAQUITS.

Whereas Grafton Estate was primarily nature as nature chose to be, the Arnos Vale featured beautifully landscaped grounds with red Ixor and Bougainvillea, Yellow Allamanda, and almond and palm trees This 400-acre estate accommodated just 54 guests housed in cottages of stucco and natural stone with verandas overlooking the beach. There was also an elegant dining room. After a long, luxurious bath, we dressed for dinner and upon being seated were presented with an extensive menu. For all the unusual, albeit interesting,occurrences at the Asa Wright Nature Centre and Grafton Estate, we were more than ready to indulge ourselves in a bit of luxury at the Arnos Vale. "It may be expensive," said I, "but I've earned every dollar of it!"

"Would you care for the fish tonight?" we were asked. But of course. The tuxedo-clad waiter appeared soon after with a tray of wedges of dolphin fish which we took to be the main course. We helped ourselves to generous portions, only to subsequently be asked if we'd like beef or pork! We were taken aback and mortified the next day when the manager teased us about eating a major portion of the fish course for all the other guests the previous night.

We played at being tourists attending the calypso, steel band, and folkdance performances at the Bucco Theater, splashed in the surf and played with the crabs, snails, and herons. Frogs continued to be omnipresent, and I began taking count each night while walking to dinner. I racked up 21 one night. At breakfast and at lunch, served on a patio beneath a flaming Flamboyant tree, we encountered a new form of wildlife entertainment, Bananaquits. These chickadee-sized little black, white, and yellow birds joined us at our table and endeavored to snatch bites from our sugar bowl if we left it uncovered. These sneaky little beauties also would alight on your glass and press their long bills into the sweet nectar of your lemonade, if given a chance. One afternoon I had a tug of war with a Mockingbird who wished to have my tea sandwich. An afternoon hike up the hill brought us to a field where Cornbirds and Anis were screeching like avian Valkyries. It's rarely quiet in the tropics!

The next day we had the experience of a lifetime for two non-swimmers. We signed up for a tour of Tobago's famous Bucco Reef, second in size only to the Great Barrier Reef of Australia. What we had not understood is that we would be taken three miles off shore and then expected to snorkel among the corals and the tropical fish to be found there.

"Nada. Not going to happen!" said I, who can't swim and is terrified of the water. But when the captain's son showed us that the water was only waist deep, he succeeded in getting us to put on snorkels and give it a try. With Alfred in one hand and me in the other, he walked us through a water wonderland that left me breathless. We were instructed to pull on his hand if either of us felt frightened, had water in our mask, or just wanted to check the water depth! I did so soon after we got underway, but when I saw we were truly in waist-deep water, I dove back in. This was a world I had never expected to see. Blue, Spotlight, Redtail, and Rainbow Parrot Fish swam all around us. There were Angel Fish, Jewel Fish, Sergeant Majors, Banded Butterfly, schools of Grunt Fish, and hundreds of other fish we couldn't begin to identify. For someone who swims like a rock and is frightened in deep water, this was truly a memorable experience.

Much has changed since our 1972 visit. These writings describe the Asa Wright Nature Centre as it was when we visited during the infancy of its development. Subsequently, it underwent major renovations and greatly expanded its staff, educational programs, and communications! It became a well-known and highly regarded site for birders and those interested in the flora and fauna of Trinidad's rain forest and a treat for anyone who just wants to see the likes of a Purple Honeycreeper! Nonetheless, in 2019 it became a victim, like so many other tourist attractions, of COVID-19. Trinidad went into lockdown, and the culture of masks and social distancing finally caused the Centre to close.

The Grafton Estate in Tobago is now the Grafton Caledonia Bird Sanctuary, but the house has been remodeled and is currently on the market for 8,000,000TT or roughly $1.6 million USD. The mot-mot may or may not be included.

Unfortunately, the once lovely Arnos Vale Hotel was abandoned; the buildings are now in shambles, and the property is closed to the public.

We were privileged to visit each of these three establishments when we did and heartedly recommend the Asa Wright Nature Centre to anyone interested in the tropics and especially to all our fellow birders. A wonderful book, *The Old House and the Dream* by Joy Rudder, provides a thoroughly interesting account of the history and the rise of the Centre to its position of global esteem. Until the onset of COVID-19, the Centre offered many educational programs and had a large staff ready to assist visitors with their questions. Since the pandemic lockdown, the Centre has been closed, but planning is underway as to how to proceed in the future.

Soon after our return home, I began presenting several natural history lectures based on our travels to bird clubs, garden clubs, photography groups, and other interested organizations. One of the most frequently requested was "Bananaquits in the Lemonade and a Motmot in the Bedroom!"

CHAPTER 3

His Name was Mr. Hu

IT WAS 6:45 A.M., March 18, 1981, my first morning in Beijing. I couldn't sleep so I got up early and went out to meet Beijing privately and on her own terms. I walked to Tiananmen Square noting women in face masks sweeping the streets with long brooms of rough branches, parents taking young children into a nearby park, and old people engaging in the Chinese exercise of Tai Chi. This was China at leisure. A dear old man walking with a cane smiled at me. He wore a faded, worn blue Mao suit and cap. Everyone wore a faded blue Mao suit and cap. I wore a new blue wool pants suit with no cap. He smiled again, and I greeted him with two of the few Chinese words I'd learned.

"Ni hao." (It meant Hello.)

"Ni hao," he replied.

He spoke little English, and I spoke even less Chinese. He told me his name, Hu, Mr. Hu. I told him mine and I gave him one of my shiny new English/Chinese business cards. We conversed slowly. I asked if I might take his picture, and he nodded his agreement. Then I discovered, in my haste, I had neglected to load my Polaroid camera. I promised to come back and meet him again the next day. But the next day, an early morning departure with our Northeastern University delegation kept me from keeping my word. It bothered me all day and continued to bother me the following morning. I had met this sweet old man, the first "unofficial" person I had spoken to, and I was afraid this kindly soul would look for me each morning. I didn't want the first American he met to be guilty of breaking a promise. After a very hurried breakfast, I raced to Tiananmen Square and to the park nearby. Trying to find one old Chinese man in a park full of thousands of old Chinese men seemed an impossible task, but there he was, and the smile that lit up his face told me he had indeed been waiting for me.

I tried to explain why I hadn't come back the day before and my purpose in being in Beijing, all the while showing him picture postcards of my university. For a while we just sat and shared the morning. Then I took out my Polaroid camera and took his picture. In an instant we had what seemed like a hundred people surrounding us watching the image appear on this magical piece of paper. I took a second picture so that he and I would both have a remembrance of our meeting. Then everyone, using the universal language of pointing a finger at themselves, wanted me to take their picture. I finally took a picture of one particularly persistent young lad, gave it to him, and while the crowd hovered around him watching the image emerge, I bid my farewell to Mr. Hu and made my escape back to the hotel. I would spend twelve days in China in official meetings and negotiations. I would see amazing sights, eat sumptuous buffet dinners, see artistic performances, engage in numerous negotiations, take copious notes for signed agreements, but most of all I cherish meeting the man I met all alone in a park on my first early morning in Beijing, and his name was Mr. Hu.

I was in China because of a ping-pong ball. For those who don't remember history, US-China relations resumed after some twenty years of Cold War because of what became known as Ping Pong diplomacy. Ever since Mao Zedong's Communist revolution in 1949, US-Chinese relations had been bitter. Then in 1971, the World Table Tennis Championship was played in Japan. The Chinese were skilled masters of the game, but the Americans were no slouches at bouncing the ball across the table either. Though forbidden to meet by both governments, an American and a Chinese player had a chance encounter. As was customary at the games, simple gifts were exchanged, and the American gave his new Chinese friend a T-shirt of the age—emblazoned with a peace sign with the words from a Beatles song, "Let it Be." The exchange was caught on film and seen by Chairman Mao. A few days later, Mao shocked the world and the US President by inviting the US Team to come to China on an all-expense paid trip. It was the beginning of the end of the US-China Cold War. In his memoirs many years later, then President Richard Nixon wrote, "I never expected that the China initiative would come to fruition in the form of a ping-pong team."

Eight years later, in September 1979, a delegation visited the United States from the Chinese Association for Friendship with Foreign Countries (YOUXIE) headed by Ambassador Wang Bingnan, former protégé and close aide to Zhou Enlai, the first Premier of the People's Republic of China. The delegation was seeking meetings with American universities. Boston was full of universities wanting to host the delegation. As Northeastern University's Coordinator of International Affairs, I wanted Northeastern to be the school selected and I worked hard to make it happen.

I had one important ace up my sleeve—Northeastern owned a beautiful mansion, Henderson House, in a wealthy suburb that could accommodate the entire delegation while giving them a place of peace and security during their visit. (Not everyone had fallen in love with China at that point.) They could walk the property and do Tai Chi on the lawn out of sight of anyone, I argued, and security would be no problem. Henderson House was used as a conference center, but at that time, a wing of the second floor was the home of our president's family, so, in essence, we were inviting the delegation into his home. Northeastern was chosen, and I set about planning a university-type "state" dinner. The night of the event, to which officials from many prestigious colleges and universities had been invited, I stood at the top of the mansion's massive winged stairway wearing a Chinese silk cheongsam dress and formally announced "Ladies and gentlemen, the Delegation of the People's Republic of China." Down the stairway they came, and at the base of the stairs, the president's little daughter curtseyed and presented Ambassador Wang with a small bouquet. It was a beautiful moment.That night, Ambassador Wang invited Northeastern's President Kenneth Ryder to bring a delegation to China to discuss exchange agreements with Chinese universities. And that is how six months later I took an early morning walk in Beijing and met my Mr. Hu.

A MOMENT OF PERSPECTIVE.

It is important to note that my diary documenting a 1980 trip to China does not reflect what China has become today. But it is equally important to see the diary as a point of reference as to what China has become in only four decades. In 1980, China had a population of 987 million. In 2020, it had risen to 1.43 billion— and it would have been even higher were it not for the Chinese government's "One Child" policy initiated in 1980. Where once Beijing's streets were filled with bicycles, there are now eight lanes of automobiles stuck in traffic daily. The older of today's population, like Mr. Hu and many of the government officials we met—including Wang Bingnan—suffered through the Cultural Revolution and the terrorism of the Gang of Four. Not so the younger generation born since 1980, who have lived in a society far more open to Western culture and now cross the street with a cell phone held to their ears.

In 1980, open sewers ran through the streets just beyond the façade of Tiananmen Square, and farmers in the countryside moved everything by human or animal power. Much of the society has become urbanized, living in a service-oriented economy. Vast differences still exist in rural areas, but great strides have been made in promoting communities with agricultural specialties, etc.

YOUXIE, the organization that hosted our Northeastern University visit to China, came into being during the Chinese "Period of Re-adjustment" when Premier Deng Xiaoping began promoting the reformation of the country's economic system and the opening up of foreign trade. I was a beneficiary of that process, and this is the story of my 1980 experience.

MONDAY, MARCH 17, 1980 EN ROUTE TO BEIJING.

We had flown from Boston to San Francisco to Tokyo and now we were en route to Beijing. The distance from Tokyo to Beijing is 1,800 miles. Our route took us across the South China Sea, over Shanghai, and then north to Beijing. After about four hours, we got our first sight of China—a landscape of brown, barren earth with the occasional meandering river.At Beijing Airport (I'm still having trouble trying to remember to call it Beijing and not Peking) we were greeted by many friends from YOUXIE, including two of the guides we had met the previous September when Wang Bingnan and the delegation had come to Boston. It was hard to believe only six months had passed since they came to us, and now, here we were coming to them!

Three special buses were awaiting our large delegation of twenty-five persons and about 2,000 pounds of baggage, including a projector, typewriter, and fourteen boxes of books and gifts. We spoke little on our way to the hotel. Everyone was exhausted, but each of us was trying to take in everything in sight—like four-year-olds at Disneyland. I remember turning for a second look at a man on a bicycle carrying two long boards on his shoulders, followed by many horse-drawn carts, one of which carried a bulging load of branches which appeared to have been cut from roadside trees. I saw goats, sheep, and a dog, of which I had heard there were few, and two soldiers patrolling along an embankment which seemed to shield nothing but a field from our view. The brightly dressed children stood out in sharp contrast to the sea of blue Mao-suited adults who walked and biked their way along the road.

We reached our hotel and were shown to our rooms with each of us toting our own baggage (no porters here) as well as a share of the aforementioned university "baggage." My roommate Ann and I shared a room in the older section of the hotel, with a high ceiling and long, somber gray drapes. Victorian furniture, an old oriental rug, a lovely large desk, and comfortable beds covered by feather ticks completed the furnishings. French doors onto a balcony overlooked the busy thoroughfare below.

There was virtually no time to unpack before we were obliged to report downstairs and board the buses again, this time to attend the welcoming banquet hosted by YOUXIE and Wang Bingnan. We met many of our YOUXIE friends there and were warmly greeted by Ambassador Wang. In addition, the guest list included representatives from the Ministry of Education, Peking Normal University (they still called it that), Peking Polytechnic, Qinghua University, and the Academy of Sciences. There were many toasts followed by the admonition "gambe" which translates into "bottoms up!" (To the amusement of many Americans, one interpreter reportedly translated it as "up your bottoms!")

Ambassador Wang surprised me by going on at great length about the Chinese Cheongsam dress I had worn at the dinner hosted by Northeastern. Although I had brought it with me, I thought it might be too flamboyant for Beijing so I hadn't worn it, much to my regret. Ambassador Wang went on to speak of how I had told him of my desire to come to China, and on several occasions that evening he dubbed me with a nickname, which when translated meant "the Diplomat!"

TUESDAY, MARCH 18 BEIJING

"Will somebody please answer that phone!" The phone rang constantly. I pulled the pillow over my head to block the noise, but there was no escaping it. Only when I got up and opened the French doors did I discover that the phone I'd heard ringing continuously was the sound of hundreds of bicycle bells on the street below.

After my morning walk to the park, I came back and had a nice western-style breakfast of toast, scrambled eggs, and bacon before we loaded up onto the buses again for our first sight-seeing jaunt to the Forbidden City or the Imperial Palace as it is also called. The Forbidden City seemed enormous and rather ominous initially, but it revealed its charm as we moved further into its courtyards, dainty rooms, and delicate gardens. It was snowing lightly as we moved about, but this added a certain beauty to the landscape.

Back to the hotel for lunch and then on to YOUXIE offices where we were scheduled to make our three-hour presentation about the Northeastern University curricula, its colleges, and its famed Co-operative Plan of Education before fourteen representatives of the Ministry of Education and several Beijing universities. The slide-show was so well received that we were pleased we had decided to lug the projector along with us. Back to the hotel we went with only 15 minutes to spare before we reported for dinner followed immediately by a visit to the Chinese Acrobatic Theater. What a schedule! For those of us staying in the far wing of the hotel, it was impossible to be on time. It took ten minutes to walk from the main lobby to our room. One roundtrip without so much as a stop in the bathroom and you're already five minutes late for the scheduled departure! The show lasted two and one-half hours without benefit of an intermission or any form of central heating. By the time it was over, we were all very tired and very cold. It proved to be the first of many 15-18-hour days ahead.

WEDNESDAY, MARCH 19

After an early wake-up call, we departed at 8 a.m. for our visit to Peking Normal University. We were suitably fortified with a warm Chinese breakfast of noodles, dumplings, cold pork, cold beef in a sesame sauce, rice gruel, and a hot cooked vegetable that none of

us could identify. At Peking Normal, a large delegation stood outside the main building awaiting our arrival. This was a pattern
often repeated. We were led upstairs in a building we were told
had been constructed in 1961, but was generally in very poor repair. I'm not enough of an expert to know if the original
construction was inferior or if there simply have been no funds for
maintenance. I suspect it may have been a bit of both, especially
inasmuch as during the Cultural Revolution the universities suffered greatly as did many of the faculty.

The briefing room consisted of a row of chairs lined up all the
way around the room with a large table surrounded by chairs in
the middle. The table was covered with a white embroidered table-
cloth on which there were numerous mugs of hot tea, each with its
own lid. This too proved to be a familiar routine in our subsequent
university visits. The vice president introduced his assembled faculty and told us of their programs, and our Northeastern President,
Kenneth Ryder, responded in kind. Gifts were exchanged, and this
too proved to be the usual ritual observed. We then moved into discussions as to how our two institutions might collaborate.

Prior to our departure from Boston, we had met with a busi-
nessman who had about as much business trading with the Chinese
as anyone at that point. He gave us several good negotiation
pointers—one of which came into play almost immediately. "Americans," he said, "abhor a lull in the conversation and think when it
occurs, it must be filled with words. That," he said, "is where you
must be careful. The Chinese negotiators will nod at the conclusion
of your remarks, but initially remain silent. Don't rush in to enhance
your offer because you think they don't like what they've heard.
They are just waiting to see if you'll offer more when they don't respond." We got very good at waiting out the silences, sipping our
hot tea, and smiling quietly.

When the formal negotiations concluded and campus visits got
underway, I was permitted to leave in order to visit the University's

Institute of Foreign Education, a research center which was presumed to be similar to the Center for International Higher Education Documentation (CIHED) I headed up at home. Other than a similarity in our respective periodical display racks, there was little we had in common. Where CIHED is the largest library on international higher education in the United States, this fledgling institute had a mere two shelves of books on foreign educational systems and only a sampling of US educational journals. Then came my big question:Did they have the ten-volume *International Encyclopedia of HigherEducation* for which I had served as Senior Editor and which had been compiled at Northeastern with a staff of fifty and 2,000 authors worldwide? No, they had not heard of it. Imagine my delight when President Ryder later informed me that "your Encyclopedia is in their main library right next to the new edition of the Britannica!"

It now being near noon, we were taken to the university dining hall where we were served a fifteen-course banquet. A whole fish was served at each table as well as giant prawns, an assortment of hot and cold meat dishes, pear strips, cooked apples, oranges, and soup, the latter always being served last in China. Ready to curl up and take a nap, we were instead bustled into our buses and driven to Peking Polytechnic University where we went through the entire ritual all over again minus the banquet.

Our first inkling of deviation in administrative authority came here when we were received not by the president or vice president (presidents are usually just figureheads) but by the university's party secretary, i.e., the Communist Party Secretary. It was he who handled the discussions and subsequent negotiations. There were frequent references to the need to obtain the approval of the "Beijing Authority" for any formal liaison, and there seemed a good deal of doubt the "Authority" would find funds to send students to the US for study. (We weren't handing out free rides!) Imagine my surprise at the end of our trip when we learned Peking Polytechnic was the first to obtain official sanctioning of an institutional liaison with Northeastern and that they would be sending two or three undergraduates and three of four graduate students to Boston in the fall.

Every negotiation session has its rare moments, but the need for better communications came out clearly when the Party Secretary asked, "What is Business Administration?" Our dean of the Business School dropped his jaw at that one, but politely described the study of business in the United States referred to as Business Administration.Later, when asked if Peking Poly taught English as a foreign language, the Secretary replied, "We have no English for foreigners, only English for Chinese." Of such moments are memories made.

THURSDAY, MARCH 20

After a quick dash to the park to look for Mr. Hu, as referenced earlier, we were on the bus at 8 a.m. again, this time to visit Qinghua University. Qinghua is often referred to as the MIT of China, and in many ways, this is reflected in the contacts Qinghua had already established with MIT, UC Berkeley, Stanford University, and the University of New York, Stony Brook. In private conversations with the Secretary-General of the Qinghua Academic Committee, I learned that these ties were primarily established with schools of which the Qinghua hierarchy were themselves alumni. So, the "old boy" network works in China too! We gained other important insights into the politics behind the scene at Qinghua as well. Our most touted work-study program known as Cooperative Education presented conceptual problems to some because work and study was a concept abused by the infamous Gang of Four. It appeared we would have to overcome that holdover concept on the part of faculty who had suffered at the hands of the infamous quartet.

I've not yet mentioned that all of our meetings were held in unheated buildings, the only available heat coming from the mugs of tea we all held tightly in our hands. We did not remove our coats and often left our gloves on as well.

Back to the hotel for lunch and "time off for good behavior" before we had a 3 p.m. meeting with the Minister of Education and members of his staff. This was a coup as many groups request an audience with the minister, but few are granted. Indeed, this was the man who signed the letter of agreement subsequently authorizing four undergraduate engineering students and two graduate business students from Peking Poly to come to Northeastern.

FRIDAY, MARCH 21

Today was a memorable day. Free of negotiations, we were going to see the Great Wall of China! The bus ride took the better part of two hours from Beijing, but it afforded us an opportunity to see the countryside. I was not prepared for the poor standard of living I saw. Homes often appeared to be little more than hovels with no modern conveniences. In 1961 I visited the Soviet Union, and in the diary of that trip I recalled the poverty of the farmlands, but I saw nothing as poor as the housing we were seeing on this bus ride. The rural populations have such a long way to go before their standard of living parallels what even the poorest of the poor have in the United States. Still, it was lovely to see how these simple people were celebrating the spring festival with brightly painted doorways. Black and White Magpies called from the courtyards and warblers sang in the trees. I'm sure it is much prettier when the trees leaf out, although I doubt these humble homes can afford the luxury of garden flowers.

We were told the Great Wall is the only man-made object visible from outer space. One is struck by its antiquity but also by the realization of how much manpower it took to build. When originally built in the third century B.C., it extended some 5,000 miles—the distance across the United States. It averages nineteen feet in width and twenty-two feet in height. Numbering in the thousands, a watchtower was erected every 450 feet. Most of the wall has fallen into disrepair, but a section at Pataling Pass has been restored to take advantage of the tourist trade.

The weather was bitterly cold the day of our visit, and it had snowed the day, before making it slippery and difficult to walk up the narrow stairs. (Chinese had small feet in those days.) I didn't think I could get my feet and ankles to bend backwards as much as was necessary to accommodate the narrow steps and steep incline. In retrospect it would almost have been best to walk up sideways!

I returned to the hotel with only 15 minutes to spare before I was receiving a very special guest. I dashed down the corridor and called to the desk clerk to please bring cups and tea to my room. I was half in and out of my clothes when the desk clerk arrived, but taking no mind of my condition, he set it down. Shortly thereafter a knock at my door announced the arrival of my guest—a man to whom I had written requesting a meeting. He was the editor-in-chief of the currently in-process, 74-volume *Great Encyclopedia of China*. To my surprise, he was carrying Volume 1 of my encyclopedia! He was accompanied by an assistant editor who spoke English.

Wearing my Cheongsam dress, I served tea, and we chatted as only two encyclopedia editors could chat. I asked if he often found that great scholars were lousy writers, and his previously placid face gave way to twinkling eyes and hearty laughter. From that point on we had great fun swapping stories, but then he had to excuse himself as he was running late for a meeting, "because I had an author who tied me up for two hours complaining about the editing of his manuscript," he explained.

Before leaving Beijing, my roommate Ann and I ducked out to a local art store to do a bit of shopping. Our selections became a community event! Between us we had selected two panda prints, each with a different pose and facial expression. Foreigners buying anything is of interest to the locals, we'd learned, and as we were having trouble deciding which one each of us would purchase, the locals decided to help! Everyone was offering their opinion, said Ann, who spoke Chinese, but in the end, we both wanted the same one. Not to upset one another, we started to walk out the door. No, no, we must come back, the crowd insisted, so back we went and bought the two prints, agreeing we'd flip a coin later to see who got which print.

SATURDAY, MARCH 22 NANKING

We awoke to a blanket of snow, and the snow-encumbered bicycle traffic made us late to the airport. The plane too was late, which put us behind schedule before we even reached Nanking. When we arrived at Nanking University, we went through what had become for us our usual "dog and pony show," but found they already knew all about us and had selected six students to be interviewed. Of course, they were hoping we were going to pay their expenses!

That evening we were whisked off to see the Peking Opera. There we froze our nose and our toes. I had to put my wool gloves on my feet during the second half of the performance. Many of our group asked to leave after the first half, but Ann and I stuck it out for the full performance, and two of the guides stayed with us so we each had our own interpreters. And interpreters one did need to understand the caterwauling that was going on. Peking Opera music bears no resemblance to Verdi or Wagner, but the acrobatic dancing is spectacular!

SUNDAY, MARCH 23

The morning schedule called for a visit to an iron ore mining and chemical production plant which I found pretty boring until we reached the foundry and saw the "hell fire and brimstone" display going on there. No EPA or OSHA pollution standards here! The air was thick with dust and smoke, and I was very grateful when we were able to take our leave. We were then separated into small groups to visit workers in their homes. My group visited a husband and wife and their two children ages 23 and 27. Their living quarters consisted of a living room, which also served as a bedroom for the parents, a bedroom for the two adult children, a pullman-type kitchen incorporated into the entry hallway, and a bathroom shared with another family. It was clear this was a "showcase" family. We noted a television set in the living room so we asked what they knew about the United States. They seemed to know something about President Carter and the forthcoming election, the American hostages in Iran, and the Soviet invasion of Afghanistan. They knew nothing of the winter Olympic Games in which their own countrymen had participated. We were surprised, as we'd heard broadcasts were being beamed back to China. We next visited a hospital that was unheated, unsanitary, and very depressing. We were taken through burn wards and maternity wards that left me uncomfortable as I really felt our "tour" was an invasion of privacy. At 9 p.m. we took off for Shanghai.

MONDAY, MARCH 24 – WEDNESDAY, MARCH 26: SHANGHAI

To paraphrase a movie released some years ago, "If this is Monday, it must be Shanghai!" Having had cold weather and little sun in Beijing and Nanking, Shanghai's sunny, warm weather was most welcome, and we looked forward to our three days here. We visited a middle school for bright students before going on to the Shanghai Institute of Technology. By now, our physics professor, a native of Changsha, China, was giving our presentation in Chinese, and having written the English script myself, I could follow along much of what he was saying. That night we were the Institute's guests for a fifteen-course dinner at the Shanghai International Club. I was seated at the head table, but I found the conversation boring as it never got beyond pleasantries.

The next day was a long day but one rich in experiences. By 8 a.m. we were on the road to the Shanghai University of Science and Technology, an hour's drive northwest of the city. Upon our arrival, we were given a typed schedule for our visit and we were off and running. Shanghai schools, it seemed, were also being approached by foreign universities, including schools from Japan, Germany, and Australia, "but the Northeastern delegation is the largest to visit us," we were told. After the usual round of discussions, lunch was served off-campus in a village inn. It was the most scrumptious and elaborate meal of our entire visit! As we were endeavoring to digest our 18-course repast, President Ryder thanked our hosts "for this simple country meal" which left everyone laughing. Much in need of walking off our heavy meal, we were taken on a stroll through the village to a beautiful Confucian Temple, an ancient Pagoda, and a stroll through Huilongtan Park and Black Dragon Pond. This was a most welcomed interlude.

While driving back to the city, we made a stop at the Malu People's Commune.One shouldn't go to China without seeing a commune! We were staggered by the numbers—69 small factories (they use the term loosely) employing 6,000 workers, 50,000 pigs, and 110 products produced by the 30,000 residents.

That night six members of our delegation were invited to the home of the father of one of the Chinese students already studying at Northeastern. When our minibus turned into his courtyard, we found the neighbors had turned out to welcome us and 50 people stood there applauding. We were ushered up several flights of stairs where more neighbors applauded us along the stairwells. The family shared three rooms, each with a bed and a couch, but the kitchen and bath were shared with other families. The presence of a color television set, a tape recorder, short-wave radio, and a telephone quickly told us this family was a cut above the average, to say the least. The dinner was catered by a local restaurant—eleven courses! I had now learned the Chinese expression for "no more" when offered seconds. We took our leave about 10 p.m. nearly incoherent under the effects of 29 courses of food in six hours!

The next day it was on to Fudan University, one of nine that the Chinese called "key universities" and an institution of great tradition and prestige. The university had 4,000 undergraduates in the first three years of a four-year undergraduate program, but since the school's reorganization after the fall of the Gang of Four, they had not yet had time to graduate a senior class. We heard this at other schools as well. Here, however, we learned of some of the atrocities and hardships that befell academics during this trying time in China's history. And once again, we were told of the need to overcome the phrase "work/study" given what that had meant under the regime of the monstrous Gang of Four.

After our visit, we were given a bit of time to just enjoy Shanghai. Three of us agreed to stop at the Bund, a famous park along the Wappo River. We had been on three different buses and the other two buses were late, so I found myself standing alone and a curiosity to the local Chinese. A blonde alone in Shanghai? My trench coat and shoes were of great interest as was my hair, which one woman reached up to stroke. Many walked up close to me and then began to discuss my appearance among themselves.When I changed a roll of film, I had twenty-five noses poking their way into the camera. Putting on a telephoto lens attracted even more attention. After my colleagues joined me, we spent three wonderful hours strolling through the city, exchanging giggles with Chinese children, walking along back streets, and enjoying a very simple meal in a small "Mom and Pop" restaurant.

THURSDAY, MARCH 27CHANGSHA

Travel day again and it was on to Changsha where a nice surprise awaited us.

The usual airport reception committee was on hand to greet us—but no hotel this time. We were taken to the "Chinese Camp David", the Rung Yuan Guest House favored by Chairman Mao, a native of this area, now reserved for visits of high-ranking diplomats. We entered through a gate under military guard. There were no other guests, and the goldfish had been dumped into the pool shortly before our arrival. Unfortunately, "dumped" is exactly what they did, and the poor fish were belly-up before lunchtime. It was a beautiful site. Camellias were in bloom around the pool, and the woodsy environment provided a very peaceful ambiance.After lunch I sat down on a mushroom-shaped stone table and listened to the bird chorus led by a Chinese Oriole. As a birder, I was picking up new species for my Birder's Life List, but handicapped by the fact that there was no field guide for Chinese birds at the time.

On to visit Hunan University, and what we found was rather pathetic. To paraphrase Winston Churchill, "Never have so many needed so much." Although Hunan had been designated one of the nine key universities for development, someone lost the key to unlock this institution from its recent bondage to the Gang of Four.The university officials with whom we met were party functionaries, not faculty, and I had the feeling I was seeing some of Mao's old chums. The place was in such disarray the faculty were ashamed to show us their laboratories or library. Repeated requests to see both were met with silence and a change of subject. We were told Hunan had 1,500 students and 1,100 professors. That's quite a faculty/student ratio! Many of the faculty seemed to be primarily involved in research rather than teaching. Some programs, directed by the First Ministry of Machine Building, could not be established for lack of qualified faculty, and they didn't have enough English-speaking faculty to welcome guest lecturers for whom a translator would be necessary. I was astounded when told Hunan had relations with 114 American universities! Further questioning reveals they meant they had received letters from 114 US universities. China relations seem certainly to be in vogue on US campuses! By now we had visited nine universities, and quite frankly we were getting tired of hearing our own voices! We were quite ready to board the plane to our final stop, Kwangchow.

FRIDAY, MARCH 28KWANGCHOW

Kwangchow was a pleasant shock. It was positively tropical.As a child I had loved the epic tale *The Cremation of Sam McGee*, who was so cold in the Artic north country that when shut into a furnace exclaimed, "Shut the door! It's the first time I've been warm." With mosquito netting over the bed, I fell asleep with the balcony doors open to the warm, night air.

Our tenth and final university visit took place at Chungshan University where flowering trees accented beautifully maintained grounds. We were ushered into a room of comfortable blue sofas with white doilies—but there wasn't enough electrical current to power the projector! After the efforts of two of our delegates, a physicist and an electrical engineer, they managed to get 200 volts into the projector and the show went on!I began my last day in China much as I had begun my first. I arose early and took a walk to a nearby park, thinking back on all that I had seen and learned in the past ten days.

We boarded our train to Hong Kong and enjoyed the modern, swivel seats that permitted us to look out at the countryside. There was even a very nice dining car. But the train lavatories were a reminder that modern plumbing had yet to arrive. The facility consisted of a porcelain-lined hole in the floor with two metal plates where one was expected to place one's feet with the open train tracks flying by below. When coupled with the swaying motion of the train, accomplishing one's objective was not easy.

As we were traveling out of China to Hong Kong, we passed by a small development called Shenzhen on the Pearl River. We were told it was the first "special economic zone" in the country created to foster productive exchanges and advanced technology between foreign firms and Chinese companies.The "reform and opening up" policy of 1979 resulted in massive foreign investment. Today that little wide spot in the road is a city of more than 13 million people with tall skyscrapers, theme parks, shopping malls, the third busiest container port in the world, and the headquarters of many Chinese multinational companies, among them Huawei Technologies. Huawei manufactures telecommunications equipment and consumer electronics. In July 2020 it passed Apple and Samsung to become the leading smartphone brand in the world. Believed to be an arm of the Chinese government and the Communist party, it is a source of cybersecurity concerns in the United States, which bars US companies from working with it. As of 2021, little old Shenzen had 138 artificial intelligence start-up companies.

Mr. Hu and I would be in big trouble today—or at least he would be—in the new Chinese Social Credit System which decides what is correct or incorrect behavior with rewards and punishments accordingly. This new artificial intelligence driven social monitoring system smacks of "Big Brother," but apparently is being accepted by Chinese society.

Our visit was concluded, and I was left with conflicting thoughts. How could this be a nuclear nation while allowing much of its population to live in houses little changed from a feudal age? China has so far to go to become a modern state, but one must admire the determination with which it is pursuing that objective. Our delegation represented a university of importance within a technologically advanced nation; therefore we were received warmly and at times with an intimacy that was almost overwhelming. Our technological expertise must have at times seemed like science fiction to a nation where there were few automobiles but you could get run down by a sea of bell-ringing cyclists and horn-blaring trucks. The outreach to us was important in Nanking and Shanghai where we saw an abundance of horse-drawn vehicles and in Changsha where we noted men, women, and children hauling and pushing heavy wooden carts with nary a horse in sight. But in Kwangchow there were high-rise buildings, modern hotels, numerous automobiles, and the Canton Trade Fair. My reflections on a 1980 visit served to illustrate how far China has come in just four decades. It's astounding and a bit alarming. China is now the second largest economy in the world and striving to become number one. It just might make it.

A 1982 ADDENDUM

In 1982, I returned to China as the head of a delegation from the new China Consortium for Educational and Cultural Exchange. Our delegation of sixteen included three college presidents and their wives, a writer, a lawyer, a Chinese art historian, a solar energy specialist, and the Assistant Commissioner of Public Health for Massachusetts. The Consortium was offering two six-month visiting fellowships of which one would go to a Chinese legal scholar and the other to a scholar or performer in the creative arts.

It was very different being the leader of the delegation. First, I now had "old friend" status with the Chinese, having been there just two years before. Secondly, my relationship with Ambassador Wang Bingnan was most definitely affording my delegation extra care. But most importantly, it meant I had to shepherd the negotiations, make polite conversation, orchestrate the negotiation pauses, and respond when questions were raised about US foreign policy, most notably as it related to the sale of military equipment to Taiwan. It also meant I was the one served a duck foot in my soup in recognition of my status!

After our welcome dinner with YOUXIE and Wang Bingnan, I asked him to do something special for my group. Having heard him speak of Premier Zhou Enlai on a personal basis, could he share some personal reminiscences about this famous man so renowned in world history?For more than half an hour, we sat listening to his stories about the man's character, his idiosyncrasies, and how he would always edit every document, every agreement, personally changing the verb structure or sentence syntax to suit his particular purpose. He also told us how Zhou Enlai would often call his staff at two or three o'clock in the morning to discuss some matter of business. The staff learned to carry their work home with them in order to be prepared for his phone calls. He spoke of the man's kindness as a human being and how he would often seek to personally befriend an individual whom he saw slighted at a public gathering.

He then spoke at length of the Americans who had sought to maintain ties with China throughout the difficult years of US-China relations. Again, he spoke in a personal vein because he knew them all—Vinegar Joe Stillwell, George Marshall, Edgar Snow. He said nothing about his own very important role, so I quoted an old Chinese proverb to him, "When you drink the water, remember who dug the well." I suggested the well had been dug well and deeply and that it would not go dry due to temporary differences of opinion or political circumstances. I then told him that this delegation had come to dig wells of friendship, but we had asked to go off the beaten path visiting institutions in cities not frequently reached by other university delegations. I then quoted one of our own New England poets, Robert Frost, "Two roads diverged in a wood and I, I took the one less traveled by and that has made all the difference." I then presented him with a picture book of New England fall foliage together with lines of Robert Frost's poetry illustrating each page. Yes, being the delegation leader made quite a difference as I would find repeatedly throughout the trip. I would also have to answer to US Taiwan relations again as well!

We met with officials at the Ministry of Education, Peking University, the Beijing Institute of Technology, and the Central Academy of Fine Arts. At the latter we watched as art students painted a male model in five different styles ranging from Picasso to Rembrandt!

We moved on to Xian, Chendu, Shanghai, and Soochow visiting institutions such as the Southwest Minorities Institute and the Embroidery Research Institute where the work is so fine, they split a single silk thread into 48 sections.

It had been just two years, but change was everywhere. The large pictures of Mao, Marx, Engels, and Stalin were gone from Tiananmen Square. We heard nothing about the Gang of Four or the Cultural Revolution. The political propaganda to which I'd been exposed previously was negligible with the exception of the issue of arms sales to Taiwan. Construction of all types was everywhere—housing, roads, highways. Construction cranes filled the skylines. It seemed as though the government had decided it was time to stop talking about the past and pontificating about the future. It was time to get the job done and to get it done now! I could not, in 1982, ever envision how rapidly China would move out from third-world status to become an economic powerhouse rivaling the United States.

CHAPTER 4

And Then There Was Joy — in Saudi Arabia

IT WAS APRIL 25, 1983 and I was having lunch at the race track. But it wasn't just any race track, it was the King Abdul Aziz race track in Riyadh, Saudi Arabia and I was the guest of a Sheik and six of his high-ranking friends at the Riyadh Equestrian Club. I was a single American woman and seven Saudi men dining together in socially segregated Saudi Arabia. As I sat there, I was reminded of the song from the Broadway show *Sweet Charity*: "If they could see me now, that little gang of mine... they'd never believe it." I looked at my luncheon companions in their long white tunics or thobes, gold-trimmed cloaks, and checkered kufiyas upon their heads, and I remarked, "Gentlemen, this looks like a reverse harem." We all had a good laugh over that one. My luncheon companions were an impressive group—the president, the vice president, and the secretary-general of the Saudi Arabian Civil Service Bureau, the secretary-general of the Manpower Council, the director-general of the Central Electric Company, the legal councelor to the King's Cabinet, and the dean of the College of Administrative Science (Business School) at King Saud University.

Quite aside from it being an impressive ambiance, it was a special moment as it indicated their acceptance of me and the research I was doing for a book I was writing on Saudi Arabian manpower development.

I should, perhaps, explain just how I ended up in Saudi Arabia having lunch with a Sheik and his friends.

While working as Senior Editor of the *International Encyclopedia of Higher Education*, I became interested in the fact that American multinational corporations were in the education business. It's a long story, but suffice it to say I wrote a book, *The Development of Human Resources: A Case Study of United States-Saudi Arabian Cooperation*. There were additional aspects of the subject that could only be written were I to go to Saudi Arabia. I asked three times. Three times my request was denied. I published my book and subsequently heard from the president of the Saudi Civil Service Bureau that they found the book of such interest and value they had sections of it translated into Arabic for the benefit of the senior staff.

"Well, now may I come?"I wrote back asking.

And then one day I walked into my office and saw a large brown envelope festooned with Arabic script and colorful stamps, and I thought, 'Oh my God, they've invited me!' And indeed, they had. In my hand I held the official invitation from the Saudi Arabian Manpower Council to come to the Kingdom to tell the story of ARAMCO's schools (Arabian American Oil Company) the role of Saudi women in the Kingdom's development and other aspects of the Saudization of the work force.

My employer, Northeastern University, agreed to give me a three-week leave of absence, and I requested and received the necessary funding from the corporate sponsors of my first book. My secretary made me long skirts, and I went out shopping for high-necked, long-sleeve blouses. Two months later I was on my way to Saudi Arabia.

My book is not bedtime reading. In fact, it is full of statistical data and would be quite boring to 90% of the general population. But it got me to Riyadh, and once there, I went to work. My days were filled with interviews. In the morning I interviewed Saudis. Their business day ends at 2 p.m. so after that hour I interviewed Americans. Then I sometimes went back and interviewed Saudis in the evenings. On the weekends I wrote up my notes, maintained a diary (excerpts from which you are about to read),prepared outlines for my morning interviews, and enjoyed some social engagements.

Prior to my visit, another woman had visited the Kingdom under the pretense of doing research, and she wrote a book that was something of an exposé on Saudi social life. I found I often had to begin my interview sessions by telling someone I was not this woman and I had a very specific and highly focused agenda. Then I would go right into my first question. It helped that I had two degrees in journalism and knew how to conduct a meaningful interview. The men, and for the most part they were all men, quickly saw I meant business and we got into substantive discussions.

But it was not all work and no play. I visited the family of a Saudi graduate student who had worked with me on my first book while in Boston, I did a tiny bit of sightseeing and shopping, I was invited to dinners in people's homes, to lunches, to an engagement party, and yes, to the Riyadh Equestrian Club with my "harem." My diary from that trip is full of names and times and discussions, none of which make interesting reading. And my social experiences came about because people believed me when I said I was not about to write a book about the décor of their homes, or their family life—a promise I must keep. But there were a few experiences I feel comfortable sharing, although all names have been eliminated.

Let me begin with a few comments about my flight from New York to Riyadh via Dhahran. I was flying Saudia Airlines, so wanting to get off on the right foot, I was dressed in a jacket, high-necked blouse, and long skirt. There were a few Saudi women on the flight, but most of the passengers were American men and a few wives. About an hour before our set-down in Dhahran, women began going into the lavatories to change out of Western clothing to Saudi apparel. Then an announcement came over the loud speaker that it is against government regulations to bring any alcohol into the country, and passengers were asked to look around their seats and collect any full or empty bottles. The stewardess then passed down the aisle to collect every trace of alcohol on the plane. I cleared passport control in Dhahran, but not without the inspector having to speak to a higher authority about the stated purpose of my visit, i.e. "research".Once on the plane headed to Riyadh, I was seated in the "family section" although I noticed women traveling with their husbands were permitted to sit with them. Now all of the Saudi women were draped in black cloaks and veils. The infamous "bourka" was everywhere. I was not so attired. I figured I had worn appropriate clothing in respect of their cultural traditions, and I hoped that was going to be enough. It was. I was asked to cover my hair only when, later in my trip, I visited a souk.

In Riyadh I got the slowest customs officer of all. He was going through everyone's bags and looking at everyone's magazines and books. The woman ahead of me had a copy of *McCall's*, a woman's magazine, which included an advertisement for L'eggs pantyhose. The customs inspector clucked his teeth and tore out the advertisement before returning the magazine to her. I was greeted by the gentleman who would be my chief aide and taken to the Hyatt Regency Hotel, told I could rest the next day as it was the Sabbath and he would come back for me Saturday morning.

I was awakened the next day by the call to prayers coming from a nearby mosque. It was earlier than I intended to rise, but I donned my "uniform" and headed to the coffee shop for breakfast. But this was no mere coffee shop. Brunch was laid out on seven tables, and although I didn't know half of the things I was eating, I found nothing that was not to my liking. The café became my oasis in the days ahead, and the staff, much interested in this American woman traveling alone, took great care to look after me.

Saturday morning, my driver came for me and took me to the Manpower Council and my new office. As I left my room, I laughed at myself in the mirror. I looked like Miss Anna with a briefcase going to meet the King of Siam in my long skirt, white ruffled-necked blouse, and peach jacket.When I met my host, the secretary-general of the Manpower Council, he wasted no time mentioning the fact that another Western woman came to the Kingdom and subsequently wrote only of negative accounts of Saudi Society. He told me with all honesty when he was told he was to sponsor my visit, his reply was, "A woman! I don't need such problems!" I promised not to give him any and I didn't.

That night I was the guest of honor at a dinner party in the home of one of the most famous families in Saudi Arabia. Mindful of my obligation to respect the privacy of my hosts, I will only say that the house was the most magnificent I had ever seen, and the buffet of Saudi and Arabic dishes was sublime. I had never tasted such tender and savory roast of lamb. This was an all-ladies dinner. The Sheika's husband did not attend. The Sheika was an American-born woman who visited frequently between her California and her Saudi families. It was a very sophisticated group of great conversationalists. Most interesting were my conversations with the Sheika's two married daughters who had very different perspectives on Saudi life and the nation's economic development. One was totally committed to her Saudi lifestyle, having a driver, but unable to go out without a male family member with her. She had no interest in learning how to drive and was happy to be taken wherever she wished to go. The other was almost a feminist. I found it interesting that two young women, brought up in the same household, would have such different perspectives.

The next day I was treated to my lunch at the Equestrian Club which, by the way, I recorded with my Polaroid camera as the men stood gathered around me seated in front of them. That's when I gave them the "harem" line! Not only did they laugh, they all wanted a copy of the photo!

There then followed two days full of meetings, most of them at the Saudi-American Bank, formerly Citibank, but now 60% Saudi-owned. Citibank had a well-developed plan for the Saudization of their workforce, i.e., replacing foreign nationals with Saudi citizens. But my discussion with both bank managers and some of their US-educated Saudi employees pointed up some problem areas which I discussed at length with both groups. I think the discussions were helpful to all parties concerned. We certainly never took a break. I was there for two days and never stopped for so much as a cup of coffee! Both nights I dined alone at the hotel coffee shop, grateful for a bit of quiet time.

The following evening, I was driven to the home of a member of the Royal Family, a prince. For nearly two hours we sat in his garden on a Persian carpet spread out on the grass as we sipped cardamom-laced Saudi coffee and mint tea and rested our elbows on large square bolster pillows. Our conversation ranged from various aspects of Saudi economic development to cultural values, the role of Saudi women, and even Saudi flora and fauna when he realized I was interested in the subject. Later he presented me with a book on the topic and autographed it for me. The prince was a very astute and very well-informed man on manpower issues. He gave me a copy of a working paper from the Woodrow Wilson International Center for Scholars in Washington, DC titled "The Manpower Problem in Saudi Arabia's Economic and Security Policy". He asked me to read it and give him my opinion. The date indicated the paper was less than one week old! When I got back to the hotel and read it, I found my own book referenced several times! My Polaroid recorded my time with the prince, but it could not capture the scent of the evening air, the songs of several birds, and the sight of a little goat nearby busily chomping on grass. The goat, he explained, was a playmate for his young son.

I returned to the hotel about 9 o'clock, but the night was not yet over. I had another party to attend beginning at 10:30 p.m.! I'd had a long day, a lengthy evening visit with the prince, and I was tired. Moreover, I was hungry and I'd been told in advance that dinner would not be served until about 1:30 a.m. I quickly dictated notes about my meeting with the Prince, ate an apple, donned a pink and silver evening dress (high neck, long sleeves and full-length skirt), and prepared to attend a Saudi couple's engagement party. I had been told this was going to be a very big extravaganza. It lived up to the advanced billing.

Saudi engagements and weddings are extremely lavish affairs. The engagement party was held in a large building designed to look like an old fortress. It was purely a functions facility, but the fact that such a large edifice was built indicates there is a market for such a facility. I've since learned many new "wedding halls" have been built since my visit to accommodate the local customs.The rental fee I was told was astronomical, and once inside, I could certainly see why. The entryway was at least 100 feet long, covered with Persian carpets, with a fountain in the center. Beautiful crystal chandeliers hung overhead. I was greeted at the door by my hostess and introduced to her family. She then led me into a hall the size of two basketball courts. A waterfall at the end of the room served as a "room divider." The women were on one side of the waterfall and the men were having their party on the other side. There were rows of chairs and sofas, auditorium style, with a dance floor at the front and an elevated stage beyond that. Some 300-400 ladies were seated in these rows dressed in the most dazzling array of evening gowns I had ever seen. One looked very much like the dress worn by Deborah Kerr when she danced with Yul Brynner in the film *The King and I*. It was, in some ways, a step back in time to an era when ball gowns, hoop skirts, petticoats, sequins, lace, ruffles, chiffon, silk, and taffeta reigned supreme in the Western world. An all-woman band of six musicians played and sang while ladies, young girls, and even children got up and down from their seats and danced to the Arabic music. The dancing was a graceful, rhythmic moving of the feet in keeping with the beat, although one number elicited some swift, jerking head movements and the tossing of the hair. I was told that these events sometimes feature bellydancers, but none were performing that night. Later my hostess told me this was Medina-style dancing, as the family was from Medina.

We sat and watched the dancing, listened to the music, nibbled on sweets, and drank sweet mint tea and Arabic coffee—for three hours! I was getting very tired and very hungry when at 1:30 a.m. the future groom came into the room seated on a chair which was affixed to a pole-stabilized carpet and carried by four men. He was taken to the front of the room where he joined his future bride. The couple sat on two large chairs on a raised dais facing their guests like a king and queen receiving their subjects. Those women who were not family members veiled themselves when the future groom entered the room. I did not put on a veil, not even having one with me.Rose petals were tossed at the young couple and many pictures were taken.

Finally, at 2 a.m. we were served dinner! We crossed a large foyer into another room where a lavish hall was filled with several buffet tables as well as tables arranged for seated dining. There was roast leg of lamb, whole turkeys, plates of salads, stuffed grape leaves, and a host of other goodies I couldn't identify, but enjoyed! By this time, I was starving, and so it seemed was everyone else because in no time at all, the food tables were reduced to scraps. Having devoured the entrees, everyone turned to the heavily laden dessert tables.These people really know how to party, I thought! It was a magnificent experience, and I was pleased to have been invited.

If something more occurred after 3 a.m., I didn't see it. By that time, I was quite ready to call it a day! My hostess called to her husband, who was celebrating elsewhere with the men, and he drove me back to the hotel. The drive back was interesting. He took his young daughter with us and asked me to sit in back with her and scooch down in the seat. In Saudi Arabia, it's not proper for a man to be out with a woman who is not a member of his family at 3 o'clock in the morning. He was very worried about being stopped by the religious police. I scooched and snuggled up close to his daughter. When I arrived at the hotel, the lobby was empty. I felt like a teenager creeping in after hours. Regardless of the hour, I immediately recorded the evening's events in my diary, and at 4:30 a.m. when I finally went to bed, the morning prayers were already being called from the nearby mosque.

Later that same morning, I flew from Riyadh to Dhahran where I stayed with the family of the Saudi student with whom I had worked in Boston. Saud and his wife, Nurten, had two little girls, ages 5 and 2 months.Saud met me at the airport in full Saudi regalia—Kufiyah, thobe, and a gold-trimmed robe or cloak as the Saudis call them. I didn't recognize him! I had only previously seen him in Western wear in Boston. A tall, handsome young man, he cut quite a dashing figure. (Think Omar Sharif in a Saudi robe). These robes can cost anywhere from $1,000 to $5,000 US dollars!

Saud worked for PETROMIN, the national Saudi Oil Company, and he lived in a company compound in Al Khobar, a suburb of Dhahran. His family had a three-level villa with access to the compound's recreational facilities including tennis courts and a swimming pool.

That evening, again dressed in my silver and pink gown, I attended a catered dinner in my honor which Saud hosted. The invitees included quite a number of local dignitaries, including the vice president of FLUOR ARABIA, one of my corporate sponsors. When the guests had all left about 1 a.m., Saud, Nurten, and I took a walk through the compound. The cool night air was relaxing, and it was good to enjoy a bit of peace and quiet. I'd done a lot of talking since I had arrived in the country, and it was nice to just relax with friends.

I spent the next four days meeting with ARAMCO and FLUOR officials. ARAMCO had its beginning on May 29, 1933 via an agreement signed with the Saudi government and the Standard Oil Company of California. Among the terms of the agreement was the stipulation that the company was to hire Saudi nationals exclusively, if they were qualified and available. From my own book I quote:

"Some Saudis were recruited initially as guides, desert drivers, camp assistants, etc., but the first instance of 'formal training' of Saudis appeared to have centered around the drilling of Dammam No. 1 in 1935. Reportedly this training involved a 'combination of gesture, grunt, shouting and an occasional indispensable word' by an American wildcat crew. *'Down'* was where the oil was, they hoped, and *'Down'* was the direction they were to drill. The Americans knew only the Arabic word for *'Up.'* The grunt, shout and point method of on-the-job training continued for the next five years as the labor force was basically illiterate. In May, 1940, the first company-operated school was created for Saudi employees. If the company was to have a literate and at least semi-skilled workforce, they were going to have to educate and train its own."

ARAMCO went on to build not only elementary and intermediate schools for boys, but in 1953 they signed an agreement with the Saudi government to build schools for girls as well. This was a radical departure from Saudi government educational policies at that time. This was the story I had come to Dhahran to learn and to write about—an American multinational company deeply involved in the business of education. It was a story that had never been told, and as it happened, the year of my visit, 1983, marked the 50th anniversary of the 1933 accord. ARAMCO was delighted to host my research and dug deeply into their archives to come up with reports and working papers to assist me.

From ARAMCO I went on to the offices of the FLUOR Company, a large American multinational construction firm operating in Dhahran and throughout the Kingdom. One day, in between my appointments at FLUOR, I got my ears pinned to the wall by a Saudi woman with a PhD thesis on"The Economic Development in Saudi Arabia and Its Impact on Saudi Women." She was, in fact, the same woman whose master's thesis I had quoted in the first edition of my book.She greeted me by telling me the Manpower Council had advised her of my trip and my mission and she was "fed up with researchers coming over to Saudi Arabia to use the Kingdom as their laboratory and Saudi women as their guinea pigs!"She then pointed to a stack of correspondence on her table from "do-gooders" who wanted to research the poor, down-trodden Saudi female. It was a great way to start an interview!

For the first time I found myself on the defensive and with another woman at that!What, she asked, did I propose to do for her? In time the conversation took a more positive note and we ended up agreeing to share materials and help one another. This meeting provided some valuable insight into the thinking of Saudi women, many of whom resent the solicitous attitude of Westerners regarding the Saudi woman's lifestyle.

I left Dhahran with stacks of materials and copious notes returning to Riyadh where the Hyatt Hotel staff welcomed me home and asked numerous questions about my visit to Dhahran.My single-woman-roving-around-the-Kingdom status continued to be of great interest to them! One of the new chapters I wanted to include in my new book concerned Saudi women, but the Manpower Council was encountering great difficulty in setting up appointments for me—they didn't have and they didn't know how to get telephone numbers for women! It is a segregated society, both professionally and socially, and women's phone numbers aren't in the White Pages. Previously, while in Riyadh, I made a connection with another member of the Royal family, a princess. I telephoned her, went to her office, and she put her staff to work researching the phone numbers of the women I wished to meet. Her Highness also reviewed and made suggestions for the questionnaire I was developing to distribute to key Saudi professional women. That night with the aid of a typewriter borrowed from the hotel, a pair of manicure scissors, and some scotch tape I'd brought along, I was able to retype, cut, and paste together a second draft of the proposed survey. (Word processing did not yet exist. Cut and paste meant exactly that!)When I finally got to bed about midnight, I was so tired I even managed to sleep through the morning calls to prayer.

The next morning, I visited the Central Riyadh Nursery run by the Ministry of Labor and Social Welfare. What an establishment! The children were from homes broken by death or divorce, and the women staff members all had college degrees in social work, education, nursing, or medicine. Yes, there were many Saudi women who were obtaining such degrees. My next appointment was at the Al 'Nahda Philanthropic Society for Women where I got a non-stop nearly two-hour running commentary by the very bubbly secretary-general about the Society's projects, classes, welfare work, etc.

My third appointment of the day was with two Saudi women who owned a boutique located in a quiet residential area. There was no sign out front, and newspaper advertising and handouts are expensive, but I was told word-of-mouth generates business for them—especially when they have a sale! I found there were many Saudi women entrepreneurs, and the Saudi-American Bank even had a financial investment and consulting service run by women for women. Today, Saudi women own many businesses and participate in many sports and charitable organizations.

Back at my office, I got word that a very special interview I had requested had been granted and the next day I would be meeting with the Saudi Arabian Minister of Petroleum and Minerals. Doesn't sound exciting? That's because you've never laid eyes on Sheik Ahmad Zaki Yamani. I had a horrible crush on him, having seen him frequently on US television. He was a handsome man with eyes that made you melt. Even my husband knew I was "in love" with Sheik Yamani.

When I arrived at his office, I found several men sitting around an outer room awaiting a call for an audience with the Sheik. It's customary when requesting a meeting with a man of his status to wait in an outer room until you are called. He calls in whomever he wants when he wants. From the empty coffee cups I saw strewn around, some had been waiting for quite some time. To their chagrin, I was ushered right in!

Sheik Yamani rose to greet me. He had a brilliant command of the English language and on "Meet the Press" and other such programs back home, he showed he was quite capable of turning a good phrase and adlibbing with great finesse. Ours was a direct question and answer exchange initially, but then he began to offer his thoughts on the limited availability of Saudi manpower and, I might add, he was very outspoken about the Kingdom's need to make better use of its woman power. He seemed in no hurry to end our conversation. When I said that I was a colleague of the man he had hired from my own Northeastern University to head up his new College of Petroleum and Minerals—to be run on the Cooperative Plan of Education Northeastern had made famous—the conversation took off in yet another direction.

I knew I ought not to presume on his hospitality, so after an hour I presented him with a special gift. Knowing of his interest in astrology and what he had termed "scientific astrology", I gave him a small pewter lion figurine hand-crafted by a Massachusetts artist. I then told him we had something in common—we were both leos! It's probably one of the humblest gifts he ever received, but I could tell he liked it. As I had done with all the men I interviewed, I asked if I might take his picture. He agreed, but allowed as how he should first put on his cloak. I left the office with a ton of notes, a real sense of accomplishment, and a photo I would forever cherish! (I was saddened when I read an article in the *Boston Globe* reporting the death of Sheik Yamani in London on February 22, 2021 at the age of 90.)

Needing a bit of a break from my round robin of interviews, the wife of the Hyatt Hotel manager had her driver take us out of the city about 10 miles northwest of Riyadh to a small oasis to see the settlement of Diriyah. The earliest settlements here date back to the 15th century, but it is most famous for its mid-18th century significance. This is the original home of the Saudi royal family. It is also were Iman Mohammad ibn Abdul Wahab established the ultra-conservative Wahabism sect of Islam to which present rulers of Saudi Arabia still subscribe. We walked among the ruins until sunset with the warm desert breeze blowing the irrigated palm trees that surround pools of water.At the time I had never heard of another Saudi who was an adherent to Wahabism, Osama bin Laden. More about that later.

I may have gone to Saudi Arabia to conduct research, but that didn't mean I was going home without going shopping!

Near the end of my three-week visit, I informed my driver that I wanted to go to the Souk, the Bedouin market. He informed me that this was the one place I must cover my hair. I wrapped a scarf around my head and off we went. Bedouin women draped in black burkas sat on the ground in 90-degree heat selling their wares—herbs, spices, powders, incense. The aroma was overwhelming—exacerbated as it was by the temperature!One woman had a heavily painted or tattooed face beneath her veil or nigal as it is termed, which indicated her tribe, I presumed. I was puzzled by the fact that some veils were so sheer you could see right through them and others so dense I couldn't image how a woman could see where she was walking. This was a place I could not take photos, which was a shame as it was a scene from old Araby. I asked my driver, Misfir, to take me to a stall selling Bedouin jewelry. Bedouin jewelry is hand-wrought silver, and much of it is massive. Misfir spoke little English, but we joked as I exaggerated the weight of one of the necklaces and hung my head low, pretending to be worn down by its weight. A laugh came out of the black bag before me. I could not see her, but she could see me and she was enjoying my joke. This was really something. I couldn't see the vendor and my driver couldn't speak English, so how was I to know the price of anything? Being creative, Misfir took out a pen and wrote the price of the necklace in the palm of his hand. But as Arabic writing moves from right to left, I read it as 5 Saudi riyals when in fact it was 50 riyals. I was then expected to barter over the price. Back went my response to my veiled vendor through the communications network of Misfir's hand.

Sensing she had a "live one", the Bedouin woman motioned for me to take a seat. I looked around and saw a bit of old carpeting draped over a box and sat down. I was then served aromatic Arabian coffee in a tiny porcelain cup. I drank the prescribed two servings while the three of us plowed through a large basket of old silver coins and bells. I managed to communicate the fact that I was looking for the oldest coin possible. The coins were from the days of Ibn Saud, the founder of Saudi Arabia, and to these coins had been welded strings of hand-wrought silver bells. A loop attached to the top of the coin would permit a chain or ribbon to be slipped through so the ornament could be hung around one's neck. Finally, Misfir assured me he had found one to his satisfaction. No bartering this time, she was firm on her price, 50 riyals (about $15). The coin was dated 1936, which pleased me immensely as it was the year of my birth.

On to another stall where I found other necklaces that were not so heavy. I really didn't want another necklace, but I found three lovely delicate pieces blending silver threads with colored beads. I bought all three, one being for myself, a second for my mother, and a third for a friend. We were having a wonderful time, and Misfir was thoroughly enjoying being my interpreter and financial intermediary.

Next, I conveyed to Misfir that I wanted a Saudi antique. That took a bit of back and forth in his limited English, but finally he got the message and he led me down a few streets to the stall of an old Bedouin man selling antique copper and brass. Now this I found interesting! I quickly spotted a lovely, blackened-with-age Saudi coffee pot of copper or brass or bronze, I couldn't tell which. It had character with its curved, covered spout and four little birds atop the lid that looked like a cross between a rooster and a roadrunner.

I knew I had to have this, but I also knew that I must first look around a bit and not show my immediate desire for something or the price would go up! Misfir began the bartering, and it went on for quite some time. Finally, he told me 80 riyals was the best he could do ($40). I took it!

I had been in the "touristy" section of the Souk. Wealthy patrons go for the Persian carpets or the gold of which there was a great deal. I knew I couldn't begin to afford a carpet, so we moved on to the gold market. What a sight! The walls of the stalls were covered with gold chains, necklaces, bracelets, and rings. Here potential purchases were weighed and then priced by hand calculators. Bargaining was out. You paid the price of the weight and that was it. I priced a simple bracelet and price it was all I did. Two hundred dollars was not what I had in mind.

I then tried to convey to Misfir the question "Do they sell tie bars?" As Saudi men don't wear neckties, we had to work awhile on this translation.I found two, one of which I felt I could afford, and purchased it for my husband. At that point, I turned my little purse inside out to show Misfir I had no more money. He thought this very funny and seemed delighted that he had helped me spend it all. In fact, I think he had as much fun that day as did I.

I was invited to a simple dinner at the home of my host that night and was pleased to meet his wife and five children. After days of formality with him, it was wonderful to sit and chat in a warm, informal setting. I think he had now decided I was not the problem he initially anticipated. But he did inform me that the Manpower Council wanted a report—before I left—of what I had seen, what information I had obtained, and what I still needed! I had my work cut out for me!

On my final day, I had a second visit with the princess to discuss the potential role of women in the Saudi work force. Then I went to my final meeting with the president of the Civil Service Bureau, a man without whose support throughout the writing of both of my books, I would never have made it to Saudi Arabia. We had a very candid conversation, and he thanked me for my observations and suggestions. Our meeting ended when he informed me that he had to leave for an appointment with the king!

As I stood to leave, he presented me with a very large, beautifully wrapped package. (I had brought him a Boston-made Paul Revere silver bowl.) Once back at the Manpower Council I opened his gift and found an absolutely magnificent, full-length, maroon velvet, fully-lined robe embroidered in gold thread. When I put it on it was a perfect fit! (Someone had to have snooped in my closet to know my size!) When I showed it to my sponsor (to whom I had also given a Paul Revere bowl), he too presented me with a gift—a desert watercolor of a Bedouin and sheep, painted in soft pastel shades of brown, beige, pink, and mauve. It had been handsomely framed in a glass and bronze frame, but how am I going to get this home, I thought. The Hyatt staff took care of that and wrapped it beautifully for my flight home.

When I got to the airport, my suitcases were so overloaded with papers and booklets my luggage was grossly overweight. I was told my excess baggage fee would be $751.72. I didn't have $751.72, so my aide went into rapid discussions with the airline personnel about the fact that I was a guest of the government and I was carrying all the books, reports, papers, and gifts it had given me. They finally gave in and let me go through without any excess baggage charges. I came back to Boston, finished writing my book, and published it three years later.

AUTHOR'S NOTE:

Much has happened within and around Saudi Arabia since my visit. The country's often alleged links with terrorism, 9/11, and the names of Osama bin Laden, and of late, Jamal Khashoggi have tarnished the Kingdom's image in the eyes of many. The media have often reported on the circumstances surrounding the lives of women and their only recently obtained permission to drive a car. I know no one in Saudi Arabia today, or if those I met are still there, they are of my age or older and not a part of today's government. This entire book is a chronicle of my life's experiences, and I had a great one in Saudi Arabia. I'm sure the same kindness I was shown still dwells within most of the Saudi population. I am grateful not only for that kindness but for the respect I was shown as a researcher who happened to be a woman. And speaking of women, I'm pleased to note that the Saudi Arabian Ambassador to the United State is a woman—Princess Reema bint Bandar bin Sultan bin Abdulaziz Al Saud. She holds a bachelor of arts degree in Museum Studies from George Washington University and has been a long-time advocate for women's rights in the kingdom and their participation in the private sector. Her very impressive résumé is proof of the emerging role of Saudi women.

It has been many years since I was in Saudi Arabia, but I have the warmest of memories as I look at my old Polaroid prints—my harem of sheiks, the prince and the princess, me in my gold and velvet robe, and, oh yes, that special photo of the Minister of Petroleum and Minerals!

CHAPTER 5

"Jambo!" The story of a Kenya safari

I CANNOT RECALL a time in my life when I did not love animals and dream of one day going to Africa. As children in Vienna, my husband Alfred and his cousin Lucy read together *Auf Grosstierfang mit Hagenbeck* (Catching Wild Animals with Hagenbeck), the tales of the famous collector and founder of the Hagenbeck Zoo in Hamburg, Germany. They would then invent games in which they too were stalking wild animals in Africa. Fate would bring Alfred and me together, and after nearly twenty-three years of marriage, we were about to fulfill our mutual life-long dreams.

In 1967 my mother gave us an anniversary present, a five-pound book by Jen and Des Bartlett, *Nature's Paradise, Africa*. Her inscription read: "To those who love: Joy and Al. A gift of love on your fourth anniversary, October 19, 1967. May it be the beginning of a wonderful adventure in new lands." Nearly twenty years later we began our plans. They, like a morning sunrise, evolved slowly and then suddenly materialized and we were swept along in a torrent of excitement.

In 1985 I decided that our adventure-loving golden retriever, Diora, should "buy" us two bush vests and matching safari shirts for Christmas! Well, I rationalized, the vests had a wonderful assortment of pockets and, when hiking, we are forever trying to find pockets for film, camera lenses, bird books, etc. When Alfred opened his gift on Christmas Eve, he looked at me with a cocked eyebrow and said, "J.D., are you trying to tell me something?"

Soon thereafter, a powerful motion picture came to our local theater—*Out of Africa*. That night we came home and began reading the safari catalogs I had collected. I don't remember our discussing whether or not we should make the trip, but like the morning's sunrise, it quickly became reality. It would prove to be the first of seven safaris to Kenya, Botswana, South Africa, Malawi, and Zambia. Each trip would be the subject of a diary. This, the first, was undertaken in 1986.

SATURDAY, JUNE 21, 1986: NAIROBI – LAKE BARINGO

Today we left for "the bush", and it was unlike anything we had expected! After many telexes between our tour company, International Expeditions, and East African Ornithological Safaris (now Origins Safaris,) we decided to add on an excursion to Lake Baringo prior to the start of the big safari. I mean, after all, there wasn't anywhere else we would have a chance to see a Mouse-colored Penduline Tit! We also decided that there might not be any other birdbrains on our safari and we'd best get some intensive birding in ahead of time. By this stage of our lives, we had become ardent birders and we were eager to do some intensive birding in Kenya.

A guide had been obtained for us who, we were told, was excellent. He was a British ornithologist and a member of the University of Nairobi faculty. We were afraid he might be a "stuffy Brit" who would look down on two American birders for whom virtually every bird in the *East African Field Guide* was going to be a new species. We needn't have worried. Adrian was a delightful chap. On our first day, we saw 63 species with Adrian calling out the bird and then giving us the plate number in the Field Guide on which we would find the bird's photo! Left to our own devices, we would have spent half our time in the field thumbing through the book trying to identify each species.

We left Nairobi shortly after 9 a.m. intending to arrive at Lake Baringo for lunch, but sightings of a Long-crested Eagle and an

Abyssinian Ground Hornbill delayed our arrival. A Long-crested Eagle isn't as large as our American Bald Eagle, but his crest is quite impressive. As for the Hornbill, well, he's pretty ugly, actually. He's about the size of our Wild Turkey, and like our turkey, he has a red and grey wattle that hangs beneath a large, thick bill. Hornbill breeding habits are rather interesting. The female is plastered up in the nesting hole, essentially imprisoned, with only a narrow slit through which the male feeds her during the incubation of the eggs. We were so taken with the rare Hornbill we almost didn't make it in time for lunch.

After lunch we began to explore the Lake Baringo area. The lake is located in the Great Rift Valley. The Rift is a geological fault which extends all the way from Mozambique to the Jordan River valley in Israel. Mile-high escarpments rise on either side of the enormous valley providing wide variations in the flora and fauna one finds in the area. Lake Baringo is one of three fresh-water lakes and as such is home to crocodiles, the hippopotamus, and many species of birds. This is not an area where lions or leopards roam, so we were free to walk about. Lake Baringo proved to be the last place we would walk to any great extent, as most of the time on safari we were confined to the safety of the vehicles.

Our afternoon excursion attracted an entourage of local children who greeted us with shy smiles and a friendly "Jambo!" (Hello). They followed us through the fields, fascinated with the gunstock on which Alfred's camera was mounted. They wore little clothing, and what they wore was ragged and torn, but they appeared healthy. Subsequently we would learn that such children often run after tourists seeking candy or pens. They cannot afford the luxury of ballpoint pens, but are eager to have them for school. But these children were not begging. They were simply going along for the fun of it. When a half dozen of them joined us, it became a bit awkward, but Adrian's knowledge of Swahili kept them from interfering with Alfred's photography—most of the time! Two of the little boys did know their birds, and one pointed out a rare Verreaux Eagle's nest high on the cliffs above us.

SUNDAY, JUNE 22: LAKE BARINGO

When the heavy clouds and rain subsided, we set out for a walk. For the next three hours, we walked through the most horrible Louisiana-type gumbo mud I have ever seen. The mud clung to my shoes, increasing its volume with every step. It wasn't long before my shoes had mud-rings the size of snowshoes. Then my shoes began to come off my feet, pulling out from under my curled-up toes. I tightened the laces, stopped at every rock to scrape off the mud, but each new step resulted in yet another build-up of mud. Now each step became a laborious effort. Alfred, with his smooth-soled shoes and Adrian in his safari boots were having much less trouble navigating the muck. I quickly saw the wisdom of the bare-footed children following us.

Today's flock of children seemed to know something about the bird life, and they began helping us with our spotting efforts. They didn't know the names of any of the species, but they knew where to look for them.

MONDAY JUNE 23: LAKE BARINGO TO NAIROBI

While en route back to Nairobi, the skies grew very dark, claps of thunder roared, and heavy rain descended on us. About 40 miles outside of Nairobi, I suddenly yelled, "Stop!" Ahead, along the road-side was a herd of about one hundred Common Zebra and easily 200 Thomson's Gazelles—and across the road some thirty Crowned Crane, the spectacular bird one often sees in travel brochures about Africa. This was a sight to be savored.

TUESDAY JUNE 24: NAIROBI NATIONAL PARK

The alarm clock went off at 5:30 a.m. and I thought we must be crazy getting up at this hour. But Adrian had insisted it was important to be at Nairobi National Park when the gates opened at 7 a.m. I was sleepy, but when a rhino dashed across the road in front of our car, I woke up quickly! Adrian had told us there was an advantage to being the first car into the park in the morning and right he was! We even had to awaken the gatekeeper to pay the entrance fee. Soon after entering the park we saw a Common Waterbuck and a small herd of Coke's Hartebeests. As we approached, the Hartebeests kicked up their heels and cavorted about like our western antelope. Two Hippopotamuses and a mongoose completed our mammal sightings on our early morning venture. At the Hippo Pools Nature Trail, Adrian said it was time to take a walk. The idea of getting some exercise was great, but knowing there could be lions had me a bit wary. Adrian assured me they had never lost a tourist here so we struck out into the bush. Our greatest danger proved to be wood ticks that hung to the tips of the grass waiting for mammals to pass by. We took turns taking them off our khaki slacks.

We returned to our Nairobi hotel and during dinner began to get acquainted with the other people with whom we would be on safari. We were prepared for the fact that we might be the only birders and might, therefore, have to confine our birding to morning and evening strolls around the lodge grounds. Birders can drive everyone else to distraction wanting to stop for "every little brown job," and we had no intention of aggravating our travel companions. Fortunately, a young lady from Cleveland's Sea World and a faculty couple from the State University of New York (SUNY) Buffalo were also interested in birds. That was perfect as there were to be five persons assigned to each combi. We dubbed ourselves "the bird brains" and immediately became a bonded quintet. Safari vans, known as combis, can seat from seven to nine people. Our group would have only five in each vehicle. They are usually equipped with sliding glass windows and a roof hatch for game viewing. Sometimes, open Jeeps have seats somewhat elevated in "auditorium" style to give those in the back clear viewing.

WEDNESDAY, JUNE 25: NAIROBI-TSAVO NATIONAL PARK

We began our journey this morning with the "bird watchers" in one combi and the others in the remaining two vehicles. Ten hours later, we arrived at Ngulia Safari Lodge in Tsavo National park. Tsavo, over 8,000 square miles, is Kenya's largest game sanctuary and one of the largest such sanctuaries in the world. It is a beautiful mixture of savannah, woodlands, rocky ridges, and lush springs.

Upon arrival in our room, we looked out on some fifty or more Cape Buffalo at the water hole as well as two warthogs. When I first stepped out onto our veranda, one old buffalo was nearly at eye level no more than fifteen feet away. He raised his head to stare at me. We contemplated one another in silence for several moments; then he slowly lowered his head and resumed his grazing. It was obvious he found me of no great interest.

We dumped our luggage on the floor, quickly washed the dust from our face and hands, and hurried out to the large open-air observation deck. A herd of ten elephants approached the water hole and immediately the buffalo backed off. Elephants don't like to share the water holes with others, and all the other species seemed to know it.

What should have been a lovely night of rest was not, simply because Alfred and I were both up and down all night checking out the grunts and snorts emanating from the darkness. We saw nothing, but our imaginations were in high gear. Hearing without seeing made it even more exciting.

We began our morning game drive once again with the birders in one combi and the others divided into two other combis. Our leader, David (whom we decided was a Robert Redford look-alike), was a native-born Kenyan of British descent.

During the morning we saw Masai Giraffe, hartebeest, zebra, Grant's Gazelle, Thomson's Gazelle, elephant, Dik-dik, Beisa Oryx, and approximately twenty new bird species. Vervet Monkeys gathered up the bread we left for them from our sandwiches. Ostensibly there were only five birders among our party of fifteen. Right? Wrong! At the first sighting of the magnificent Crowned Crane everyone put their cameras into action.

THURSDAY, JUNE 26: TSAVO TO AMBOSELI NATIONAL PARK

A morning drive to the Shitani Lava Flow was interesting, as it was 500 years old, but still devoid of vegetation. We remembered our trip to Iceland where we had seen vegetation coming to life on lava fields much younger. But the amount of rainfall is far less here than in Iceland, hence the difference. As much of the park is without water, Mzima Springs is quite astounding gushing 50 million gallons of clear water daily from the volcanic cinder cones nearby.

A dusty, very dusty drive then ensued as we headed to our lodging at Kilimanjaro Buffalo Lodge in Amboseli National Park. As we approached the lodge, we saw in the distance the snow-capped peak of Mt. Kilimanjaro. One of the rare photos of the two of us got taken that day with Kilimanjaro in the background. It was here that Ernest Hemingway wrote *The Snows of Kilimanjaro*. I bought the book in the gift shop as it seemed an appropriate time to reread a classic.

After dinner David gave a very enlightening lecture on Amboseli, its ecology and history. He also talked about how the Maasai people were over grazing the area, cattle being a sign of wealth. The more cattle you could obtain, the wealthier you were perceived to be. The Maasai's large herds of cattle, sheep, goats, and donkeys have eaten the grasses to stubble denuding the land to little else but red clay and a sage-brush-looking plant. It's a complex problem wrought with native tradition and modern-day politics, but it is the land that suffers as well as the great game herds it struggles to support.

FRIDAY, JUNE 27: AMBOSELI NATIONAL PARK

This was only the third day of our 22-day safari, but it was so memorable I didn't know how things could get any better. We arose to a clear blue sky with the peak of Kilimanjaro glistening in the sunlight. Although the mountain actually sits in Tanzania, it dominates the entire surroundings with its elevation of 19,340 feet. Our lodge stood at 4,300 feet meaning that we would looking at a 15,000-foot rise—straight up.

On the road at 8 a.m. and we soon encountered a stately giraffe, beautifully outlined against a backdrop of Kilimanjaro. A little further down the road, a herd of zebra and wildebeest were likewise positioned. Next came the elephants, those majestic creatures that seem the very essence of all that is Africa. Elephants, we have observed, walk very quietly, perhaps because they walk on their toes. It is quite possible to be among them and barely hear their movements. That's not to say they can't tear down trees and trumpet loudly, but they can move almost noiselessly in spite of their enormous size.

We crossed a terrain that was incredibly bleak—a salt flat created by the drying up of vast portions of Lake Amboseli. In the midst of this barren dustbowl, we came upon a swamp so filled with elephants, wildebeests, gazelles, zebra and Cape Buffalo that Alfred, in retrospect, said it was his most memorable moment of the entire safari.

People always ask, "What did you do about rest rooms out there in the bush?" The procedure was simple: boys to the right of the vehicles and girls to the left and no peeking behind the bushes! When there were no bushes, or when lions could be lurking in tall grass, we learned to hold your water until the driver could find an open spot with an unrestricted view. Then you made a mad dash behind the van, ladies first. If there were two combis, they turned and faced each other, and the occupants retreated to the rear of both. The system worked perfectly.

When lunchtime arrived, we discovered how magnificent a "Bush Box Lunch" could be. The Kilimanjaro Lodge had packed us cold chicken, cheese, salami, tomatoes, potato chips, banana bread, watermelon, bananas, and soft drinks. After lunch Alfred and I took a stroll to the observation hut on a nearby hill. We needed to digest—not just the food but all that we had seen.

I mentioned the word "digest" as there were often times when each of us privately went off by ourselves to come to terms with the grandeur of what we were observing. At other times we talked among ourselves about how privileged we were to be seeing some of the true wonders of the world. Everyone in the group felt grateful that we had come while it was still possible to see great herds of animals roaming free. You can never feel the same about an elephant, for example, once you have seen it moving about in the wild. It can never again be a circus performer or a zoo specimen in the eyes of one who has seen it living free. The experience does not leave you as it found you, and, I think, you come away a richer human being.

We began the late afternoon game drive in search of lion and soon found a pride of five some distance off the road. We knew park rules required drivers to stay on the roads. The terrain is fragile in a dustbowl, and tires quickly destroy sparse vegetation. But it seems there are some who don't care about such concerns.

As we were admiring the lions from a distance, other vehicles pulled up, saw the lions, and headed right up alongside, the dust flying in their wake. The scene was ugly—German and French tourists shouting loudly and a dozen combis racing across the land. And there the lions lay in the midst of the dust, noise, and chaos.

Some tourists, our guide told us, will press large bills into the hands of the drivers to break the law. We took down license plate numbers to record the offenders. This was *not* the Africa we came to see. Combis were everywhere; dust clouds and dust devils blew across the landscape.Shortly thereafter, another cluster of combis had gathered around a stump. As we pulled past, we saw a bewildered Bat-eared Fox looking out at the horde of vehicles that had surrounded it. Back on the road we saw a dead cobra. Some driver had very obviously gone off the road just to run over it. The dead snake lay there with tire tracks across its neck. Everyone in our group was silent. Why, we asked one another, did such ugly behavior have to come to a tranquil place like this?

At this point, David shook his head in dismay and turned off on secondary roads to get away from the other vehicles. Suddenly the terrain changed and we were in brush and deep grass. "We're going off by ourselves to look for rhino," he said quietly. In the mid 1970s, he explained, there were 20,000 Rhino in Kenya. At the time of our visit there were only 350 left. Poachers had killed them for the high price their horns would bring. In places like South Yemen, a rhino-horn dagger could bring as much as $15,000. (By 2021 conservation efforts have brought the population back to about 800, but they remain threatened by poachers as we were later to see.)

Then suddenly, there they were—a rhino cow and her calf! And we had them all to ourselves. Slowly, silently, we edged toward them. We stopped about seventy-five feet away. The cow started toward us. Would she charge us to protect her calf? We all remained silent. No one spoke. No one moved but for the occasional motion of a finger pressing a camera trigger. We froze as she came close. She stopped, lifted her head to smell us. She looked hard at us, no doubt straining her notoriously poor eyesight to take us in. After what seemed a very long time but was probably only seconds, she accepted our presence and turned back to rejoin her calf.The one-ton Mama gently "kissed" her calf, lovingly reassuring it that all was well. Tears welled up in my eyes. Alfred reached over and squeezed my hand tightly. This was a moment never to be forgotten. Quietly, David our guide said, "We're going home now." Silently we all nodded in agreement.

Later that afternoon, Alfred returned from a short birding walk inquiring if I had had a good rest. He knows I'm not good at taking rests and he was really asking,"What have you been up to?" In fact, I had gone to the observation post where the previous night we had seen several nocturnal species. I found a Rock Hyrax sunning itself, and I spent the next hour photographing his every move. It's hard to look at this little "rock rabbit" and realize this little fellow is one of the closest living relatives of the elephant!

While enjoying my private moments with the hyrax, a handsome German gentleman, who seemed very much at home in these surroundings, asked how I was enjoying my safari. I waxed poetic about the quality experiences we were enjoying. But then I told him about the ugly incident the day before when several combi drivers had left the road to tear across the park in order to get close to the pride of lions. Recalling the incident, I let my anger flow about such behavior. He agreed that the action was wrong, but said the drivers were fiercely competitive and working for good tips from satisfied customers. I let go another tirade about the preservations of the park for future generations and the error of harassing animals and destroying the terrain for the gratification of the moment. Imagine my surprise when, later that evening, I learned that I had been lecturing the owner of the African Safari Club whose drivers and guests had been the very same offenders that so angered us! Well, good, I reasoned. Let him hear what some other tourists think of that kind of conduct! David had told him of our displeasure, but somehow, I think my spontaneous "lecture" from a paying customer may have had a greater impact. At least I hope so.

Dinner was lively, as usual, with much good humor and storytelling. As our group was in three different vehicles, there were always many "what did you see today" exchanges. Dennis, our North Carolina SWAT team policeman, had us all laughing hard when, in his Southern drawl, he said, "This animal watching business is a lot like an early morning police stake-out!"

The writing of a diary while on the road is not easy what with early mornings and late evenings. This particular evening, I felt the need to write extensively while my memories were fresh. I retreated to a distant part of the lounge and began to write.

After a while, Alfred brought me a cup of coffee and asked, "How's it going?" Seeing that I had stopped writing, David came over and said something I will never forget. "The emotion you showed today," he said, "and the obvious appreciation you have for the wildlife, gave me the greatest enjoyment I've had on safari for more than a year." Safari guides meet all types, I guess, and it matters deeply when they have guests who really care.

SUNDAY, JUNE 29 AMBOSELI NATIONAL PARK
BACK TO NAIROBI

As we retraced our steps back to Nairobi, I realized I had written nothing about the geography of Kenya. It has been said that Kenya is a country about the size of Texas with the topography of Colorado. That's true in part, but it doesn't look anything at all like Colorado. Our first two parks, Tsavo and Amboseli, were located along the Tanzanian border, south-southeast of Nairobi. The remaining areas we were to visit lay west and north of Nairobi. If one wanted to make time, the best route was to go back to Nairobi and head west on a major highway.But we had three hours of dirt road to traverse before we reached the main highway. At one point today I photographed the road—25 miles of dirt road lay before us—straight as an arrow.When at last we reached our hotel, I washed the red Amboseli dust from my hair and watched the red clay swirl its way down the shower drain.

MONDAY, JUNE 30: NAIROBI – MAASAI MARA
GAME RESERVE

It is 10:30 p.m. as I write this and we are in the bush, in a tent, three feet from the Mara River bank, and the game trail is right outside our tent door.

We left Nairobi about 9 a.m. and traveled for about two hours on asphalt roads, crossing the Great Rift Valley. Then the pavement ended and once again, we were back on bumpy dirt roads. There were times my fanny bounced out of the seat so often I felt like a tossed salad in the making.

We had a picnic lunch, sitting on the ground, for lack of any logs or rocks, while five Maasi children stood some distance off observing us. Dennis's wife, Mary, a school teacher, decided we should all stretch our legs by engaging in some Jane Fonda workout exercises. I'm sure those Maasi children thought we had some very weird dances or post-dining traditions!

We continued on our way and mid-afternoon began to cross a high plateau. Soon large herds of animals came into view including a new species, the Topi, an exceptionally beautiful member of the antelope family. The wildebeests came next, then the zebra and the gazelles. This Kenyan extension of Tanzania's famed Serengeti Plain is the richest game park in all of Kenya. The reserve covers 700 square miles and is home to the "Big Five"—lion, leopard, buffalo, elephant, and rhino. It is also, of course, the place where we hoped we might be lucky enough to catch a glimpse if the annual wildebeest migration out of the dry Serengeti and into the rich grasslands of the Mara.

I haven't adequately described our ubiquitous travel companion—the dust. It is red and it is everywhere. Every day it is on our clothes, in our hair, and all over the cameras and binoculars. We try to protect the latter two by carrying them in plastic bags, removing them only to take photos. The combi drivers always stop when someone needs to change film; nevertheless, every night we must carefully wipe the equipment clean. And every day it gets dirty again.

The Mara River Camp was owned at the time by East African Ornithological Safaris, our tour host. Alfred and I have done a great deal of camping, but this camp is unlike anything we've seen before. Our tent, approximately 10 feet by 12 feet, is completely covered by a picturesque thatch-peaked roof. We have an elevated wooden platform with steps leading to our "front porch". Two chairs invitingly provide seats for game viewing. Inside, the tent is equipped with two twin beds, a night table, electric lights, and two comfortable deck chairs. And the bathroom is only a zipper away. A permanently attached bathroom behind the zippered canvas features a flush toilet, a modern sink with running water, a full shower, and a large dressing area. This is luxurious camping!

As we prepared for bed, we listened to the hippos snorting in the river just a few feet away. A generous pile of droppings right outside our door made it obvious that they don't always stay in the river. This was corroborated when an armed guard escorted us to our tent after dinner and advised us to stay put until dawn. But no hippo came near, and eventually we drifted off to sleep. Lest you think we were unduly alarmed, be advised that more people are killed by hippos than any other animal in Kenya. It isn't that they are so vicious; it's just that they see poorly, panic easily, and stampede readily. It's curtains if you happen to get in the way.

TUESDAY, JULY 1, MAASAI MARA GAME RESERVE

I suppose we'd be emotionally saturated if every day was absolutely spectacular, so I guess today served its purpose. It was a downer. Our morning game drive resulted in the people in two of our vehicles getting close-up shots of a leopard up in a tree. By the time we got there, however, the leopard came down almost immediately out of the tree and disappeared into the bush. Photos of leopards are not easy to come by, and when Alfred tried to get off a shot, someone's head seemed to always be in the way. Later that day, one of the combis went back and found the leopard had killed and hauled a Thomson's Gazelle up into the tree. We missed that photo opportunity too.

The one saving grace of the day was finding a young male lion lying alone under a tree. I have a real thing about lions, so I waited and waited until finally the lion turned his head and looked at me. He gave a big sigh as if to say, "Are you through now?" and yes, I was, but I had wanted that head-on shot. You always want to get the animal's eyes in your photo. It turned out to be my most favorite shot of the entire trip. Amazingly, when we got home, we discovered that Alfred had, in fact, gotten eight quick shots off of the leopard, and one of them was his best photo on the trip as well. All's well that ends well.

WEDNESDAY, JULY 2, MAASAI MARA GAME RESERVE

When we were first looking at safari company literature, we spent considerable time trying to decide where we wanted to go. Both Kenya and Tanzania looked inviting. Tanzania offered such wonderful attractions as the Olduvai Gorge and Ngorongoro Crater, both noted for spectacular game areas. Tanzania also hosts the world-famous Serengeti Plains, home to hundreds of thousands of wildebeest, zebra, gazelles, and other plains animals. The Serengeti gets dry in their winter months (our summer) however, and the vast herds migrate north into the northern extension of the plains, Kenya's Maasai Mara. Television documentaries on the migration show spectacular scenes of the wildebeest, especially as they mass along the crocodile-infested riverbanks waiting to make the plunge—a plunge that ends in death for many.

With this as a background, we were ecstatic when David told us there were reports that the migration was three weeks early and heading north into the Mara! The grasses of the Serengeti apparently had turned brown early this year and some1.5 million wildebeest and a half-million zebra were on their way into the Mara.

We set off early in the morning in hopes of finding the herds. When we found them, it proved to be a sight we will never forget. We never saw them crossing the Mara River, but what we saw was an awesome spectacle—thousands upon thousands of wildebeest as far as the eye could see. If you can imagine being in the midst of a thousand Texas cattle drives, just maybe you get some idea of the magnitude of the migration. But there is no way to describe the noise! For nearly an hour we sat in the midst of the milling herds, watching, listening, and marveling at the sight.

We have decided the wildebeest, otherwise known as gnus, are the clowns of the plains; their motto seems to be "If you can run, don't walk and always chase any intruder who crosses your path." The result is a constant galloping about going nowhere in particular with cow-pony chases at break-neck speed by one bull after another.

Then the roles reverse and he who was being chased turns and become the chaser. Make sense? No, well it doesn't when you watch them either. On one occasion, a wildebeest pranced by us with the flashy high steps of a Lipizzaner horse performing in the Vienna Spanish Riding School. We applauded the performance. "Oh," he seemed to say, "you liked that?" Back he came in the opposite direction with the same dancing steps. We applauded. He reversed his direction and pranced by for a third time. This continued for six "performances." He appeared to be playing to his audience.

A small pride of lions, together with their recent zebra kill, consumed our attention for quite some time, but when we prepared to leave, we found we were stuck. The combi was hung up on a rock and the lions were only a few feet away.

Now what? At this point we learned something of the laws of the Mara. Other combis were in the area, also observing the lions, and when they saw our predicament, they swung into action. Two combis came around and formed a wedge between our vehicle and the lions. A third combi pulled up behind us and the driver attached a tow line.

It was fascinating watching the reaction of the lions. The presence of our four combis, and some twenty people therein, didn't seem to faze them. They had feasted on the zebra, their bellies were full, and they were very sleepy—until David and another driver got out of their vehicles. Instantly the lions were alert. Their eyes followed the men's every movement. Those once sleepy eyes came alive with interest. Lions can move with amazing speed, and these drivers knew it!

After the tow was attached, David rocked our combi back and forth and eventually worked us free. The wedge of combis remained in place while the tow line was retrieved and all drivers were safely back in their vans. A short time later we came upon another combi with a flat tire. This time our three vehicles stood guard until the tire had been changed.

THURSDAY, JULY 3: MAASAI MARA GAME RESERVE – LAKE NAIVASHA

"Did you know there was a hippo grazing right outside Dennis and Mary's tent last night?" someone asked. No, we hadn't heard a thing. Dennis came over to tell us the story. "We were awakened by something tearing up the grass. I looked outside the tent and saw a Mack truck parked alongside the tent and it was eating grass," Dennis enthusiastically explained. "It must have come up out of the river right by your tent," he added. How could we have slept through the march of a hippo six feet from our beds! Maybe hippos walk on their toes as elephants do, but evidently their "table manners" are noisy enough to wake the neighbors!

Today we visited a nearby Maasai village where our guide had negotiated a "group rate" with the village chief that would allow us to photograph the residents. The Maasai were not shy; in fact, they were quite eager to pose for pictures and to sell us their handcrafts. We observed one cultural phenomenon which I'm sure Eastman Kodak never expected to become a by-product of their film. The Maasai deem it fashionable to make holes in their lower ear lobes and to stretch these openings ever wider to accommodate numerous arrays of beads and other adornments. Kodak film canisters make good "stretchers", and someone in our group gave our guide an entire bag of 35mm film canisters to distribute as he saw fit. Earlier in our trip we had encountered more than one Maasai warrior—men follow this custom too—wearing a Kodak film canister in each ear. (They must be having to recycle them in the current digital age!)

We were invited into one of the cow-dung huts and were surprised to discover it carried no odor and was cool and dry. In summer the dung keeps out the heat, and in the winter, it serves as a good insulator against the cold. The rooms were small, but each served a particular function. There was one room into which young livestock are brought at night to protect them from predators.

Cattle, goats, and sheep are often brought into the village at night. The villages are usually enclosed by dense walls of brush and thickets, called bomas, piled high to keep out predators.

After our visit to the Maasai village, we embarked on a long dusty road and finally at 4 p.m. arrived at Safariland Lodge on the shores of Lake Naivasha. After three nights in tents in the bush, it was great to be in a beautiful lodge with over 100 acres of land-scaped grounds complete with a duck pond, fountains, hedges of bougainvillea, poinsettias, and a host of other flowers.

FRIDAY, JULY 4, LAKE NAIVASHA

It is nearly 8 a.m. and I am still in bed! What luxury! This is an un-programmed morning and we are free to do as we please. This luxury of sitting in bed writing in my diary, when I am fully rested and not subject to a schedule, permits me to reflect on some of the impressions we have been gathering regarding the wildlife we've seen. I've already commented on the wildebeests, but I want to record a few impressions of some of the others.

The little Thomson's Gazelle is a delicate antelope with a tan coat, a white belly, and a black streak along its sides. It also has a short black tail that "wags" continually with the perfect rhythm of a metronome. If you are familiar with the tune "The Syncopated Clock," hum that to yourself at a slightly sped-up tempo, and you've got the pace and precision of a Tommy's tail. We dubbed it the "windshield wiper".

The warthogs must have been the inspiration for the expression "high-tailing it". They are skittish and often run when our vehicles stop. As they run, they stick their long, skinny tails with a tuft of hair at the end, ramrod straight, giving a comical air to their de-parture. (On later trips to Botswana, we were told the locals think their tails look like antennae so they call them "Radio Botswana.") By the way, a group of warthogs is called a sounder—a great word to remember when playing Scrabble!

The giraffe are graceful creatures moving along with a long, lanky gait covering great distances with each step. They look down on you with long, slowly flickering eyelashes that would cost a mint at Macy's.

The elephants operate in family groupings, and the extended family take great interest in their young with all the aunts, sisters, cousins, and grandmothers looking after the infants. The nursing mothers are so gentle as they position their front legs so as to permit their babies to nurse. Elephants, we were told, are the only mammals who have their mammary glands located between their front legs. It's important to read an elephant's body language when on safari, and the guides are very good at this. Mock charges by young bulls trying to show off can be both benign and dangerous. If they are just trying to show off their macho personality, they'll always stop and back up after trumpeting a bit and endeavoring to scare you. But there are times when their inexperience can lead them to actually charge. The guides know how to tell the difference—most of the time—however, we did have one experience on a later safari where the guide read the animal wrong and we had to step on the gas and get out of the territory quickly!

Among the impalas we noted continuous attempts by single males to displace the King of the Harem. The dominant male must keep a constant vigil over his herd of females. Young males, we noted, often gather together in "bachelor's clubs".

And then there are the lions—my very favorite of all. Unless they are getting ready to hunt or looking after their cubs, they appear to do nothing but lie around all day snoozing. But there is such a majesty about them.

JULY 5: LAKE NAKURU NATIONAL PARK

After a scrumptious buffet lunch, we left Safariland to drive a short distance to Lake Nakuru, and our next night's lodging, Lake Nakuru Lodge.

Lake Nakuru is home to 2 million Pink Flamingos. There are reportedly five million worldwide, three million of which live on the soda lakes of the Rift Valley. Lake Nakuru is often referred to as the host of the greatest bird spectacular in the world. These alkaline lakes would be fatal to most other bird species, but the flamingos are able to eat the algae in the lakes without ingesting the lethal liquid. Both the Greater and the Lesser Flamingo live here, although from a distance it's often difficult to tell them apart. Small crustaceans also live on the shallow lake bottom providing food for the Cormorants, White Pelicans, Marabou Storks, and Egyptian Geese. The pelicans feed on the alkaline-tolerant tilapia fish, which were introduced and have flourished in the lake.It was interesting to learn how well the birds had adapted to a seemingly hostile environment.

JULY 6 LAKE NAKURU TO MOUNTAIN LODGE, MOUNT KENYA NATIONAL PARK

We headed off to Mountain Lodge Sunday morning stopping en route at Thomson's Falls where we looked at wood carvings at the shops of talented craftsmen. One couldn't look without buying, so Alfred and I chose lovely Thomson's Gazelle and rhino carvings, both beautifully made.

We then began the long climb into the dense vegetation of the cloud forest of Mt. Kenya National Park arriving in time for lunch at a lovely treetop hotel. The lodge was encased in drifting fog as we toted our cameras and luggage up the muddy path to the main entrance. The rooms were tiny and the bathroom was down the hall, but each room had its own balcony looking down on a large water hole. The water hole view made it a five-star accommodation in our book! The lodge appeared to be built of an assortment of tree trunks strapped together in a rustic but firm manner. The large open-air observation lounge on the second floor gave a great view of the surroundings. We began exploring our new accommodation like a pair of tracking dogs on a scent. We discovered more observation lounges and, beneath the ground, a cement bunker where we came eyeball to eyeball with Giant Forest Hogs. Back upstairs we found between 30-40 Sykes Monkeys making their way from one balcony to another looking for food or objects they found interesting. I watched one monkey slip through the louvered windows of the room next door and come back out with something wrapped in waxed paper. There goes someone's sandwich, thought I! I really understood the warning signs when I saw a teacup go flying off the observation deck followed by a flying saucer!

At Mountain Lodge we were at 7,000 feet, and by late afternoon the damp, foggy air sent us back to our rooms to put on every layer of clothing we could muster. Throughout the afternoon, we alternated our viewing site from the lounges to our room to the underground bunker. What a feeling it was sitting in the bunker and watching an elephant walk by and finding yourself only a few feet from its toes!

Our visit here gave us several wonderful hours of watching animal behavior. Here we learned that there is homosexuality among male elephants, two of which were at the waterhole. These same two young males put on a good show when confronted by an old Cape Buffalo who refused to honor the elephants' desire to keep the water hole to themselves. For more than an hour, we watched the two scheme and bully and make mock charges at the battle-scarred old buffalo. His only reaction was to look up and with a disgusted grunt give the young ones what must have been the buffalo equivalent of "Buzz off,kids." In spite of my anthropomorphic analogy, the frustration of the teenage elephants and the determination of the old veteran buffalo was a wonderful insight into interactions among species.

We also observed some other interesting elephant behavior. When an elephant has an itch, it uses whatever is available to scratch it. One elephant proceeded to a tree stump, turned, and began to slowly rub his rump back and forth until he'd resolved his itch. Once while in the underground bunker, a male elephant got an itch just as he walked past our vantage point. For some reason, the male was displaying a large erection (a male elephant's penis can weigh as much as sixty pounds) so he curled his instrument up to his tummy and proceeded to scratch his itch! I was too dumbfounded to even think of taking a picture of that one!

We spent the next two days in Mount Kenya National Park, hiking and birding and taking advantage of the photo opportunities from the balcony and the bunker. The afternoon yielded an incredible parade of wildlife—several elephants, five Cape Buffalo, eight Giant Forest Hogs, a group of Bush Pigs, two Spotted Hyenas, a large Spotted Genet, a Black-tipped Mongoose, Bushbucks, Sun Squirrels, Hamerkops, African Black Ducks, and Marabou Storks.All we needed was a partridge in a pear tree!

Next it was on to the Samburu Game Reserve, a very different habitat from that of Mountain Lodge.

WEDNESDAY, JULY 9 SAMBURU GAME RESERVE

It's often said good things come in small packages, and the Samburu Reserve and its counterpart across the Uaso Nyiro River, the Isiolo-Buffalo Springs Reserve,prove that true consisting of less than 128 square miles. Nonetheless, there are species here such as the Gerenuk, Grevy's Zebra, Reticulated Giraffe, and the Somali Ostrich which are not readily seen anywhere else in Kenya. It was fascinating watching the gerenuk with their elongated necks standing on their hind legs, their delicate forelegs balanced against the bush on which they were feeding.

At Samburu Lodge we were at an elevation of 2,000 feet, and for the first time I was wearing a sleeveless blouse. It felt good to be free of sweaters and bush vests, and I was pleased we would be staying here three days. We were all struck by the beauty of the Samburu region and the diversity of the terrain. At times, I was reminded of Utah's Zion National Park, and then, a short distance away, we would encounter the uniquely African grassy savannah with flat-topped acacia trees adorned by Weaver Bird nests swinging from the branches. I've not mentioned the large termite nests we have seen along our way, but the Samburu termites get an A+ for creative design. Some mounds look like large sand castles, others like multi-family condominiums and still others like tall chimneys.

On an afternoon game drive, we got word that a leopard had been spotted together with her cubs. She was magnificent, lying on a high rocky ledge playing with her young ones. Three other combis were already on site, and soon there were fifteen! We decided to wait them out and we were rewarded for our patience. After about thirty minutes the other combis left, the sun began to set, and we were alone with the leopards. This was another instance of waiting it out to have quality time with the animals. Patience is so important if one is going to have meaningful experiences on safari. One can't take the "been there, done that" approach as many tourists we saw seemed to be doing.

Here we also met members of the Samburu Tribe, cousins of the Maasai. They too measure their wealth in cattle and maintain ancient tribal traditions including the education of their warriors. The Samburu have less aversion to photography, and we were treated to an afternoon performance of their dances which we were permitted to photograph. The women wore as many as twenty necklaces around their necks which they bobbed in time to their sing-song chants as they danced, dances that centered around various cultural customs. The men had colored their hair with bright red ochre and wore very elaborate hairstyles.

We were sorry not to see the Somali Ostrich, but our guide told us, "Anyone who loves this country and animals as you do will return." Little did he—nor we—know, this trip would prove to be only the first of Alfred's and my seven safaris.

LIKE A POTATO CHIP, ONE IS NOT ENOUGH!

When we returned home, we told everyone we met about our magnificent adventure. We talked about it so much that one day the director of the Northeastern University Alumni Office asked if we'd agree to lead a safari for Northeastern alumni. We enthusiastically agreed to do so, and soon had a group of sixteen university alumni, staff, and personal friends ready and eager to go.

As leaders of this tour, we decided to take the group for three days to Amboseli Park, three days in the Maasai Mara, three days in Samburu Park, and then on to Meru National Park, which Alfred and I had not visited previously.

Our Amboseli visit was highlighted by viewing two young, inexperienced cheetahs stalking and attempting, unsuccessfully, a zebra kill. A zebra kick sent one of the cheetahs flying!

During our approach to the Maasi Mara, we encountered a very muddy and very heavily rutted road in which the lead combi quickly got stuck. Everyone got out to lighten the load, but the van remained a victim of the mud. There was naught to do but push, so our hearty bunch of Yanks put their shoulders to the back of the vehicle. The wheels spun, the mud flew in all directions, but finally, the first van was free. Unfortunately, the second and third vans got stuck as well. As six of our merry band of travelers were already covered in mud, our experienced "pit crew" pushed the other two vehicles through as well. We had some pretty tough-looking "mud puppies" in the wake of all that, but everyone took it with great humor.

The Mara visit highlight was viewing the mating of two lions, a process which occurs about every fifteen minutes for about two days! No wonder the lion is called the King of Beasts!

In Samburu we observed a herd of elephants cross the river and watched for some time as a very tiny baby learned how to crawl up a muddy bank. It took several attempts, but he finally made it.

Our final stop, Meru National Park, is renowned as the home of Joy Adamson, author of the book *Born Free* and her famous lioness, Elsa. Here we found something most unusual—nursing twin giraffes, one of which was an albino! Then it was on to see the Park's five White Rhino protected by armed guards. White Rhino are far more docile than Black Rhino, and I was permitted to walk up and place my hand on the gentle giant's snout. (A week after we returned to Boston, I opened the *Boston Globe* and read of the slaughter of those same five rhino as well as their guards. Murder by poachers!)

When the safari was over, Alfred and I stayed on for another two weeks on our own. With a private driver/guide we spent our time in Buffalo Springs Game Reserve (near Samburu), the Mara, and the Langata Bird Sanctuary in Nairobi. Our highlight was spending an entire day discreetly following a cheetah and her cubs and finally seeing her make a kill to feed her very thin young ones. Cheetah, unlike the lions and leopards, hunt by day, taking advantage of their great speed, but the rush of tourist vehicles has interfered with their hunting, and many of their young die for lack of nourishment.

We returned to Kenya yet again two years later, leading a group of ten on a tented safari. It too had its moments. At one site we saw nearly 1,000 Thomson's Gazelles migrating and silently, from 100 feet away, observed the birth of a baby "Tommy" as they are called. We met Safari Ants up close and personal, and took bucket showers. We topped things off with a stay at the renowned Lewa Downs Sanctuary, then a private home that had just opened three cottages for guests. Today it is a much larger establishment and a prime eco-tourism destination.

Alfred once asked our favorite guide, David, if he ever got tired of going out day after day and he replied, "No, because it's never the same. You never know what you're going to see." Indeed. Perhaps that is why we returned to Africa so many times. After four safaris in Kenya, we went on, in subsequent years, to South Africa, Zambia, Malawi, and multiple times to Botswana.

Why? Because you never know what you're going to see!

CHAPTER 6

Tigers, Trains, Cranes,and Hot Curries

Authors note: *Alfred, my husband is the guest author of this chapter.*

In 1989 Joy received a phone call from the Executive Director of International Expeditions (IE), a travel company with which we'd worked frequently. India was trying to encourage tourism, and IE was trying to market its trips to India. A joint effort followed, and a few of IE's previous tour leaders were being invited to go on a "Fam Trip" to become familiar with India and, hopefully, agree to lead a tour there. One of us was invited to participate. Joy elected me.

Our tour members represented science museums, zoos, museums of natural history, an aquarium, maritime center, and Northeastern University where I am employed.

This trip would turn out to be very different from our previous journeys. First and foremost, Joy and I had always worked as a team, and now I would have to work both cameras myself, keep track of our wildlife observations, maintain a bird check-list, and, for the first time, be the one responsible for keeping a trip diary. I hate to write diaries! Therefore, I carried a tape recorder (remember, this was 1990) into which, each night, I dictated an account of the day's adventures. I hate to dictate.

Upon my return, Joy transcribed my rambling recordings, and a long process of editing ensued. She had to remove my rather infantile commentary reminiscent of "See the cat. The cat is brown. The cat is on the other side of the street." Please bear with me. I promise never to write a diary again! But I hope you enjoy it!

Alfred Viola

TUESDAY, MARCH 27,1990 DELHI

I was awake by 5 a.m., but I waited to go down to breakfast until 7 and then found everyone else was already in the dining room. No one could sleep. At 10 o'clock, our Indian Tour Leader, Pradeep Sankhala, gave us a briefing. He is the son of Kailash Sankhala, the former Director of the Delhi Zoo and the Founder of Project Tiger. This is a young man who has grown up surrounded by animals and he appears to be very knowledgeable.

He began his remarks with a few key points:

- Eighty to ninety percent of the visitors to Indian national parks are Indians.
- The parks get few foreign visitors. Those few who come are serious naturalists. The Indians, much less so.
- Wildlife is coming back into the parks now, and observers have found that most are diurnal. There being few nocturnal species, there are no night safaris.
- There is no walking in any of the national parks. We must stay in the vehicles except at the bird sanctuary where no cars are allowed.
- We will visit the "Golden Triangle"—Delhi, Jaipur, Agra—the most heavily visited centers in India. The rest of the tour will be to areas rarely visited by either Indians or foreigners.
- Photography is unrestricted, but no video cameras are permitted in the Taj Mahal. (One fellow had a camcorder and had to pay heavy fees to take it into the parks as equipment of that sort is considered commercial!)
- The Indian greeting is accomplished by placing one's hands together in front of the chest and saying "Namaste".

On that note we headed off to the Delhi Zoo. It was a once-over-lightly briefing, but I noted a lot of free-flying birdlife and I kept wishing I could hang around and do some photography. Well, it's only the first morning. I guess I'll see a lot of birds later.

We drove through Old Delhi, and it was teeming with people and traffic. It's hard to describe the masses of humanity and the diverse means of transportation. There were rickshaws, motorcycles, bicycles, cars, buses, lorries (trucks), and in the midst of all this chaos, two cows were standing in the middle of the road, quietly chewing their cud. The traffic just moved around them. The cows were the only thing that was quiet. The people seemed to navigate by horn in a pushy, close proximity pattern. And this was a major highway, you have to understand.

At lunch, I had my first taste of Indian curry. A little too spicy for my taste. We toured Delhi, which, like Washington D.C., is a planned city with a long promenade featuring the House of Parliament at one end and the President's House at the other. We visited old Delhi, the "first city" as it is called, which is a ruin somewhere between 800 – 1,200 years old. Then it was on to the site of Mahatma Gandhi's cremation, which is now a shrine. We noted numerous shrines and temples throughout this area. Next on our agenda was a guided visit to the Red Fort, built in 1639 with 70-foot high walls that extend for a total circumference of one and a half miles. As I looked at this massive complex, I couldn't help but think that this was built about the time the Pilgrims landed on our Massachusetts shores and built their simple abodes.

After a brief wash-up at the hotel, we attended a cocktail party at the home of the recent director of the Delhi Zoo. (In India, we were told, one can only hold a specific job for five years and then one must move on.) He and his wife were charming and served a variety of snicky-snacks which were very tasty. We next moved on to an Indian restaurant for dinner. Our guide ordered for us, and the food was hot! Spicy, spicy hot! Even the marinated meat was hot and there were no vegetables, just rice. Afterwards we were offered ice cream or rice pudding. I ordered ice cream to put out the fire!

WEDNESDAY, MARCH 28 DELHI TO JAIPUR

It was a six-hour ride to Jaipur via a two-lane highway with a great deal of traffic. There were motor-driven three-wheel vehicles, camel carts, horse carts, cattle carts, and people carts. The main draft animal was, without a doubt, the camel. I had no idea there were so many camels used for so many different purposes in India. The roadside scenery was diverse. Once we left the populated areas of Delhi, the region became semi-arid and it was very arid by the time we neared Jaipur. Long bridges over dry riverbeds suggest that there are heavily flooded areas during the monsoon season.

We passed through several bazaars (groupings of small shops) and several truck stops with rest areas for the drivers. These rest stops consist of a number of bed frames with a cloth lattice, no mattresses, no blankets, no anything. The drivers rent the bed frames for a set period of time. Nearby there were often deep wells where the drivers could wash up and their bathing was totally public—a sight that surprised some of the women in our tour.

Jaipur had teeming populations in the streets. One has to see this population density to believe it. We arrived at our hotel at 3 o'clock and were told there was a city tour at 4. I begged off in order to go to my room and record my observations. (I'm trying to take this diary-writing business seriously.)

THURSDAY, MARCH 29 JAIPUR

The highlight of the day was a visit to the home of Kailash Sankhala, the founding Director of Project Tiger. He talked at length about the conservation issues in India and what is being done to address them. We were delighted to learn that Kailash would join us for the rest of our tour. He's a fascinating fellow.

Project Tiger was started in 1973 with the banning of all tiger hunts. By the late 1960s, it had become obvious that the tiger was rapidly headed for extinction. Over a period of several years, fifteen tiger reserves were established in various regions of the country. In the ensuring fifteen years, the tiger population has increased dramatically, and other species such as the One-horned Rhinoceros, numerous species of deer, and various plants and invertebrates also have flourished in the newly established reserves.

After dinner I went to the hotel bookstore to get reference materials, i.e. the *Insight Guide to Indian Wildlife*, and the *Book of Indian Birds*. The latter I found better than the birding guide I had brought from the States.

FRIDAY, MARCH 30 JAIPUR TO RANTHAMBHORE

It is now 11 o'clock at night, and I'm sitting on the veranda of the ex-hunting lodge in which we're going to be spending the next three days, about two and one-half miles from the Ranthambore Tiger Preserve.

The day started in Jaipur very, very early. Our first stop was the Palace of the Winds—which didn't impress me—then on to an astrological observatory created in the 18th century to take advantage of the position of the sun during the day to show time precisely in a variety of ways. There were devices for each sign of the zodiac and for astrological observances via the exact location of the sun.

The Amber Fort was the next stop, an enormous 10th century marble and sandstone complex which sits on a hilltop and extends for about two miles. It was built by a maharajah for his twelve queens. At the Amber Fort we had our first elephant ride. We got on the elephants at the bottom of the hill and rode to the top via a series of switch backs. The boarding process was interesting. They have an elevated cement platform which one climbs via a few steps. They then move one standard-sized elephant alongside, and one simply sits down on a wooden platform atop the elephant's back.

A metal pipe is put in front of you as a safety bar. Two people sit on one side, then the elephant very nicely turns around and moves his other side up against the platform while two more people get aboard. At the top of the hill, there is another platform where you reverse the process to disembark. I found photography impossible from the back of an elephant. I don't know how this is going to work when we are riding elephants through a game park later in the trip. (Note: These elephant rides are no longer permitted.)

The Indian government department in charge of this "Fam Trip" obviously wants us to see all facets of Indian culture, even though our focus is natural history, so from the Amber Fort we went to a rug manufacturing area to see how rugs are made. A few members of the group actually bought rugs and had them shipped home.

We made fast tracks after that, and I must commend our driver. There are enormous traffic jams and there always seem to be a herd of goats or sheep or cattle—in the road or crossing the road—and the drivers go along with a blind faith that they're not going to hit anything. I asked what happens if the bus does hit something, and I was told, "Oh, they do a lot of damage to the cars so the drivers don't want to hit anything." And so, we maneuvered our way through and around the livestock. The drivers have no fear of getting close to other cars either. There have been many times when I'm sure we had no more than six inches of clearance between our bus and another vehicle. Boston driving will seem tame when I get back home!

A dusty, bumpy road led to Ranthambhore National Park and Tiger Preserve and the lodge within. The park is the former hunting grounds of the Maharaja of Jaipur. It's hard to judge the size of the park, because it sits on the downslope of an escarpment with a valley between the escarpment and a rise on the opposite side. The valley, or fold as it's called, is what is apparently of interest to the tigers. The area gets very little rain, only about 20 inches a year, but there are permanent waterholes which are, of course, what attract the wildlife. Although the vegetation is rather sparse, it sustains large herds of deer, and that, in turn, attracts the tigers. There is a gate with a small parking lot, the importance of which we would learn later.

When we reached Tiger Moon Lodge, no one unpacked. We all just grabbed our cameras and went directly to the small Jeeps awaiting us. I lucked out as I was in a Jeep with both Pradeep and his father, Kailash, as well as Pradeep's eight-year-old son.

The preserve is very impressive and has an abundance of wildlife. We had been inside the preserve less than ten minutes when we spotted a tiger. It was walking away from us so Pradeep turned the Jeep around only to be surrounded by other Jeeps—just like our experiences in Kenya. When asked why he had stopped, Pradeep said, "Well he may be headed to the waterhole, and if so, he might cross somewhere around here." Just at that moment, the tiger appeared out of the woods, walked towards our Jeep and across the road about six feet in front of us! What a magnificent sight. He appeared to be the size of the large male lions we saw in Kenya—about 500 pounds. Seeing him within six feet and within ten minutes was an impressive start to our day.

We saw a large herd of Chital Deer before arriving at a waterhole that had an abundance of waterfowl: Cormorants; Brahminy Ducks; egrets; Grey, Green, Night, and Purple Herons; White Ibis; Moorhen; Wood Sandpiper; Green-winged Teal; swallows; terns; and a White-necked Stork. What a day!

FRIDAY, MARCH 30RANTHAMBHORE NATIONAL PARK

The day began at 6 a.m., and by 6:30 we were all in the dining room for a cup of coffee and "bickies." By 6:45 we were in the Jeeps and headed to the park in order to get there before the gates opened. First, the animals were most likely to be more active in the cool morning hours, and secondly, and most importantly, only nine vehicles are allowed in the Park at any one time. Come late and you have to sit in the parking lot and wait until someone comes back out. The Jeeps are supposed to stay only 90 minutes. We stayed close to three hours.

This morning we saw Wild Boar and Chital Deer, as well as the larger and impressive Sambar Deer. Two small ponds yielded more bird sightings. Birds are everywhere in the park and around the lodge, but there isn't a great deal of time to do any real concentrated birding as Pradeep keeps wanting to keep the show on the road. Pradeep's focus was on the tigers, and he was looking for a female with two cubs. I guess his focus is to be expected of a son raised by a father who is the Tiger Specialist of India!

After a late breakfast, some of the group left to visit the villages and others went to see the other lodge. This is a "FAM" trip, and part of that obligation is checking out the accommodations.Apparently, we aren't staying at the lodge of choice for some reason, and while it is okay and all the amenities are in place, there are no screens on the windows, the room is hot, and the electricity intermittent, so the ceiling fan worked only some of the time. We left the windows wide open so we soon had a little gecko in the bathroom, but Greg, my roommate, and I decided to leave him alone. He eats mosquitoes!

The food is ample but somewhat starchy and only passable. Given I'll be expected to lead a group from Northeastern University here, I feel it important to mention that accommodations, food, and the means of game drive transportation is not what my previous charges have become accustomed to in Kenya and Australia.

During the afternoon game drive, I was in a Jeep with one of the local driver-guides and he was an excellent birder, so I was able to add several new species to my list, many of which augmented my Birder's "Life List." While I got birds, my colleagues in one of the other Jeeps saw two leopards—a mother and her cub—which is rare, so it was quite a treat for them.

SATURDAY, MARCH 31: RANTHAMBHORE NATIONAL PARK

The same 6 a.m. wake-up call, coffee, and biscuits and we were on our way. Today we were put into a lorry with two rows of bench seats. This had us sitting up higher, the better to see, but it made it difficult to tell the driver to stop when we saw something. Again, we saw a great deal of birdlife, Chital, Sambar, a large Indian Mongoose, and our first Nilgai, a large member of the antelope family.

I'm not an expert on trees—in fact I wish I did know more about them, as there is quite a variety of species ranging from acacias to absolutely gigantic Banyan trees.

Our afternoon game run sparked a tiger jam. Just before the park entrance, we saw two Jeeps pulled to the side of the road where they had just seen a tiger walking. We stopped, other Jeeps that came behind us stopped, and soon there were nine Jeeps trying to maneuver into a viewing spot along a one-lane road. The tiger eventually came into the clearing, but seeing nine Jeeps, she decided the crossing was not to her liking and she turned and walked away from us, disappearing behind some bushes. Fortunately, I managed to get off a few photographs before she disappeared. Although the first viewing had been much closer, today's sighting was in better light.

It took a while to untangle nine Jeeps, but eventually we got underway and entered the park. Today all of the drivers were looking for that leopard with her cub. Two of the Jeep drivers, including mine, gave up and left, and, of course, the one that stayed behind saw the leopard and its cub. Well, we've seen that sort of thing happen in Kenya too. Always a good idea to sit quietly and wait.

That night we had another lecture by our tiger expert, Kailish, on how to obtain an accurate tiger count. This man's expertise is phenomenal. It's been an honor having him with us.

We had breakfast at the Jogi Mahal, a rustic hunting lodge within the park. The large pond alongside the lodge attracted a large number of birds as well as a Mugger Crocodile. I especially enjoyed seeing the Tree-Pie, a species similar to our Magpie but even more colorful.

After breakfast we climbed about 700 feet via several switch backs to reach the ancient fort I mentioned previously. At the entrance we passed through a massive wooden door, the outside of which was covered with large wooden spikes, with those at the lower level blunted. This, it was explained, was to keep the elephants, who might be led by an attacking army, from trying to butt open the massive door, while allowing horses to enter uninjured. The fort was less a fortress and more a fortified city. In its heyday it was populated by 20,000 to 25,000 people. Some in the group entered a Buddhist temple while others explored the shopping stalls of those who dwelled here. A little boy smiled and waved. I smiled and waved back and took his picture. He smiled and waved again. I can't say enough about the warmth and friendliness of the people.

Our days are long, rising at 6 a.m. and extending until dinner around 9 p.m. The evening's entertainment starts around 10 o'clock. Dick, the IE representative, says this is only because it's a "Fam Trip" and the tour leaders cram in every experience possible so that we, as American tour leaders, can pick and choose which activities we might wish to include in the tours we lead. I gather tourists are usually given a three-hour afternoon rest. But I do think it is an Indian custom to dine late, so this is something about which I need to warn my colleagues.

SUNDAY, APRIL 1: RANTHAMBHORE TO KEOLADEO NATIONAL PARK

It is now 9:45 p.m. and I'm in my hotel room in Keoladeo National Park and Bird Sanctuary. It has been another long day and I'm tired. Most of the group is still in the dining room, but I came upstairs to record my diary for the day and get some badly needed sleep. As usual, the day started at 6 a.m., but our morning game drive was unimpressive. Lunch was bad—lots of chopped up pieces of lamb or chicken with the bones included, white rice, a very highly seasoned lentil soup, and a potato dish of some sort. This trip will not be memorable for its food.

We left Ranthambore shortly after this so-called brunch and drove to the train station. This was to be another "experience" for our Fam Trip and it certainly was such! The railway station was mobbed. The train was mobbed. Everyone wanted to be the first to board. As the Indians shoved and pushed, we were swept up in the flow of human traffic onto the train. We had a second-class compartment, a so-called sleeper compartment, which consisted of two bench seats on top of which were twofold-up ledges that served as beds and were intended to sleep four. There were six of us in the compartment, which was actually quite roomy. It was not terribly clean. Many in our group thought it was exciting and even romantic to ride on the train. I'm afraid the romance got lost on me. We looked at all the facilities, including the tourist class where people were jammed in like canned sardines. It was not possible to walk through the tourist car as one would have to step on bodies sitting and lying everywhere. The first-class sleepers we were told were being phased out, but other than having more modern seating and air conditioning, they weren't much better than the second-class compartments.

Soon after leaving the station, we had a mishap. The train hit a man on a bicycle. The brakes came on, the train stopped, people began running alongside the tracks, and the train had to back up almost a half-mile. The man was killed, and the train crew had to wait for proper authorities to come claim the body before the train could continue. In a nation of such dense population, I'm not surprised accidents happen, and, in fact, we've seen many crunched and abandoned cars and trucks along the roads.

We disembarked in the town of Bharatpur, forced our way through the crowded station and out to the street where we were led to a line of horse-drawn rickshaws. The rickshaws were in tough condition, but some of the poor ponies were in even worse shape. After our arrival at the hotel, the zoo contingent of our group went to the local Indian guide and registered a loud protest about the condition of the horses. He was told that any tours these people were likely to bring over would include people who were very sensitive to the care of animals. One group had to even shout at the rickshaw driver to stop beating his horse! I think the guide got the message that Americans won't be party to animal abuse!

After a 40-minute rickshaw ride, we entered Keoladeo Park and Sanctuary. When we arrived at the lodge, we checked in quickly, dumped our gear, took our binoculars and cameras, and went for a bird walk. It was nearing dusk so we knew we didn't have much time. A park ranger came with us to help with species identification. The path we were on was an elevated dike, he explained, and the fields we were viewing would be flooded during the monsoons. I was reminded of Bear River National Wildlife Refuge in Utah, one of my favorite birding sites. Unfortunately, darkness came upon us quickly, and we saw only five new species before we had to head back for dinner.

MONDAY APRIL 2: KEOLADEO NATIONAL PARK

It is now 10:30 p.m. as I try to dictate today's activities. Another long day as we were awakened at 5:30 a.m. We traveled down the road about a mile on rickshaws, and from there we had to hoof it. Our objective was a series of ponds bordered by levees, but most of the ponds were dried up. In addition, the expanding population, we were told, has diverted much of the water for agricultural purposes. The result has been a great reduction in the amount of wildlife in the Park, but that made for interesting bird sightings at the ponds still filled with water. We saw the one Siberian Crane and the one pelican in the park, but then there were hundreds and hundreds of spoonbills, egrets, heron, jacanas, plovers, sandpipers, storks—the whole gamut. A flock of Sarus Cranes flew in and they were spectacular. We walked back to the rickshaw rendezvous site and arrived back at the lodge for breakfast at 11 a.m. I was starving!

That afternoon we were shown two other lodges so we could specify which one we wanted to use when we brought our own tour groups over. One was still under construction, but it is quite close to the park entrance. But to me it had zero character. The other was the Golden Palace, the place where the Maharajah put up his hunting guests. It was a good-sized lodge, and most of the group thought it had real character. I was totally turned off. There are hunting trophies everywhere. Wherever you looked there was some poor tiger's or leopard's head hanging on the wall, and I found it really bothered me. I guess once you've been doing a bit of travel and you've seen these beautiful creatures in the wild, it seems sacrilegious to see their heads hung up as wall décor.I mentioned my feelings to one of my colleagues and was told I simply didn't appreciate the history of the place. No, I guess he's right. I didn't. Beyond that, the place was not clean, the furniture was in disrepair, and a steep staircase led to the upstairs rooms which I knew some people in our travel group would have trouble negotiating. Well, that's why we were being shown three accommodation options.

After lunch we were told we were being taken to a local fair. One of the other fellows wasn't interested, so the two of us opted to hire a rickshaw driver, a very personable young man, who took us to a spot where we could see a Rock Python. And sure enough. There he was sunning himself on a rock—just where a Rock Python should be!

Lunch was not served until 4 o'clock when the bus brought the others back from the fair. Dining is on a very irregular schedule. My stomach is not. I moseyed around the lodge grounds looking for birds and found a Little Green Bee-Eater, Red-whiskered Bulbul, a spectacular Paradise Flycatcher, and a Red-breasted Parakeet. My bird list is really expanding.

That evening Kailash Sankhala gave a lecture on the Indian custom of arranged marriages. He showed us a page from the Delhi Sunday paper where "marriages wanted" were being posted. He went into considerable detail and it was fascinating, especially inasmuch as I've had Indian graduate students who were the products of arranged marriages. Some were good, some not so good. But I guess that's true of all marriages.

TUESDAY APRIL 3, BHARATPUR TO AGRA

Boy, I'm behind on my diary, and this has been quite a day. We had an early morning bird walk before leaving the lodge, a tour of two forts—Fatehpur Sikri, a visit to the Taj Mahal, and a bus ride from Bharatpur to Agra some 35 miles away.

Our two-hour bird walk didn't yield much, so that was disappointing. But the visit to Fatehpur Sikri was outstanding. This is a fortified city built in 1571 of red sandstone by another Maharaja. (There seems to have been a lot them.) Although 25,000 people lived within the city's walls, they lived there for only a few years, after which the water supply ran out and the residents all moved back to Agra. That's why the fort is in such good condition. No one has been around for centuries. It was a magnificent complex complete with a separate series of apartments for the Maharaja's three major queens. Wife No. 1 presented him with a son so she had the most sumptuous quarters. The other quarters were slightly smaller, but I'll tell you, royalty really knew how to live! The splendor is almost unimaginable. Of course, those who served the royals lived in abject poverty. We got into a discussion on this topic after dinner and were comparing those days of yore with today's Indian population where dual living standards are still very prevalent.

When we got our first glimpse of the Taj Mahal, I was astounded. The Taj is difficult to describe it is so magnificent. It is built of white marble inlaid with beautiful semi-precious stones. The Taj was erected by the Shah Jahan in memory of his favorite wife, who died in childbirth while delivering her fourteenth child. She was then just 34 years old. It was constructed by 22,000 artisans and laborers. The interior walls are marble inlaid with 28 types of precious and semi-precious stones including sapphire, jade, jasper, turquoise, and lapis lazuli. When erected, some of the Shah's followers objected to the amount of money being spent on this marble tribute.At this point, his son generated a coup and overthrew his father. The old man spent the last seven years of his life in the Red Fort where he could see the Taj from his window. The actual arrest and imprisonment were carried out by his grandson, we were told. I think today we'd call that a dysfunctional family.

The white marble of the Taj is so bright in the sunlight that it defies photography, so we made two trips to see it, the first in late afternoon and then again the following morning.

There was quite a bit of panhandling going on at both the Red Fort and the Taj, and it got rather obnoxious. We were told not to make eye contact and not to speak as they would then know what language you spoke—and I suppose the price goes up if you're American!

There was a jewelry store in the hotel so that evening I did a bit of shopping for my wife, having seen some nice items that other members of the tour had purchased.

WEDNESDAY, APRIL 4: AGRA TO DELHI

We had a 5:30 wake-up call, a quick cup of tea, and then it was on to the Taj to be there at sunrise. It was really breathtaking to see the Taj materialize out of the first rays of the morning sun. We stayed here for about an hour before returning to the hotel for breakfast. Not having had a chance to talk to my wife for some time, I managed to get a call through. It lasted 21 minutes and cost $121! I guess she'll have to hear about the rest of the trip when I get back home.

That evening we had a critique of the tour, and I voiced my concerns about some aspects that I knew would be difficult for some of my tour group—the train ride, the steps at one hotel, the number of passengers per Jeep. Initially, my comments got brushed aside by the young hotel tour guides, but then Kailash spoke up and said,

"Listen to what he has to say." Their society reveres age and as Kailash said, "with age comes wisdom." I liked that philosophy.

THURSDAY, APRIL 5: NEW DELHI TO KAZIRANGA NATIONAL PARK, ASSAM PROVINCE.

It was a long, long journey to the Forest Lodge at Kaziranga National Park. We had a two-hour flight to Assam, most of which was in heavy clouds. Breakfast consisted of sliced apples that were tasteless and a hot dish with some kind of wrapped Indian goody that was incredibly spicy. There was also a piece of bread that was tough as shoe leather. I had three cups of coffee to drown my sorrows and that was my breakfast. At one point, however, the pilot made a sharp turn and headed north so we could see the Himalayas. They are magnificent!

Upon arrival in Guwahati, the capital of Assam, we were taken to the home of the local manager of Dynamic Tours, our Indian tour company. As she was recently widowed, she was not allowed to leave her home for 40 days, so she graciously welcomed us into her home. The walls were constructed of bamboo that was filled in with a light cement-like material and the roof was corrugated metal. I was reminded of the Asa Wright Nature Centre in Trinidad as the general architectural layout seemed similar. We were served tea and an assortment of baked goodies that were delicious. It's her custom to meet each tour group and escort them to the Lodge, but, of course, custom prohibited her doing so at this time. She gave each of us a gamocha, a welcoming scarf which is a piece of cloth neatly embroidered. It has a number of uses, we were told. It can be tied around the head, used as a scarf, or used to tie a tripod onto the seat on the back of an elephant!

We had a six-hour drive some 150 miles to the Forest Lodge in Kaziranga National Park. Assam is lush and green and seems to have, in general, a higher standard of living. The Brahmaputra River flows through this province and goes into heavy flood during monsoons. The soil is rich, therefore, and is used to grow all manner of fruits and vegetables between the heavy rains.

We made a couple of stops to break up the travel, and at the second one we had a good view of the Brahmaputra flood plain. Then someone spotted a tiger! It was quite some distance off, but with binoculars we could see it was stalking a herd of Hog Deer. While we were watching, a second tiger came into view and then a third. The latter two were cubs, and they were much more interested in play than deer stalking.

Although it was only 7 p.m. when we arrived at the lodge, it was totally dark and we could see little of our surroundings. The lodge was a bit run down, but it was the best available, so no one was complaining. We were just very pleased to be able to visit Assam and Kaziranga.

FRIDAY, APRIL 6: KAZIRANGA NATIONAL PARK

We were awakened at 4 a.m., being told all of India is on one time zone—hence our early morning wake-up call and the fact that it was dark at 7 p.m. last night. Someone turned on a radio at 4 a.m. with Indian rock music—extremely loud. If that didn't get you up, the siren that went off a 4:05 certainly did! At 4:15 someone came down the hall and pounded on each door. That did it. We were all downstairs at 4:30 for tea and bickies. We piled into our bus and a short time later reached our destination in time to see the arrival of the elephants and their handlers, known as mahouts. We were going to go riding atop elephants in search of rhinos! Now how were we going to ride an elephant this time? Well, the elephant very nicely kneels down to let the handlers put the saddle on them and tie it in place at the tail, the front legs and under the neck. The handlers then marched their procession of elephants to another area and we were instructed to follow. There we climbed up about ten feet into an octagonal cement gazebo. There were two protruding platforms, one on each side. We walked onto one and then right onto a seat on the back of the elephant. The elephant is then turned around, and passengers board from the other side. We'd done something similar earlier, but these people really had the system down pat.

Once everyone was on board, the elephants started out into the morning mist. Elephants walk with surprising evenness. We entered a swampy area where, at times, the elephants sank into the ooze up to their knees, but I didn't feel a thing. The big, flat pads of their feet cushion the ride, but I did occasionally hear a "shlurp" suction noise as the elephant's foot came out of the muck. We saw ten or twelve rhinos as we made our way through the elephant grass. This stuff is indescribable. Here we were sitting atop the elephants and in some places the grasses extended up over our heads. It didn't seem to deter the elephants at all, as they just walked right through it.

Suddenly right before us there was a rhino with a calf and a third rhino nearby. One of the adults came towards us, looked us over, and grunted a bit, whereupon the elephant raised her trunk and trumpeted. The rhino immediately decided retreat was the better part of valor. The same thing happened when we came upon a herd of Water Buffalo. One of the buffalo made a mock charge.The elephant raised her trunk and trumpeted, and the buffalo backed up, quite literally with his tail between his legs.

As we proceeded through the grass, we saw several more rhino, including one with a Cattle Egret standing on its back! When photos were wanted, the mahout would stop the elephant to give people on one side the chance to take a picture and then he would turn the elephant around for the sake of the photographers on the other side of the saddle.

We came to a rather flat plain with short grasses and found a mud hole in which no less than three rhino were basking. Next came a couple of Hog Deer, followed by a herd of 20-25 buffalo. There was a great deal of bird life as well.

After about three hours, we returned to the lodge where we were served an excellent breakfast of papaya juice, English porridge with milk and sugar, eggs with an extremely delicious toast—a lot of which was consumed—coffee and tea. This was the best breakfast we'd had on the entire trip.

This afternoon we took a Jeep ride into the park. The Jeeps were in poor condition, and the entire floorboard of the one in which I was riding was loose. I could see the motor housing shaking underneath. Interestingly, we were accompanied by an armed guard here, just in case we had any kind of an animal attack. When we approached a pond, we saw several birds including drongos, doves, egrets, Teal and Purple Heron, quail, and a spectacular Indian Roller. There were also elephants and buffalo in the distance. An elevated treehouse blind enabled us to look out over two ponds where we saw some new species, but no quantities of anything.

As we neared our elephant-ride departure area, we saw a herd of about twenty buffalo accompanied by two anhinga swimming across the entire width of a lake. Apparently, as the buffalo swim they stir up the bottom of the lake and they stir up the fish as well. This makes fishing easier for the anhinga!

When we returned to the lodge, we had an after-dinner lecture by the superintendent of the Park.

SATURDAY APRIL 7: KAZIRANGA NATIONAL PARK

We got to sleep in until 4:30 this morning! Then it was tea, coffee, and peanut butter cookies! This morning's elephant ride wasn't that spectacular, although we did get a better look at the rhino cow and calf. I continue to marvel at the 16 to 18-foot tall elephant grass here. Back to the lodge for breakfast and then out for a bird walk. Here, we were told, it was a leech-infested area. We tucked our pants inside our stockings and sprayed our shoes, ankles, and pants with insect spray.

We entered a dense forest accompanied by Bobby, a new local guide who just received his bachelor's degree in physics and was about to start on his master's degree in solid-state physics. As he grew up here, he earns some extra money working as a guide in the summer. He and I had an interesting conversation about the educational system in India and the US. In addition to Bobby, Kailash was with us, along with our gun-bearing ranger, the bus driver, and his helper—so five people looking after 12 of us. We hadn't gone 20 yards before Kailash pointed out leeches to us. Other than a concern about these inch-worm-like critters, it was a pleasant three-mile-walk. We saw Hoolock Gibbon, considered quite rare, a Capped Langur, Asian Giant Squirrel, and a number of forest-dwelling birds, including a Brown Fish Owl, a Collared Scops Owl, and a Spotted Owlet. At the end of the walk, we entered a tea plantation. It was a bit nerve-wracking walking among the 2 to 3-foot tea shrubs as we were warned about the prevalence of snakes.

Lunch was chopped lamb curry again, rice, and the same vegetable dish we've had every night.

Our afternoon Jeep tour took us to the western portion of the park where we'd not yet visited. Here we saw an Assam Monkey, so we've now seen all three monkey species in the park. We reached the lake and were enjoying the tranquility of the scene, the waterfowl, and an osprey flying overhead, when suddenly along came five Jeeps carrying some potentate and all his aunts, uncles, cousins, and kids. There was also a lorry full of bodyguards and paramilitary personnel. Fortunately, they only stayed about 30 minutes and then we had peace again. Their visit certainly shattered our quiet reverence, however.

When we returned to the hotel, Kailash got the group together for what he termed our "Last Supper." We had a good exchange about the tour and Indian history and culture, about which I have learned a great deal.

In the midst of our discussion, a young man suddenly appeared and motioned to Kailash. It seems there is no telephone communication between the park and Guwahati, and this poor fellow spent six and one-half hours traveling to our lodge to tell us our flight for tomorrow was cancelled! The flight available would be at 9 a.m. the next morning and we needed to be there an hour early. This meant leaving the park at 2:30 a.m. Kailash decided it was too tight a schedule so we would leave at midnight, drive to Guwahati, check into an airport hotel for breakfast and a wash-up, and then leave for the airport. Considering the fact that we'd been up since 4 a.m., this wasn't happy news, but there was nothing to do but make the best of it.

SUNDAY, APRIL 9: KAZIRANGA TO GUWAHATI TO DELHI

Everything went as planned today. We left Kaziranga at midnight, got to Guwahati at 7:30 a.m., shared a couple of rooms so people could freshen up, and had some juice, coffee, and toast at the hotel before departing for the airport.

When we arrived in Delhi, we were given our schedule. We had been traveling for 13 hours and had been up all night. Most of us just said no to the planned activities. We'd worked hard on the "Fam Trip", but we still had a long flight back to the US and we were quite ready to call it quits.

We've seen two widely different ecosystems on this trip. The Delhi area is hot and dry, although Delhi itself has morning fog and mist. Assam has lush green vegetation and deep forests. When the monsoons come and the Bramaputra River floods, the temperatures in Agra and Ranthambhore will hit 120 degrees. Kaziranga National Park closes from the end of April to mid-September as the flood plains fill with water and the animals migrate to higher ground. The Keoladeo Bird Sanctuary is best from January to March. The birding and the wildlife viewing is terrific, but you have to be prepared for some rough travel and accommodations en route. Clearly, it is not yet as developed for tourism as is Kenya.

We have also seen three different historical ages during our tour. The Amber Castle is of an ancient era. Ranthambhore is about 1500-1600. Fatehpur Sikri is in in that same time period, and the

Red Fort and Taj Mahal are of the 1600s. While the country has built many fortified cities, shrines, temples, and monuments as well as modern cities, many people live in poverty and animals roam freely. Cows that no longer give milk are released to the "public welfare." Sanitation is in the dark ages, while VCRs are the current rage. Mechanical maintenance is not a high priority.

The wildlife and the birds are spectacular, and the government does seem to be trying to protect them and their environment. In that regard, the tour lived up to its billing.

Our final lunch in Delhi consisted of, you guessed it, lamb curry, and the meal between London and New York was lamb curry as well. My wife, Joy, was at the airport in Boston to greet me and drive me home. I was very tired, but not too tired to have a wonderful, home-cooked cheeseburger before collapsing into bed. And that is my story of a Fam Trip to India, a land of many contrasts.

Alfred Viola

CHAPTER 7

Love Those Boobies!

"IT WAS THE BEST OF TIMES; *it was the worst of times"*

So wrote Charles Dickens. I know he did not have a Galapagos tour in mind, but his words aptly describe our adventure.

It was the best of times because we have never had such close encounters with mammals, birds, and reptiles that know no fear of man—a phenomenon that permits incredibly close observation and photography.

It was the worst of times because we spent twelve days taking cold showers in brackish water, adapting to the ways of pump toilets, cramming ourselves into narrow bunk beds, adjusting to a small ship that bucked and rolled simultaneously, making do with small meals that always seemed to include fish, and endeavoring to remain cordial in a 12 foot by 12 foot lounge with 18 other people, including three children who thought the lounge was their private playroom.

We have camped, we have hiked, we have traveled on horses that were belly-deep in snow and ridden Zodiacs in the Bering Sea, but we have never experienced anything like our visit to the Galapagos Islands!

FRIDAY, AUGUST 19, 1988: MIAMI TO QUITO, ECUADOR

It is 4:37 a.m. and we have just taken off from Miami International Airport bound for a journey back in time.Our destination is the "Enchanted Isles", the string of volcanic outcroppings six hundred miles off the coast of Ecuador, on which Giant Tortoise, Sea Lions, Marine Iguanas, Fur Seals, Galapagos Penguins, Magnificent Frigatebirds, and Blue-footed Boobies make their home.These are the rocky outcroppings from which Charles Darwin, in 1835, collected and studied specimens which he then discussed in his book, *On the Origin of Species.*

Evolution—the very word conjures up so many images.Before our journey I did some reading on Darwin and on the origins of the Galapagos themselves.I was amazed to learn that Darwin was a 22-year-old medical school drop-out when he set sail on the H.M.S. Beagle to serve a five-year hitch as the ship's scientist. He had no idea that the specimens he gathered on one island would prove different from those collected on another, or that the bills of finches would prove different according to the foods upon which they fed.

Since 1959, the Galapagos archipelago has been a national park, administered by Ecuador. Tourism has expanded greatly in recent decades. At the time of our visit, the number of visitors was restricted to 24,000 per year, and there were only three hotels on the island of Santa Cruz and none on any of the other islands.Today, nearly 300,000 visitors come each year, but fortunately, most tour only the two inhabited islands. Visits to the uninhabited islands are strictly controlled. Many visitors use tour boats as their floating hotels, and many make only three to four day tours. But ours was a twelve-day journey to many islands rarely visited.

There were some attempts in the past to establish settlements on some of the islands. Unfortunately, there were a variety of domestic animals brought in by these early settlers, and when the settlements were abandoned, so were the domestic animals. Since there are virtually no predators on the islands, these feral animals multiplied freely. Some of the islands now harbor substantial populations of donkeys, goats, cats, pigs, rats, etc., which compete with the natural populations for the limited food supply. The tortoises often fared poorly in this competition. In recent times major efforts have been made to control the feral species, some more successfully than others.

Although the Galapagos Islands lie on the equator, the climate is temperate and comfortable, with an average temperature in the 70s (Fahrenheit). The reason for this is the powerful influence of the Humboldt Current, which originates in the Antarctic, parallels the coastline of South America, and then turns west at the equator and the South Equatorial Current which flows through the island archipelago. The Galapagos are located at the confluence of these two currents.As we were to discover, these currents also have a profound effect on the ease of travel between islands. When the ship was moving with the current, the passage was very smooth, but when it was bucking or crossing the current, the passage could be very rough indeed.

Once again, we chose International Expeditions (IE) as our tour company, booking early. Subsequently, the remaining cabins on the twenty-passenger ship were reserved by the Nature Conservancy. This gave us an extra guide, Dr. Bruce Stein, which was most beneficial.

When we arrived in Quito, we immediately became aware of the city's 9,000-foot elevation. One didn't run up the stairs here. One walked slowly, and even then you were likely to find yourself out of breath. Slow and easy were the instructions for the first 24 hours.

SATURDAY, AUGUST 20: QUITO TO OTAVALO

Before heading out to the Galapagos Islands, we were slated to visit the famed Indian Market at Otavalo, north of Quito.We arrived after a three-hour bus ride during which time our guides gave us interesting bits of information about the altitude, the life zones in Ecuador, and the culture of the indigenous people.

There are twelve major languages—not dialects—actual languages spoken in Ecuador.People from many areas migrated into the area in centuries past, worshiping the sun and looking for those sites that appeared to offer the highest elevations in an effort to get closer to their Sun God.Hence the diversity of languages and cultures today.The peasants' manner of dress also reflects diverse origins. Men and women alike wear a fedora-style hat—the color denoting the home region.Both men and women often wear one long braid of hair down the middle of their back, and the men wear woolen ponchos over their white pants.The women dress in richly embroidered peasant blouses, skirts of deep reds, purples, and other bright colors with embroidered edges, and, often, elaborate head dresses are wrapped atop their heads. The people seemed to be quiet and unassuming, and, at the marketplace, even those who begged and the merchants who tried to sell their wares did so in a quiet, gentle manner.

The market was a dazzling array of gaily dressed peasants and brightly colored woolen weavings.The Indian Market is held each Saturday morning, and tourists and natives alike come to buy and observe.Stalls were filled with beautiful woolen goods hanging on display for would-be buyers.Other vendors spread their goods on the ground in a giant "fleamarket" style. In some sections, I felt as though I were walking through an art gallery, viewing the beautiful designs and patterns on display.

SUNDAY, AUGUST 21:OTAVALO TO QUITO

Another early morning departure, this time en route to the 11,000-foot alpine meadows of the Andes.During the night it had snowed on the 16,220-foot peak of the dormant volcano, Mt. Cotacachi, and the snow was sparkling in the sunlight. After about an hour's ride, we reached the meadow, disembarked, and made our way through a herd of grazing cows to a ridge where we could look down into the caldera of an extinct volcano.A lake, known as Lake Cuicocha, filled the caldera, and a small island could be seen in the center. The surrounding meadow was filled with wildflowers. I lost no time in getting out my macro lens and proceeded to belly-flop my way around the meadow taking photos of red, white, yellow, pink, blue, and purple blossoms.Some were of the lupine family; others were of the daisy, clover, figwort, and blueberry families. All were new to me, but not to Bruce, the Nature Conservancy guide.A Ph.D. botanist who specialized in the flora of the region, he rattled off the Latin names of everything I was photographing.He was a real asset to our tour. The meadow, the crater, and the lake are all part of Cotacachi National Park, a reserve financed in part by the World Wildlife Fund.

After lunch there was a bit of native-crafts shopping for those who wanted local souvenirs.Here in the high Andes, the Indians are superb weavers of woolen rugs, sweaters, wall hangings, and other such goods.There are three different styles of weaving, and we were driven to two homes—not shops—where two different weaving techniques were being practiced.At the home of the second weaver we visited, the ancient art of the back-strap loom was practiced.As this is a far more time-consuming type of weaving, the artisan had only a few articles for sale.

Before our departure, Senora Maldonado, the weaver, took us to her kitchen where she proudly pointed to her second "cottage industry"—guinea pigs!Nearly 40 were running around the dirt floor. When she brought in an armful of hay, they squealed their delight and came running out from under their various hiding places.One little baby was no more than four inches long! The Ecuadorian Indians consider guinea pigs a form of table meat, and many people raise them to sell as food.

MONDAY, AUGUST 22:QUITO TO THE GALAPAGOS: BALTRA AND SANTA CRUZ ISLANDS

We began the day with a flight to Guayaquil, where we changed planes and then flew on to the Galapagos.

When we arrived on the Island of Baltra, there were hundreds of tourists milling around, all waiting to go on Galapagos tours.I began to worry about how crowded these "remote" islands were going to be, but felt relieved when I heard that most people would be on short tours, while we were going to have twelve long days of island-hopping!

Our vessel was "intimate"—a 76-foot boat which we shared with eighteen other passengers and seven crew. Once aboard we were shown to our quarters. Our cabin was only about 8 foot by 8 foot square.There were bunk beds with six drawers built into the base of the lower bunk.A five-foot storage box with a lid held our life vests and provided a storage place for small suitcases or duffel bags.We had a private bathroom with sink, toilet, and shower stall, where a cold trickle of water spewed forth sporadically.We had a sliding window in the cabin and in the bathroom, which opened to provide fresh air. The cabin certainly was not spacious, but it was adequate.

The upper deck consisted of four cabins, the bridge (adjacent to our cabin), and an open deck that accommodated two rows of four lounge chairs each. Around the periphery of the deck were a number of benches, inside of which were located some of the tanks containing fresh water for the journey.The main deck consisted of the dining room furnished with four tables for five persons each, the kitchen, a small bar, the purser's cubicle, and a library/lounge consisting of cushioned seats around the periphery with the stairway to the lower level in the middle. There was a small deck at the back of the ship from which a ladder went down to an embarking platform.There one boarded the dinghy for excursions ashore.

The lower level consisted of eight cabins and the crew quarters. These cabins were smaller than ours and did not have window ventilation.We were very glad we were on the upper deck!

The ship's crew consisted of the captain, two sailors, an engineer who doubled as cabin steward, a dining room steward, and two cooks. (Note: International Expeditions uses a much larger, more commodious ship today.)

After a pleasant lunch served on linen and china, we were given a brief lecture by our Galapagos Park Guide, Rodrigo, about the rules of the ship and the Galapagos National Park. When we were told we had about one half-hour to get unpacked, change our clothes, and load our cameras for our first island visit, Santa Cruz, everyone "exploded" out of the dining room and into their cabins to get prepared.

It was a wet landing, meaning that one swung one's legs over the side of the dinghy and waded ashore in ankle-deep water.The dinghy was a Boston whaler, which Alfred assured me was virtually unsinkable.That was comforting, inasmuch as there were no life vests in the dinghy and neither of us can swim!

We landed on a shore of lava rocks where we encountered a black Marine Iguana, posed as though he were the official welcoming party. The Marine Iguana is smaller than we had expected, with few specimens exceeding eighteen inches in length. With their relatively diminutive size, they did not seem to be the ferocious-looking beasts popularized in Japanese science fiction movies.

While we endeavored to dry our feet and put on our sneakers, a Yellow Warbler came running by, scurrying across the sand at water's edge in search of the insects dislodged by our feet.As we walked along the beach, dozens of Magnificent Frigatebirds soared overhead, their great wings slowly beating as they circled and rode the air currents. A short distance from the shore we came upon a lagoon where two Greater Flamingos were feeding.As we walked back to the sandy beach, we stopped to admire a brightly colored Sally Lightfoot Crab, a dazzling crustacean of red, yellow, and blue.

Back to the ship and within a half hour we had sailed to another section of the island where a Mangrove Hammock awaited our exploration. We climbed back into the dinghy and set off for a leisurely cruise into and around the mangrove trees. Our goal, we were told, was to see Green Turtles and sharks!We found both—three large turtles and three Blue-tipped Reef Sharks.As the sun set and the cool evening breeze came up, we returned to the ship, weary, ready for dinner, and ready for an early night of rest!

TUESDAY, AUGUST 23:ESPANOLA ISLAND

What a night! I was up every hour checking the white caps on the water,wondering if I should get out our life vests in anticipation of the ship going down.We are not seasoned sailors, and perhaps more accomplished boatmen would have realized that this was simply a small ship going against a powerful current. But I was scared to death we were going to sink!

We pulled anchor about nine o'clock and traveled all night at what I thought was high speed, although we later learned the ship can only do about 8 to 10 knots. The water was rough. As a result, we pitched forward and back and rolled from side to side endlessly.It was a challenge to climb the ladder to the upper bunk while the ship was dipping and rolling up and down with the waves, but gradually I began to learn how to bounce with the motion of the ship and belly-flop across the top bunk. Once there, however, it was impossible to sleep. We appeared to have both currents hitting us simultaneously. With one we rocked and with the other we rolled.

About 8:30 a.m. we reached the island of Espanola, some 60 miles to the south of Baltra where we had landed the previous day. Breakfast conversations seemed to suggest that we may have had it worse because we were on the top deck and in the bow of the ship, where the pitching motion was at its worst.On the other hand, we had windows that we could open wide and those below had only sealed portholes. It seemed an even trade-off.

After breakfast we boarded the dinghy for a tour along the high cliffs of Espanola Island.In the dinghy we got our first good look at sea lions who playfully swam alongside, seemingly happy to have our company.There also were thousands of birds roosting on the cliffs—Blue-footed Boobies, Swallow-tailed Gulls, and Magnificent Frigatebirds.Audubon's Shearwaters swam in small flocks ahead of our dinghy, scattering as our boat drew near.

Back to the ship for a little quiet time and then the ship moved around the island to a sandy beach where some thirty sea lions were sunning, swimming, and even lazily surfing at the water's edge. They were so wonderfully curious and trusting—with the exception of the big bulls who would occasionally chase us away from their harems—barking loudly in the process.

At 2:30 p.m. we were again scheduled to go ashore on yet another section of the island, but we found three ships already at anchor there.As the bridge is adjacent to our cabin, we could overhear a prolonged and somewhat agitated conversation (in Spanish) over the ship's radio.We didn't understand a word of it, but then we watched as our captain boarded the whaler and was driven over to the other three ships. We surmised that they didn't have clearance to be there because they all skedaddled after his visit.We do know that the National Park Service controls public access to the islands, and I think ships have to "file flight plans" in advance to avoid having too many tourists ashore at any one time.

By 3 p.m. we had the place to ourselves, and we went in, after another wet landing, for a three-hour hike.What a walk!We stepped around snoozing sea lions and Blue-footed Boobies—the latter mating, courting, and rearing young of all ages—often in the middle of the trail!We next encountered Masked Boobies and Waved Albatross, also with young.

It was a difficult hike over lava rock, especially as I had a knee replacement only a few months previously. But I managed to keep up not wanting to miss a thing.

WEDNESDAY, AUGUST 24: FLOREANA ISLAND

We got in three hours of sleep before we set sail for Floreana Island.Then, about midnight, the sideward rolling motion began with such force I sometimes felt as though I were going to fall out of the upper bunk!We were not going against the current, however, so at least we didn't have the up and down motion that characterized our first night. When we awoke, we were quietly anchored off Floreana Island with its volcanic cones rising into the mist.Sea lions were sunning themselves on the beach, and Blue-footed Boobies and frigatebirds soared overhead.

Our morning hike proved to be a botanical expedition.Floreana has more than 50 volcanic cones within its 80 square miles.After greeting the sea lions and Yellow Warblers on the shore, we began our hike inland.I photographed several plants, both indigenous plants native to the Galapagos and endemic species found only in the Galapagos. The Scalesia Villosa were particularly interesting. Often referred to as the Darwin Finches of the plant world, the genera, or family, is indigenous to the islands, but sixteen species have evolved over time and all are endemic.

While I concentrated on photographing the flowers, Alfred spent his time photographing Darwin Finches.The Darwin Finches were a key part of Charles Darwin's theory of evolution. There are thirteen species in the Galapagos. All are grey, brown, or black sparrow-sized birds and similar if not virtually identical in plumage. The bill is key to the identification of each species as their bills have adapted to specific food sources. After a while, we made our way back to the shore and sat among the sea lions while we awaited the arrival of the dinghy. As our crew had been fishing for our lunch, the ship was surrounded by about thirty frigatebirds, circling overhead, looking for food as the crew cleaned the fish and tossed scraps into the sea.

Late afternoon we pulled anchor and headed for the Devil's Crown, a rocky volcanic outcropping off the coast of Floreana. The ominous appearance of the rocks was made all the more striking by the cactus silhouettes that stood out against the sky. With no apparent soil or water, the cacti have sprouted from crevices in the rocks and now march like sentinels across the craggy ridge.

This area was reputed to be especially good for snorkeling, and several members of the group donned masks and flippers to investigate the waters.

Shortly after four o'clock, we set sail to Santa Cruz Island, and by dinner time we were rocking and rolling on the high seas once again!

THURSDAY, AUGUST 25: PORT AYORA, SANTA CRUZ

We had a fascinating morning ashore at the Charles Darwin Research Station on Santa Cruz Island. The Research Station Exhibition Hall had several well-designed displays, photos, and text on the history and development of the islands and the historic impact of man.The Giant Tortoise, for which the islands were named (galapagos is the Spanish word for tortoise), suffered greatly when pirates and sailors of the 19th century filled their ship holds with live tortoises and kept them there for up to a year without food or water.The tortoises survived but were gradually eaten for fresh meat.So many were killed in this manner that some islands became devoid of tortoises altogether.

The Darwin Research Station is raising young tortoises and incubating eggs in order to protect the latter from rats, feral pigs, cats, and dogs—all remnants of man's intrusion on the islands.In one corral, people are permitted to enter and touch the giant beasts.As I sat down, one old boy walked over and was proceeding to pass right on by, until I reached out and gently stroked his forehead.He stopped, slowly turned his head toward me, and arched his neck a bit.I moved my hand down and began to stroke his neck, then caressed his throat.He closed his eyes in ecstasy as I continued to stroke his throat and cheek for a good five minutes.He never moved.When I stopped, he would open his eyes and look at me—much as our golden retriever does when she wants the petting to continue.There was no doubt that the old boy was enjoying his caresses—and so was I!What a thrill to stroke such a gentle giant.

Rodrigo told us a number of interesting facts about the tortoises—how their shells differ in size and shape according to the feeding habits on the particular island from which they come. Those on arid islands, for example, have smaller shells, and the shell is shaped so as to permit the tortoise to raise its head high when trying to reach scarce food supplies.Those in wet areas with dense foliage have larger shells that curve downward all the way around.It was not difficult to understand Darwin's observation that species evolved in structure and appearance according to the food supplies that governed their survival.

The most famous of the Giant Tortoises is Lonesome George, the last of his species, the Pinto Island Tortoise. George was discovered on Pinto Island in 1971, most all of his food supply having been destroyed by some 40,000 feral goats on the island—all descendants of three goats dropped off there in 1959. George was taken to the Darwin Research Station where he lived another 40 years. Several attempts were made to have him mate with females of other species, but none of the matings were successful. (George died in 2012 when it was thought he was over 100 years old. His body was preserved by taxidermists and it is on display at the Darwin Center in an exhibit dedicated exclusively to the life of old George. His species is now extinct.)

Charles Darwin recorded his own encounter with these Giant Tortoises in somewhat less enthusiastic terms. He wrote in 1835:

> *"As I was walking along, I met two large tortoises, each of which must have weighed at least two hundred pounds: one was eating a piece of cactus, and as I approached, it stared at me and slowly stalked away; the other gave a deep hiss, and drew in its head. These huge reptiles, surrounded by the black lava, the leafless shrubs, and large cacti, seemed to my fancy like some antediluvian animals."*

I think Darwin should have tried caressing one on the throat!

On the grounds of the Research Station, we saw several new bird species, some of which were so tame they came right to the trail's edge as if to welcome us and chat awhile. The plant life here on Santa Cruz was unusual too. Giant prickly-pear-like cactus with thick tree-like trunks, looking almost like the trunks of pine trees, lined the trails. This Opuntia Cactus forest, as it is called, appeared to be home to several bird species.

Our afternoon siesta was interrupted by the sounds of water splashing alongside the ship.Once again, the crew was cleaning fish for dinner and throwing the debris over the side.More than a dozen Brown Pelicans were fighting over the fish while the frigatebirds swooped in to steal tidbits.Frigatebirds, we learned, do not fish for themselves.They are excellent flyers and often steal their food from the beaks of other birds in flight.As another large piece of fish flew through the air and into the water, a Blue-footed Booby dove for it.The boobies are magnificent divers.Straight as an arrow, they dive deep, but often, we noted, come up empty-handed.

Our afternoon destination was to be two of several volcanic calderas that in years subsequent to their formation had sunk several hundred feet.As we hiked along one caldera ridge, we were struck by the lush vegetation on Santa Cruz—cactus forests, dense hardwoods, and tall grasses.The top of the volcano is covered with ferns as the winds and currents are such that this particular island gets a good deal of rain.

FRIDAY, AUGUST 26:
SANTA FE AND SOUTH PLAZA ISLANDS

What a sight awaited us on Santa Fe! Some 200 sea lions lay on two sections of sandy beach and the rocks between them.It was incredible walking ashore among them, seeing them so relaxed, nestled against one another, while others, primarily bulls, fought over "territories" whose boundaries our unknowing eyes could not discern.

We had been advised that morning to bring sneakers, as we had a bit of a hike ahead of us. Fortunately, I made a last-minute decision to tie my Swiss hiking boots around my neck instead—and was I ever glad when I saw the trail! Rocks, boulders, lava rocks, high steps, steep inclines, and, as we neared the top, a narrow ledge to which we clung by our fingertips as we made our way up the last 100 feet.

When we finally made it to the top, we were rewarded with our first view of Land Iguanas.This particular species is endemic to this island.We saw four, but most were off the trail and the guides were strict about our keeping to the trail. Unlike the Marine Iguana, this species is quite large, and some individuals we saw were up to 5 feet in length.

This trail was overrun with tourists.For the first time in our five days of touring the Galapagos, we were meeting scores of other tourists on the trails; the harbor was full of ships, and the "wilderness" feeling of the other localities we had visited was missing here.Diego, our new guide, advised us that people who fly out from Quito often go only to the closest islands—Santa Cruz, Santa Fe, and South Plaza.I couldn't help but think how very different—and distorted—our view of the Galapagos would be if we were only to see these tourist-infested regions.

The trip back down the Santa Fe Trail was worse than the route up, but with the help of Diego, Bruce, and Alfred, I made it back down even though I was the last one off the trail.

Our next island, South Plaza, turned out to be a little gem.The island is really only an islet, but it is beautifully covered with Red Sesuvium, a ground cover that sets off the gray lava rock and the cactus forest somewhat as red cranberry bogs set off the scene during a Cape Cod fall. As we climbed the gradual rise to the high cliffs at the back of the island, I felt as though we were climbing the moors of Scotland.Perhaps it was the Red Sesuvium, perhaps the wind, the cliffs, and the gulls, but it was a wonderfully cheery kind of place.Along the cliffs, Swallow-tailed Gulls were nesting, and a beautiful aerial ballet was taking place against the wind with gulls, frigatebirds and tropicbirds in performance.

We found Land Iguanas as soon as we arrived, and they proved to be curious fellows who seemed to enjoy company.One scurried over to me as I knelt down to take a photo.It was much too close to focus as it sat by my knee, so we had a little "eyeball" conversation for a while.

The ubiquitous sea lions called, barked, grunted, and sneezed continually.In fact, as I was writing this diary at 10:30 p.m., I could still hear them on the beach.The bulls were loudly claiming their territory and running off would-be intruders even in the black of night. At one point along the path today, three bulls started vocalizing and chasing one another, and four of us got caught in the middle of a "Mexican stand-off".There was naught to do but wait until the bulls had sorted out their differences.

It was nearing midnight when I finished writing about the day's adventures, and I knew tonight would be another long journey— some seven hours or more—to our next destination, Genovesa Island.

SATURDAY, AUGUST 27: GENOVESA ISLAND

A smooth overnight trip enabled us to sleep well and be ready for another day of adventure and discovery. It was thus on Genovesa Island this morning.The Great Frigatebirds, the second of our frigatebird species, on their nests with young were easily approached, as were the Red-Footed Boobies. Alfred found four migrant species, a Wandering Tattler, Ruddy Turnstone, a Whimbrel, and a Yellow-crowned Night Heron close at hand too.

The walking, however, was difficult.Although the trail was relatively flat, it was a lava boulder scramble and the hiking was very rough.

Genovesa Island is the smallest, eastern-most, and most remote of the northern cluster of Galapagos Islands.Its lava rock is only sparsely covered by low bushes and shrubs, most of which seem to provide nesting sites for frigate birds and boobies.

I decided not to go on the afternoon excursion after I took one look at "Prince Philip's Steps" up the side of a lava cliff. This was not for me!

I was so glad I had turned back, as I spent a delightful afternoon alone on the upper deck reading and making notes on Charles Darwin's book, *The Voyage of the Beagle*, published upon his return to England. Reading his comments and observations, while in the midst of noting and writing my own, provided a much-needed period of quiet reflection—something there has been little time for in this heavily scheduled trip. In Darwin's words, "It is the fate of most voyages, no sooner to discover what is most interesting in any locality,than they are hurried from it."It would appear that even Darwin was frustrated with ship schedules many long years ago.

Thinking back on our own experience, I marveled at how closely we approached the birds and how many species were intermingled.In one photo I captured a female Great Frigatebird, two color phases of the Red-footed Booby, an immature Swallow-tailed Gull, and the ubiquitous Marine Iguanas.Darwin didn't seem to care much for the latter, writing:

It is a hideous-looking creature, of a dirty black color, stupid, and sluggish in its movements...Their limbs and strong claws are admirably adapted for crawling over the rugged and fissured masses of lava which everywhere form the coastline. In such situations, a group of six or seven of these hideous reptiles may often times be seen on the black rocks, a few feet above the surf, basking in the sun with outstretched legs.

Either Darwin didn't visit Genovesa Island or the iguana have greatly increased in numbers since his day, as we saw about forty basking in the sun together—a mass of tangled feet, legs, tails, spiny backs, and horny heads. Although Darwin found them hideous, I am fascinated with the Marine and Land Iguanas.They, like the Giant Tortoises, seem such symbols of prehistoric times.

The proximity of birds and animals on these islands leads to some interesting problems at times. One can get so immersed in one's photography as to lose sight of other objects near at hand.At one point, while focusing on a male frigatebird and young, I failed to notice the Yellow-Crowned Night Heron sitting in the brush less than three feet from where I stood.I felt the need to apologize to the bird, ignoring it as I had and very nearly stepping on it while my eyes were focused on a more distant target.Trusting baby Red-Footed Boobies craned their necks to look at us as we passed within a few feet of their perch, and immature Swallow-tailed Gulls ran to our feet crying for food as though they somehow expected us to deliver a fishy tidbit.What a privilege it is to experience such close encounters with these creatures.

SUNDAY, AUGUST 28: BARTOLOME AND SANTIAGO

As I write this, it is 4 p.m. and Alfred and I are alone on a beach on Santiago Island.I really should not say we are alone, as we have a bull sea lion sleeping on the sand nearby, six Galapagos Penguins are cavorting in the water near shore, a Brown Pelican is swimming close by, a Whimbrel and a Wandering Tattler are feeding on the rocks at shoreline, a pair of Yellow Warblers are flitting around the bushes, a Brown Noddy is circling overhead, red, yellow, and blue Sally Lightfoot Crabs are climbing over the rocks at water's edge, and little Lava Lizards are scurrying in and out of the rocks against which I am leaning.The beauty of it all is that we have all this to ourselves.The rest of the group is taking a hike over a recent (150 years ago) pahoehoe lava flow, but we stayed behind to sit at the water's edge and quietly await whatever might come our way.Oftentimes, this is the best way to enjoy the natural world.

It has been a delightful day.We awoke this morning to the spectacular sight of Pinnacle Rock, a 150-foot craggy monolith off the starboard bow.After breakfast, we boarded the dinghy and traveled around the rocky shore looking for endemic Galapagos Penguins.We soon found them swimming and feeding.We made a dry landing by scrambling up a rocky embankment after which we climbed up an ashy trail some 400 feet to a spectacular overview of both Bartolome and Santiago Islands.This view is probably the most photographed in all the Galapagos and appears on every Galapagos travel brochure one sees.

We returned to the ship, changed into our bathing suits, and returned to the beach for a swim.What fun when the penguins decided to come over and play! They swam between us—one coming within a foot of my legs as I stood near the shore.Three sea lions came to cavort with us too. I remembered a childhood song I used to sing when playing alone on my backyard swing: "Playmate, come out and play with me"—to which I now sang, "and bring your penguins three to splash and swim with me!"

MONDAY, AUGUST 29: ISABELA ISLAND

When we awoke this morning, we were cruising along the west coast of Isabela Island, by far the largest of all of the islands in the Galapagos archipelago.This J-shaped island, which is about 70 miles long and 40 miles wide at its base, consists of six large coalescing volcanoes which rise up to 5,600 feet. The west coast is rimmed by high cliffs that are covered with tens of thousands of Blue-footed Boobies, Masked Boobies, and Brown Noddies.

Our morning expedition was a cruise along the coastline observing the roosting birds. When we came around a bend, we found ourselves at eye level with about 100 Brown Noddies roosting on a ledge.The only distraction was the myriad of flies—they were horrible—on everyone's face, hands, and body.The sun was hot, and presumably the bird guano was thick and so, therefore, were the flies! We began swatting ourselves and one another to the point where all photography ceased.We entered a cave, and the flies enveloped us.We had to beat a retreat.I would guess that the breeding colonies of noddies attract the flies here, but on the other hand, we have been in other rookeries where there were no such problems.Why here?Another mystery of the Galapagos, it would seem.

After a pleasant three-hour cruise—the first lengthy daytime travel since our first day at sea—we arrived at Tagus Cove, about mid-point on Isabela Island.Tagus Cove is a lovely circular, well-sheltered cove used by pirates in the days gone by, and by cruise ships and fishing vessels alike today.We had a dry landing with a rock scramble up the cliff and then a flat two-and-a-half-mile hike along a volcanic ridge to a water-filled caldera.

TUESDAY, AUGUST 30:ISABELA ISLAND

We began the day with a visit to Urbina Bay on Isabela Island.This fascinating location was the site of a geological uplift in 1954. About three miles of coastline, inward for up to one mile's distance, rose up some thirteen feet. The ocean floor heaved upward as well, and thousands of marine animals were left stranded—literally high and dry.Today one walks on coral reef and observes lobster carcasses and sea shells that stand as macabre testimony to this astounding event only a few years ago.

The area is now home to a nesting colony of Flightless Cormorants—another species altered by time and circumstances.Of the twenty-nine species of cormorants the world over, only those in the Galapagos have lost their ability to fly.It is presumed that a lack of terrestrial predators, coupled with the close proximity of feeding grounds, resulted in the birds having no need to fly and gradually losing the ability to fly, i.e., the "use it or lose it" phenomenon.Today's birds have small vestigial wings that serve no real purpose.

We were able to approach the cormorants closely, although those on nests with eggs or with young squawked their protests.Others stood quietly, curiously watching as we walked within two feet of them.As there are only 700 - 800 pairs of this endemic species, it was wonderful to see them.

WEDNESDAY, AUGUST 31: FERNANDINA ISLAND

We spent the night in Tagus Cove with the rhythmic sound of the ship's generator reverberating off the steep circular walls of the cove.

About 5 a.m. the engine started up, and we sailed about an hour across the channel that separates Isabela and Fernandina Islands. We boarded the dinghy but found the island was not an easy access as the tide was out, the water was shallow, and the lava and coral were scraping against the bottom of the boat.For three hours we explored the coastline and the lava flow from La Cumbra volcano.In 1968 most of the volcano's four-mile floor collapsed some 900 feet.The lava flow is expansive, and yet the island was full of life where we came ashore.

Our destination this morning was the largest colony of Marine Iguanas in the Galapagos.The Marine Iguanas are the only seagoing lizards in the world.Their swimming and diving abilities are phenomenal.They feed on algae and have an interesting ability to excrete consumed salt through salt glands, located above the eye, that connect with the nostrils.Frequent sneezing expels the salt and, on several occasions, we observed the sneezing/salt ejection process.

At first, one doesn't even notice them—their black motionless bodies blend in completely with the black lava rock.But as we began to walk inland, we suddenly realized that we were surrounded by clusters of a hundred or more iguanas scattered here and there across the rocks. What a place for an Indiana Jones film, I thought. Reminiscent of *Raiders of the Lost Ark* in which Indiana dropped into a pit of vipers, Hollywood could drop Indiana into a caldera full of iguanas. The iguana colonies presented several photo opportunities. Two iguanas that I found were having a territorial dispute. After a good bit of squabbling and rapid head bobbing, a territorial behaviorism, the smaller of the two males backed off.

As the sun began to move higher and the morning mist began to burn off, some of the larger males began to move to the water's edge to feed on the tiny red-brown algae growing on the tidal rocks.I watched closely as one appeared to use his tough lips to pull the algae free.Another waded into the shallow water and began pulling up green seaweed.This was the first time I had ever seen these fellows feeding.

Fernandina Island also seemed to be a sea lion nursery with pups everywhere, their bleating filling the air.We watched for nearly a half-hour as one young pup tried to make his way over the lava rocks to his mother only ten feet away.

A short way up the trail, two Sally Lightfoot Crabs were endeavoring to mate. Our approach interrupted their courtship ritual, and they seemed determined to wait until we left before resuming their dance.What a shame.There was so much to see, but one needed time to just sit down and let time and nature take their course.

There were not only iguanas and sea lions on Fernandina, however.The island also was teeming with bird life.A Galapagos Hawk, another endemic species, flew overhead carrying a large stick to its nest.Two Ruddy Turnstones circled the area; a Semipalmated Plover fed at the water's edge as did a Whimbrel and a Wandering Tattler.A Blue Heron and a Lava Heron were fishing. Brown Pelicans, Blue-footed Boobies, penguins, and cormorants swam off shore.Mockingbirds sang loudly and followed us about as though they were pleased to have company. The Yellow Warblers were everywhere—we've now seen them on every island.

We returned to the ship, and the captain set the course for a twelve-hour journey to our next destination, James Bay on Santiago Island.

The going got rough, in part, the captain explained, because we had used up much of our stored fresh water and the ship was now much lighter.At dinnertime, the ship was really bouncing around. Things were flying off the tables and the kitchen was a disaster. I managed the main course. Alfred ate only the soup and dessert. My Viennese husband is never too sick for dessert!

THURSDAY, SEPTEMBER 1:
SANTIAGO (JAMES BAY) AND RABIDA ISLANDS

This morning we boarded the dinghy to re-visit Santiago Island from the James Bay side of the island.Once ashore, we encountered another sea lion nursery, but this one with very young pups, including some judged to be no more than three or four weeks old.Further along the cliffs we came to a Fur Seal colony. How beautiful the Fur Seals are with their large, luminous, soft brown eyes.Whereas sea lions feed by day, Fur Seals feed at night, and we were clearly disturbing their daytime rest. What yawns! Every time I'd get ready to take a Fur Seal's photo, it would give me a jaw-breaking yawn. Many chose to sleep and ignore us. Some would wake up momentarily, give us a look-over, yawn, and lay back down again.Some wouldn't even open their eyes when I spoke to them!

Back to the ship for a three-hour run to Rabida Island, and our afternoon excursion. Landing, it seems, was going to be tough.There wasn't a foot of unoccupied sand on the entire beach. It was a solid mass of sea lions—more than one hundred in all. When we finally found an opening, I disembarked and waded in. Alfred was right behind me, I thought, but no. He was flat on his whatsis in the water—with the camera! Just as he was getting out of the dinghy, it seems, a wave came in and the dinghy lurched forward knocking him into the water. Fortunately, his camera was in the special waterproof bag we had purchased. The bag was totally submerged in the water when Alfred went down, but the camera and his telephoto lens stayed dry!

As we sat on the beach drying our feet and putting on our shoes, two sea lions flopped their way toward us. I grabbed the camera and stepped to the side to watch the action. One came forward and began to sniff Alfred's sneaker. It then stopped and looked up at Alfred with a quizzical expression. A second came along to have a sniff and pose the same question. Maybe they were trying to figure out these strange creatures that put their flippers on and off? Here on Rabida Island we found our first young featherless pelicans in the nest, and I watched as one mother regurgitated food for her young.

Back to the ship and we set off for Seymour Island—the last stop on our itinerary. Packing seemed in order, but it wasn't easy with a rocking ship tossing me and the clothes around the cabin as we plowed full steam against the current.

FRIDAY, SEPTEMBER 2:
SEYMOUR AND BALTRA ISLANDS TO QUITO

The now-familiar routine began once more—in the dinghy and on our way at 8 o'clock. Before going ashore, we cruised the coastline looking for male frigatebirds with their red pouch inflated. The male inflates his pouch and spreads his wings during mating season in an effort to attract a female.Once ashore we came upon a large breeding colony of frigatebirds, and, to our delight, about seven or eight males were in their courtship display with their bright red distensible throat pouch fully inflated.

Our next encounter was the "Booby Hatch." After scrambling over rocks and up a cliff, we walked through a nesting area of Blue-footed Boobies.And when I say "through", I do mean just that.The boobies were everywhere including the middle of the path!The young were in every stage of down and plumage. The Blue-footed Booby courtship display is quite elaborate. The male points his neck and tail skyward and then performs a slow dance raising his bright blue feet up and down before the female. I thought of Elvis and his song "Don't Step on My Blue Suede Shoes."During his display, he may also offer the female gifts of small pebbles, their future nest being little more than a scraping on the ground lined with pebbles and guano.

Back to the dinghy and back to the ship for last-minute packing while we sailed back to Baltra airport

SATURDAY, SEPTEMBER 3: QUITO

I began the morning with a hot tub bath in our hotel room.Such amenities are so appreciated after cold showers with brackish water aboard ship!We had a luscious breakfast at the hotel buffet and then bought a newspaper and three news magazines for reading aboard the long flight to Miami. The Republican National Convention had concluded during our sojourn to the south, and there was much to catch up on in the national and international news. Hurricane Gilbert was coming out of the Caribbean and heading for the Mexican/U.S. mainland. Seoul was gearing up for the summer Olympics, and the Boston Red Sox were making a run for the Eastern Division championship. What a different world from the islands we had so recently left behind!

The plane made a stop in Guayaquil and then continued on to Miami. Eight of us convened for dinner that night after which there followed a candid discussion of our respective assessments of the journey. As I said on the opening page of this diary, it was "the best of times" and it was "the worst of times", but they were all fascinating times.

Quoting from his own diary on *The Voyage of the Beagle*, Charles Darwin wrote:

> "The natural history of these islands is eminently curious, and well deserves attention. Most of the organic productions are aboriginal creations, found nowhere else; there is even a difference between the inhabitants of the different islands; yet all show a marked relationship with those of America, though separated from that continent by an open space of ocean, between 500 and 600 miles in width. The archipelago is a little world within itself, or rather a satellite attached to America, whence it has derived a few stray colonists, and has received the general character of its indigenous productions. Considering the small size of these islands, we feel the more astonished at the number of their aboriginal beings, and at their confined range. Seeing every height crowned with its crater, and the bound-

aries of most of the lava streams still distinct, we are led
to believe that within a period, geologically recent, the
unbroken ocean was here spread out. Hence, both in
space and time, we seem to be brought somewhat near
to that great fact - that mystery of mysteries - the first
appearance of new beings on this earth."

A visit to the Galapagos is a journey back in time, but it is also
a hopeful promise for the future. It is a place protected by and, to a
considerable degree, undisturbed by man. Upon checking with International Expeditions in 2021, I found there are still numerous
restrictions on ship and visitor traffic.

Each ship is limited by permits called cupos for the number of
passengers allowed on a specific ship. If new ships come in, old ships
must leave. Most vessels are small yachts accommodating only 16-
20 guests. There are a few that take 30 or 50 guests and an even
smaller number that accommodate 100 guests. No ship can visit a
single island more than once every fourteen days, and there are
large fines for any deviations. As during our visit, there must be a
registered Galapagos guide for every 14-16 people, and no tourist
can be on an island without a registered guide. In fact, if for some
reason someone is on a trail with a group and needs to turn back,
a guide must go with them. If no extra guide is available, the entire
group must turn back.

The Galapagos Islands are a natural jewel to be treasured by all
and for all. We were privileged to walk among these ancient species
where Darwin and his scientific observations brought new insights
into the natural order of life. There are journeys one takes in life that
leave an indelible impression on the soul. This was such a journey.

Wandering Albatross,
South Georgia,
Antarctica,
Alfred Viola

Gentoo Penguin,
Port Lockroy, Antarctica,
Joy Viola

Polar Bear,
Cape Churchill,
Manitoba Joy Viola

(TOP) *Koala, Alfred Viola*
(BOTTOM LEFT) *Kangaroo with Joey, Joy Viola*
(BOTTOM RIGHT) *Wombat, Joy Viola*
Australia

(TOP TO BOTTOM)
Lion, Joy Viola
Cheetah, Alfred Viola
Leopard, Alfred Viola
Maasi Mara, Kenya

CHAPTER 8

Kangaroos, Cockatoos, and Chump Chops!

In 1989, my husband and I led a tour of twenty adventuresome folks to Australia. During our visit we managed to (a) cuddle a koala, (b) pet a kangaroo, (c) boil the billy, (d) eat Whichetty Grub soup, e) savor kangaroo steak, (f) cruise through crocodile infested waters, (g) learn to sing "Waltzing Matilda," and (h) have dinner with the real Crocodile Dundee! Let me tell you all about it!

FRIDAY, JUNE 23:ON BOARD QANTAS AIRWAYS

It is 4:23 in the morning Boston time, and we have just finished dinner—our second—since beginning our journey from Boston to Brisbane, Australia.The upside-down dining hour is in preparation for our journey to the Land Down Under where a Boston morning is the next day in Australia, where their winter comes during our summer, and where there exist real people who actually look, live, and speak like Crocodile Dundee!

We began talking about an Australian tour when veterans of the Kenyan safari tour we led gathered on Cape Cod to share photos. "Where are we going next?" someone inquired. Well, as Alfred spent a sabbatical leave in Australia and traveled around extensively… the words were barely out of my mouth when someone said, "Good, let's plan a trip to Australia."

Several months later, during a pre-departure briefing, we introduced the group to a few Aussie facts and figures, as well as some Aussie slang.

G'day, Yanks! I'm going to *take the mickey out of* (tease) all of you *within a coo-ee* (the sound of my voice) today with some Aussie words and phrases to *stir the possums* (liven things up).

> By the time I've given you all this *bullswool* (nonsense) you may not know if you're *Arthur or Martha* (coming or going) and you may think I've got *kangaroos in the top paddock* (bats in the belfry). *Not on!* (no way).
>
> Now, as you know, we're going to arrive in the *Banana Republic* (Queensland) like a bunch of *sundowners* (itinerants who arrive at night looking for a meal and a bed, having done naught to earn it), and in spite of all the *tucker* (food) you'll already have had, I suppose you'll still want *Billy Tea and bickies* (tea and cookies) before you go to bed.After *Brizzie* (Brisbane) and O'Reilly's Guest House, we'll head for *Steak and Kidney* (Sydney). And when we wander the *never-never* (Northern Territory) or go off to *woop woop* (the boonies), we'll have a chance to *be as game as Ned Kelly* (ready to take on anything as per a famous Aussie outlaw).
>
> We hope you'll all be good travelers.We don't want you *getting farther behind than Walla Walla* (falling behind) or *flogging the cat* (complaining a lot).

This quiz seemed outrageous when we gave it, but when we got to Australia, we heard people using these terms! The Aussies have such an extensive slang vocabulary that you sometimes wonder if we really speak the same language.

MONDAY, JUNE 26:
BRISBANE TO LAMINGTON NATIONAL PARK

After a long series of flights from Boston to Los Angeles to Fiji to Vanuatu, we finally arrived in Brisbane, Australia. We were met by Greg of Australian Wildlife Tours and transported to our hotel where we all fell into bed exhausted.

In the morning, we set off for the Lone Pine Koala Sanctuary located along the Brisbane River, a short distance out of the city. There, virtually all of us became classic tourists and paid the requisite $5 to cuddle a koala and be photographed with same. Within this privately owned sanctuary, I found the maternity ward especially interesting.Here "mothers-in-waiting" were feeding on eucalyptus leaves with their front paws resting on their distended tummies!One little mother-to-be looked like she was ready to pop momentarily as she sat, uncomfortably, on her little bum, awaiting the birth of her offspring. I spent so much time in the maternity ward that I barely had enough time to pet an Agile Wallaby and a Red Kangaroo.

Some of our group had flown in from other US cities and one friend had come from England to join us, but by late morning everyone was packed up and ready to go. "Has everyone been to the bathroom?" I unceremoniously called out. "Two hours straight to O'Reilly's with no stops. Use the one here at the hotel before we leave." Being a tour leader has its moments!

With that task taken care of, we headed out of the city and up into the mountains toward Lamington National Park and O'Reilly's Guest House, a world-renowned rainforest retreat. Hairpin turns led to narrow roads and then even narrower roads with Greg wheeling our Deluxe (the name of the company) 36-passenger coach at what seemed a preposterous speed.I'm sure we gave more than a few cars a scare when they saw this behemoth coming toward them! "They quit serving lunch at 2!" Greg shouted out, as he set his jaw in a determined manner and propelled us up the mountain. Greg seemed to know this road well, but for those unfamiliar with the climbs and curves, it was a bit hair-raising.

And then the road entered the rain forest and wound its way among the "forest primeval." I recalled the scene in the *Star Wars* movie when Luke Skywalker was piloting a mini-rocket through the forest of ewoks and other creatures.

At 1:45 Greg proudly declared that it was the first time a big coach had made the run in two hours! And he did seem to know the route well. Once off the bus, we were led directly to lunch. Lunch? After that ride? But no one could refuse the warmth of the O'Reilly family. "We've been holding lunch for you. Come sit at your reserved tables! Are you tired? We'll get you to your rooms right after lunch!"

The rooms were frigid, and the windows were wide open! We closed the windows, turned on the electric heater, and lay down for a few moments of silence! Queensland would be warm, we thought, but it was the Australian winter and we were in the Green Mountains.

O'Reilly's is a privately owned lodge located in the midst of Lamington National Park. But it is much more than that. Since 1918, it has been a retreat for birders, hikers, and all manner of nature lovers who want a chance to experience the magic of the rain forest and the warm hospitality of the O'Reilly family. In 1911, eight O'Reilly boys from two families moved from the Blue Mountains area northwest of Sydney into the MacPherson Range country that now encompasses Lamington National Park. Selecting 100-acre sites, they expected to set up a dairy business. Later that same year, all remaining land was withdrawn from "homesteading options" as we knew them in the U.S., and the establishment of a national park was proposed. In 1915 the park was, in fact, established. The O'Reilly lands were now isolated. There was no hope of roads being developed, and pack horses had to be used to bring in supplies via a track (trail) completed by the O'Reillys themselves. Visitors began to venture up the track (we call such things "trails"), and in 1918, O'Reilly's received their first guests. The dairying idea was abandoned, a guest house was erected and opened for business in 1926, and those adventurous enough to travel two days on horseback from Brisbane came to the new establishment. In the mid-1930s, a road was built between Brisbane and the village of Canungra, but the remaining travel had to be done by horseback until 1947 when the final link of roadway was constructed. All things considered, our coach journey was pretty tame compared to having to travel that terrain via horseback.

Alfred had visited O'Reilly's during his sabbatical leave in Australia, and as he was eager to share the place with the members of our tour, he announced a 4 p.m. bird walk. Vince O'Reilly learned of Alfred's previous visit, and the wildlife-loving nature of our group, and therefore decided to show up at 4 o'clock and lead the walk himself! We were delighted. We set off like the Pied Piper and his band of children, following Vince across the lawn.

Vince knew how to start off a tour with pizazz. Flocks of red and blue Crimson Rosella Parrots and red and green King Parrots were feeding on the front lawn. They flew eagerly to any outstretched hand offering food. You didn't have to be a birder to enjoy this scene!

His next stop was a place frequented by the spectacular black and gold Regent Bowerbird. He held out a bit of grated cheese and the bird flew to his hand. He suggested we return to the spot at our leisure for photographs, and then he led us a short way further to the bower of the Satin Bowerbird, a deep indigo blue bird with a unique means of courtship. A bower, a bowl-shaped nest, is built on the ground, with two, foot-high walls. His "front door" is decorated with blue feathers, blue wildflowers, blue bottle caps, pens, and anything else blue the male can find! The male endeavors to attract the female to his bower and then to "display" for her with song and dance in the hope of convincing her to stay and mate. Males who do the best job of interior decorating win the females!

During dinner that night, the Brush-tailed Possums and the tiny Sugar Gliders came to the spot-lit feeder in front of the dining room bay window.The moment they appeared, several of our group bolted from the dinner table and went outside to try their luck at nocturnal photography.

After dinner there was a six-projector slideshow presented in a newly constructed audio-visual room filled with about 100 large, comfortable chairs that invited weary guests to relax so much that some dozed off to sleep! Others took a nocturnal walk to the glow worm grotto where millions of glow worms hung on a cliff wall like twinkling stars. These luminescent critters aren't worms at all, but larvae of a small primitive fly.

TUESDAY, JUNE 27:O'REILLY'S GUEST HOUSE

At 6 a.m. our alarm clock awakened us, and we hurriedly dressed, gathered up our cameras, binoculars, and bird books, had a quick cup of coffee and a bite of sweet roll and headed out to the front lawn for a 6:45 bird walk.I expected to see only a handful of people responding to Peter O'Reilly's early morning invitation, but found, instead, some 40 people—including almost all of our group of 22—dressed in warm layers and ready to go. King Parrots and Crimson Rosellas were already on the front lawn entertaining the birders.

Peter O'Reilly was overwhelmed by the turnout and called in brother Vince for support. Each man took half of the group and we started out in two different directions. It was a pleasant walk of nearly an hour before Vince announced it was time to head back for breakfast. (Coffee, tea, and small nibbles of sweet rolls, or some such eatable, were set out each morning for early risers with a large buffet breakfast being served in the dining room at 7:45.)

At breakfast, Tim, a younger generation O'Reilly, came around to tell us what activity options were planned for the morning: (1) an all-day hike of some 5 miles, (2) a half-day bird walk of 3 miles, and (3) a bus ride and short walk to a scenic lookout. Our group split in all three directions with some electing to do each of the suggested activities. Alfred and I decided to take a private hike to Moran Falls, and one of our group, Patty, decided to join us.

It was a lovely walk to the falls, and en route we heard, and Alfred finally spotted, an Eastern Whipbird—a large black bird with a white cheek patch whose call is the sound of a sharp, cracking whip.I watched the bird as he called and marveled how so much sound could come from his small throat.The three of us bounded, bumped, and crawled along the trail, photographing sunlight filtering through the canopy, crow's nest ferns, and staghorn ferns growing on tree trunks. Lichen and fungus were sprouting from the warm, rich earth, and bird songs filled the air.

There were several alternative paths back from the falls so we opted not to return the way we had come. Better, we thought, to explore new paths. That proved to be a questionable decision!The path meandered through a eucalyptus forest into an open meadow where cows grazed on the hillside and butterflies fed on the flowering Yellow Groundsel. Then we saw the creek that lay ahead and there was nary a bridge by which to cross. The three of us caucused about the route to follow.Patty and I decided that the rocks were too far apart for us, so we sat down and began removing our shoes and socks.Better to go barefoot and roll up our pant-legs, we reasoned, than to fall in and get our shoes soaked. I had just gotten one shoe off when I looked up and saw Al on "all fours" on the rocks halfway across the stream.He was stuck and his gunstock and camera were hanging from his neck dangerously near the water.Quickly, I pulled off my other shoe, rolled up my pants, and waded in to help him get upright. Together, we got across the stream.But Patty was back on the other side holding my shoes and hers as well as her camera and binoculars.Nothing to do but wade back across in my muddy, wet, stocking feet. Patty and I tied our shoes laces together, hung our shoes around our necks, and then, draped in shoes, cameras, and binoculars, started back across the creek—the third crossing for me.The water was cold! The mud oozed between my toes.The rocks were hard on my feet.It felt wonderful when we reached the soft grassy slopes on the other side.We later learned this is considered a classic Australian bush crossing!

We sat down in the sun for a bit, feeling like a pair of Huck Finns, and just enjoyed the warm sun and the scene around us. Alfred, as usual, was off chasing birds with his camera.

I finished the rest of the hike in shoes, minus socks—the latter drooping along behind me, tied to the strings of my jacket like dead fish on a line. Wearily, we arrived in the dining room for lunch five miles and four hours after our departure.I returned to the room to write in my diary laying atop an electric blanket (they put them under you in Australia) and beneath blankets and bed spread with a sweater draped over my shoulders, wearing a flannel nightgown and a cotton robe, with the electric heater, mounted on the wall above me, belting out heat. It was cold at O'Reilly's, but it is best to visit during the Aussie winter as the summers are unbearably hot.

WEDNESDAY, JUNE 28: O'REILLY'S GUEST HOUSE

We woke to a cloudy morning, but by the time breakfast was over, the sky was beginning to clear. Again, our group split up in pursuit of different options—some taking a second guided five-mile hike, some taking a bus trip to a lookout, and some taking long or short hiking options of their own choosing. Alfred and I decided to concentrate on photography with the beautiful bowerbirds as our prime objective.For three hours we sat on the ground opposite the Satin Bowerbird's bower.Our patience was duly rewarded.

I had been advised by one of the locals that the Satin Bowerbird, who decorates his bower with all matters blue, has a distain for all things yellow. I decided to experiment. I cut two strips from a yellow plastic bag, placed them in front of his bower while he was away, and stepped back ready to record the bird's reaction. It was decisive! He did not like yellow, and he promptly removed the offensive decorations. I tried it a second time, and once again he removed the yellow intrusions in his bower display of blue feathers, blue flowers, blue bottle caps, and blue plastic straws. And then the female appeared and entered his bower. The male promptly began his courtship—strutting, clucking, calling, chirping, and dancing.

These birds are fed at O'Reilly's, and, of course, they were checking me out to see if I had anything worthy of their interest. Fortunately, I had a box of raisins that Qantas Airlines had given us, which I had thought to bring along. I decided to try to lure the birds out into the sunlight where I might have a better chance of capturing their beautiful colors on film. I tossed a half-dozen raisins out on the ground. Whoosh! In an instant, the area was filled with birds.We spent the next hour sitting on the ground, enjoying 11 species of birds—of which we were able to photograph the bowerbirds, the White-browed Scrub Wren, the tiny Superb Blue Wren, and the brilliant blue and red Crimson Rosellas. Would they take food from my hand, I wondered? Slowly, I stretched out an upturned palm filled with raisins. The male Regent Bowerbird lit on my fingers and began to feed. Obviously, this was not a new experience for him, but it certainly was for me! As he ate, I turned him slowly, watching the iridescence of his jet-black feathers and the movement of his golden crown in the breeze. What a jewel I was holding in my hand! What a memory I was holding in my heart.

THURSDAY, JUNE 29:
LAMINGTON NATIONAL PARK TO SYDNEY

Greg drove up a small safari bus with just 22 seats to take us back to Brisbane. The luggage was piled into a little blue trailer that bumped along behind us as we wove our way back through the trees, around the horse-shoe curves, and back down the mountain into the city. The air was cold, but our 22 bodies were generating a great deal of heat.The result was fogged-up windows that we were perpetually wiping in order to view the passing scene. A few Pretty-face

Wallabies and Red-necked Wallabies provided some excitement along with the sighting of four or five new birds. There was much hilarity over Greg's identification of some "Pile-headed Rosellas" which we finally determined was his Aussie pronunciation of Pale-headed. However, our date with an Ansett Airlines flight at 9:45 kept us moving right along. We boarded our flight to Sydney, and as our 6:15 a.m. breakfast was wearing thin, we were glad to be served an ample snack on board.

At Sydney Airport we were met by the much-heralded John Dare—a consummate professional guide about whom we'd heard rave reviews. He was a fairly tall man with a girth that suggested he enjoyed his food. His brown Aussie Akubra hat sat at a jaunty angle on his head. He was accompanied by Keith Johns of International Expeditions, who was in Australia scouting out some new sites not previously on their itinerary. This included several of the places we were about to visit at Alfred's instigation.

John and Keith gathered up our luggage, directed us to the large, Deluxe bus (more about that later), and the driver promptly took us on a lengthy tour of Sydney and its immediate environs. Sydney is a beautiful city. It has handsome architecture, beautifully appointed gardens and parks, lovely homes—and that gorgeous harbor with its 150 miles of convoluted shoreline. We had a quick walk about the Sydney Opera House, a UNESCO World Heritage site, then it was back to the hotel for dinner at the Sydney Tower, at 1,063 feet, the tallest building south of the equator. The revolving dining room gave us a magnificent 360-degree view of the city. That evening some of us attended a concert by the Sydney Symphony Orchestra at the Opera House.

FRIDAY, JUNE 30: SYDNEY TO MELBOURNE

We began the morning in Sydney with a very early walk through "The Rocks." Today it is a fashionable section of shops and restaurants, but in 1788, it was the site of Australia's original penal settlement. Initially, it was little more than a village with a store, hospital, prison, and barracks. It became a tough district and eventually a slum, and it was not until 1968 that the Sydney Cove Redevelopment Authority was established to restore and renovate the area to its present status as a major tourist attraction.

Then it was down to the dock, where we boarded a harbor cruise boat, which we had almost entirely to ourselves! We roamed from topside to the inside cabin tables where coffee and bickies were waiting. The Sydney harbor is truly a jewel with so many little inlets and coves that host everything from shipyards to multi-million-dollar mansions. Moreover, it is a working harbor with extensive commercial shipping passing through.

But penguins were calling, and after a little more than an hour's flight, we arrived in Melbourne and immediately departed, in another Deluxe 30-passenger coach, approximately 90 miles south to Phillip Island and the famous Penguin Parade.

The Fairy Penguins, or Little Blue Penguins as they are also called, are the smallest members of the penguin family and are found only in Australia and New Zealand. Slate blue and white in color, they call out with a high-pitched bark as, each evening, they waddle out of the sea and onto the sandy shore to their grassy burrows.

The penguins were coming ashore earlier this time of year, so it was important we get to the viewing stands on time. We were well rewarded for our efforts.Although it is very hard to take accurate penguin counts when they come ashore in small groups all along the beach, a canvass of our group came up with an estimate of about 400 penguins seen in the course of the evening.

Each penguin group we saw had its own personality.They bobbed around in the sea for a bit, washed ashore, scurried along the water's edge, dashed back out to sea when some imaginary danger spooked them, then, led by one brave little soul, finally began their dash up the banks to their burrows in the tall grass.

They feed at sea during the day and come ashore to their grassy burrows after sunset when darkness protects them from predators such as foxes, dingoes, and feral cats. They return to the sea before dawn where they must avoid predator seals to survive.Although the night air was cold, there was no wind, and we were not overly chilled during our hour-long vigil at the beach. Earlier I referred to viewing stands, and stands there are, like bleachers at a high school football game. But these bleachers face the dark sea, and people huddle together under blankets, their eyes focused outward, binoculars in hand, watching and waiting.

Silence prevails as the little fellows waddle their way up the beach in the full glare of floodlights and onto well-worn paths from which their human observers are fenced off. Hundreds of observers of multiple nationalities watched in whispered awe.

As we walked back along the boardwalk toward the parking lot, we stopped to enjoy the penguins "socializing" at their burrows. What a racket! They call back and forth as if inquiring of one another's health and the catch of the day. On the boardwalk we could stand directly above them, see at close range and observe their comical ways.

We were quite ready for dinner by now, and John Dare had made a reservation for us at a small restaurant on the island.

"To the penguins," rang out the first toast of the evening.

"To the first penguin," replied another happy soul, who then gleefully reminded everyone that this left 399 more to be toasted!

We had thought we were the only patrons in the establishment, but when we noticed another couple, we felt embarrassed, and Bob, a member of our group, went over to make our apologies.

"No, indeed," they said."Are you enjoying your visit to Australia?"

"Oh yes, very much," he replied.

"Where are you from?" they asked.

"Canada!" said Bob—not wanting them to think us a bunch of boisterous Americans!

When they said they hoped to visit Canada someday, Bob assured them there were many beautiful places to see and urged them to make the trip. We all kept a straight face until we got outside the restaurant and then burst out laughing. Feeling we should now sing the Canadian National Anthem, we loudly sang out "Oh Can.. a..da...."and then realized none of us knew the words despite hearing the anthem at our many Boston-Montreal hockey games!

That night gave rise to the birth of The Penguin Society, but more about that later.

SATURDAY, JULY 1:
MELBOURNE TO HALLS GAP, GRAMPIANS NATIONAL PARK

We are all eating much too much food!

Once again, we started the day with a big cooked breakfast of eggs and the option of ham, bacon, sausages, tomatoes, and, of course, juices, cereals (hot and cold), fruit, toast, croissants, coffee, and tea! Bob ordered an omelet that, when delivered, prompted him to comment that it was either a four-egg job or a two Emu-egg creation!

We then began our morning drive southwest toward the Great Ocean Road along the southern coast, a drive that was reminiscent of the U.S. Pacific Coast highway.

Midmorning, Dick, another group member, said how much he wanted some really good lamb chops at some point on his Australian journey. John Dare decided he knew just how to fulfill that desire, so he stopped the coach in the seaside town of Lorne, and John gave the local butcher a yarn to talk about for months to come.

"G'day, mate"

"G'day to you. What can I do for you?"

"Have you chump chops today?"

The butcher picked up a pair and placed them on the scale.

"How many will you be wanting?" he asked.

"About 50 should do it," was John Dare's matter-of-fact reply.

The butcher stared at him in total disbelief.

"You're kidding."

"No, I'm not. Well, can you do it or not?"

"Well... I guess so," came the bewildered reply.

And with that exchange—followed by a great deal of sawing and cutting on the butcher's part—John had the makings of a cook-out lunch for the next day. Chump chops, by the way, come from the place where the leg of lamb meats the loin. They are known to be lean and meaty.

At lunchtime, Alfred and I caucused with John and our driver, Mark, and reworked our route to the Grampian Mountains.The coastal route was taking much too long, so we agreed to turn north after Port Campbell and cut through back roads. At Port Campbell National Park, we beheld the spectacular "Twelve Apostles", twelve giant monoliths standing in the water just off shore, the remnants of eroded sandstone cliffs. (We've since learned that many have subsequently been eroded by the Southern Ocean tides.)After a lengthy photo opportunity, we turned inland. The driver had never traversed these roads, but the map looked good, so off we went.We left the coast at 4:00 p.m., and two hours later we were sitting in a sheep rancher's front yard—totally lost.

The front door opened, and a bewildered rancher walked slowly toward the bus sitting in the middle of his front lawn. In the dim twilight, the huge white coach, adorned with rainbow-colored strips, large letters spelling out D-E-L-U-X-E, and American and British flags must have seemed an absurd apparition.

"Ya got the Billy on?" Mark called out cheerfully.

The rancher stared at us in amazement.

"Reckon we made the wrong turn," Mark suggested.

"I reckon you did," the rancher replied, still scratching the hair beneath his battered Aussie Akubra hat.

"Guess we should have gone the other way at the intersection."

"I guess you should have," came the reply.

Slowly, we backed out of his yard and disappeared into the failing light.

"He'll head to the pub for sure tonight, telling everyone about this big white bus that drove into his yard with a load of lost Yanks," John said, "and the story will probably get better with every telling."

"And if he meets the butcher who had to cut 50 lamb chops to order, they'll all think we're crackers for sure," Mark added.

Well, we made a couple more wrong guesses on unmarked roads, but eventually at 7:00 p.m. we arrived in Halls Gap in the heart of Grampians National Park. We were given deluxe accommodations complete with queen-sized bed and a jacuzzi in the bathroom. Dinner began with a toast: "To the Twelve Apostles!" We then spent the rest of the dinner trying to name, and toast, each of the twelve apostles, the Seven Dwarfs, Santa's eight reindeer, and the lineage of Adam and Eve and Cain and Abel! This group may be a bunch of lawyers, nurses, scientists, professors, and other professionals, but it got very silly in the evening!

SUNDAY, JULY 2: GRAMPIANS NATIONAL PARK

It was a foggy, rainy morning in the mountains, but everyone was out early to watch the kangaroos feeding in the field behind the motel.Breakfast was delivered to our room by means of the Aussies' wonderful "silent butler" system, whereby breakfast orders are placed the night before and then delivered at the prescribed time through a small trap door into each room.

Soon after 8 o'clock we departed for the new Grampians Visitor Center for a special presentation of the Center's audio-visual program on the history of the Grampians, its flora and fauna. Grampians State Forest became a national park in 1984, just a few months before Alfred and I made our first visit there during his sabbatical leave. We had so enjoyed the area and its wildlife that we had added it to this year's itinerary, although International

Expeditions had not previously included the park on their tours. The area is well known for its 900 species of wildflowers, including 100 orchids, its more than 200 bird species, its 60 miles of craggy granite mountains—one of which rises to 3,831 feet—and its rivers, waterfalls, and escarpments. I thought the area looked somewhat like the White Mountains of New Hampshire.

John Dare had arranged for a local couple, Ian and Thelma McCann, to guide us through the Grampians. Both are long-time residents of the area, and Ian is the author of several books on the Grampians. We drove the back roads with Ian directing us down one dirt road after another in search of koalas, kangaroos, and emus, all of which we found.

At lunchtime, John and Mark built a fire and grilled our 50 chump lamb chops, together with large sausages that John referred to as "growlers". (They lie in your stomach and growl was the explanation!) They were actually very good and coupled with a bit of bread, lettuce, tomato, and celery constituted a most tasty lunch. We ate with our fingers, and no lamb chops ever tasted better.John Dare "boiled the Billy", the local expression for making tea, swung the pot in a vertical circle three times—in the prescribed ritual—and served us Billy Tea to wash down our meal. It was a wonderful bush picnic.

When we had digested our lunch and each was on his own for a bit to wander about the area, Bob, a non-birder, came back into camp to tell us he had found a pair of spectacular red and gray birds he thought might be Gang Gangs, a colorful member of the cockatoo family. Several of us followed him to the spot where he'd seen them, and indeed they were Gang Gangs—a new life-list bird for both Alfred and me.

Shortly thereafter, we came around a bend in the road, the coach stopped, and there were squeals of delight from everyone on the bus. Kangaroos were everywhere!Everyone grabbed their camera equipment and headed out of the bus. "You knew this was coming, didn't you!" said Ruth with a wink as she rushed past. This was Zumstein's, a site where kangaroos have been studied and fed for generations. For our group, like many others, it was the first opportunity for close encounters in the wild with the symbol of Australia.

When we returned to Halls Gap, the village green was filled with the cries of Corellas coming in to roost in the trees. Hundreds circled overhead, and Alfred and I stood transfixed for several minutes. The Little Corella is a large, white-crested cockatoo with a pink face and yellow bill. In flocks of hundreds they are an impressive sight. They fly out in the morning to unknown feeding destinations only to circle back to their roots in the late afternoon.

MONDAY, JULY 3: GRAMPIANS TO HEALESVILLE SANCTUARY,MELBOURNE

We awoke to a cloud of Corellas flying and squawking overhead, a koala feeding in the tree above our roof, and kangaroos once more feeding in the nearby fields.There is so much wildlife in the Grampians.

But there was no more time to dawdle as we were programmed for a long drive to Melbourne and on to Healesville, a good five hours away.

Healesville is a unique location. The Sanctuary was established in 1921 as an animal medical research station specializing in the breeding of native animals. In 1928 the Sanctuary was taken over by the Government of Victoria. A wonderful maze of trails leads through a natural bush environment where one sees wallabies, kangaroos, koalas, emus, wombats and 200 native bird species. White Ibis were hanging around the picnic tables for handouts, and the Brush Turkeys were everywhere, as were several free-flying bird species. There was a special enclosure for the endangered Tasmanian Devil, the largest carnivorous marsupial in the world. A most unattractive fellow, with a temperament to match his puss, he looks very menacing with his fangs protruding from his lips!

Alfred and I went our separate ways at times.I, for one, got totally entranced with a little brown furry "lawn mower" who wouldn't stop eating. More properly known as the wombat, this pudgy little guy was grazing on the grass in his large enclosure as if he hadn't eaten in days. His ample girth was solid evidence to the contrary, however. Wombats are fairly common in southeastern Australia, but like most Australian mammals, they are nocturnal and not often seen.They have broad, blunt heads, rounded ears, and a coarse fur. Although they can weigh up to 65 pounds and grow to a length of 40 inches, this fellow was considerably smaller. The sun was on him nicely, his fur had a beautiful sheen, and he was a most photogenic subject.

TUESDAY, JULY 4: MELBOURNE TO ULUHRU KATA TJUTA NATIONAL PARK

The alarm went off at 4:45 a.m., but I didn't mind as today we were flying to the Australian Outback! Our flight across the Simpson Desert was spectacular. Everyone on the plane—Aussies and tourists alike—were drawn into conversation about the scene below. The red clay soil, normally a monochromatic landscape, had been blessed with rain and was now red, brown, green, blue, and aqua. The red clay beds, filled with water, yielded the brown muddy pools.The salt-lined beds produced blue waters, and those with algae growing on top were aqua. One could spend an entire tour exploring the Outback! Australia is nearly as large as the forty-eight contiguous states of the U.S., and one just can't do the continent justice in a single three-week trip!

We arrived at the Alice Springs airport with only a few minutes to spare before our flight to Uluru Kata Tjuta some 275 miles southwest. Since 1873, this area was known as Ayer's Rock and the Olgas; however, since our visit in 1993, the names were changed to reflect the original nomenclature of the Aboriginal people who reside in the area. There is now an official dual/name policy although the original names are generally preferred within Australia.

When we arrived at Yaluru airport, we were taken to our hotel in the Yaluru complex. In earlier years, the hotels and campgrounds were located at the base of the Ulura Rock. Now, a new resort complex is located a short distance from the Rock, and the Rock itself has been given back to the Aboriginal people.

Both the Olgas(Kata-Tjuta) and Ayer's Rock (Uluhu) are remnants of an ancient mountain range, but Kata Tjuta's 36 large domed formations are formed of a boulder conglomerate whereas Uluru is a sandstone monolith, Uluru meaning an "island mountain".We took a short walk into one of the gorges, but all too soon it was time to "report back." John Dare, in his consistently thoughtful manner, greeted us at the coach with slices of fresh watermelon. After all, it was Independence Day and he'd heard Americans eat watermelon on July 4th! It was a much-appreciated gesture, and we bit into the juicy fruit and spit out the seeds in true-picnic fashion—wondering if in a year's time some future visitors might find watermelons growing here!

When we reached Uluru, each of us sought our own special place along the sunset-viewing trail to film the renowned color transformation of the mountain when illuminated by the setting sun.

We returned to our hotel and "dressed for dinner" at John Dare's suggestion. We soon saw why! It was July 4th and three huge American flags were hanging from the dining room ceiling. Small American and Aussie flags, mini firecrackers, and "New Year's Eve" horns were at our specially-reserved tables. Another couple from Maryland joined in our celebration, and then a table of Aussies stood up to sing us a rousing version of "Waltzing Matilda." We all joined in to the best of our ability.

WEDNESDAY, JULY 5: ULUHU TO ALICE SPRINGS

Uluru is a sacred place to the indigenous people, and their cave paintings are full of sacred tales, fairy tales, and stories of everyday life. Much of the Rock is associated with the Dreamtime—the people's story of the Creation.

The cave drawings can best be likened to the kind of simple road maps we often draw for friends—a few lines accompanied by much verbal embellishment and references to landmarks along the way. So it was with the cave drawings—a few lines accompanied by a Dreamtime story, a legend, or even an explanation of a sacred rite.

First, it is important to understand that the Dreamtime is the Aboriginal version of Genesis.It is their designation for the period when the Great Father Spirit and the tribe's totemic ancestors journeyed through a territory, creating its landscape and entrusting it to their descendants. Each group had its own name for the Great Father Spirit, and each had its totemic ancestors responsible for creation, as the group saw it manifested in their own local environment. Uluru, for example, was formed, according to Dreamtime stories, when Mala the Hair Wallaby stood over a pile of sand, cut a vein in his arm, and let the blood pour over the sand. The sand turned to rock—Uluru—and to this day, its red color is attributed to the blood of Mala.

The Dreamtime stories of the various groups reflect the environment in which the groups lived.The Rainbow Snake, for example, was the symbol of rain and water, without which life could not exist—especially in an arid region such as Uluru, for example.The Rainbow Snake caused the rivers to flow and the clouds to rain, and, as a life-giving symbol, also was associated with fertility.

After spending the morning exploring Uluru, we began a 275-mile coach drive back to Alice Springs. John Dare had suggested we travel via coach rather than fly as per our original itinerary, to permit us a more extensive look at the Outback. We had agreed.And although long, it was an informative ride, noting as we did the rapidity with which the landscape changes from treed hills to barren flats. There were times when the passing scene reminded me of eastern Montana and other times when I would have thought myself in the rolling hills of Iowa. Rivers lined with tall trees were found in some spots while only dry, flat flood plains or dry washes existed in others. Throughout our journey, a magnificent sweeping pattern of cirrus clouds stretched for miles across the sky.

At 4 o'clock, we rolled into Alice Springs and were immediately driven to an opal shop where John had made arrangements for a short lecture on the mining and grading of opals. Ninety-five percent of the world's opals come from an area 500 miles south of Alice Springs. I was amazed to see and learn how the pure white opal gemstone with its inner "aurora borealis" of lights can be made dark blue and dark green through a painting and layering technique of doublet and triplet layers of thin opal gemstone, although solid opals are the most valued.

That night John Dare took us to a small restaurant noted for its local cuisine. We were served a very nice cream soup with some sort of small nutmeats, it seemed.Only after we had eaten it did John tell us we had just consumed our first bowl of Witchetty Grub Soup! The Witchetty Grub is a fat white grub, about 4 to 5 inches long, which the indigenous people consider a delicacy. So do Aussies who live in the Outback! Those weren't nuts I had bitten down on.They were toasted grub bits! I decided not to think a great deal about this subject. The soup had been very tasty. Now, what was the entree? Kangaroo steak, of course.

THURSDAY, JULY 6: ALICE SPRINGS TO DARWIN TO KAKADU NATIONAL PARK

There are many romanticized descriptions of Alice Springs. None of the tourist guidebooks, however, advise visiting the sewage plant. Eight of us got up at the crack of dawn to go there!

It was a bit chilly, but the sun was warm. Layered in sweaters and jackets, gloves and hats, eight birders joined forces and by combining our skills, managed to find and positively identify 27 species of birds during our two-and-a-half-hour walk around the sewage ponds. The rest of the group visited the headquarters of the Royal

Flying Doctor Service and took a brief tour of Alice Springs, including the original town site some distance from the present settlement.

Our loveliest sight was a flock of about 75 Galahs, those soft gray and raspberry-colored cockatoos, who flew in and landed near us to drink in a quiet pond. Their lovely images were mirrored in the still waters, and their plumage was "aflame" in the first rays of the morning sun.

And then it was on to the airport where we boarded our flight to Darwin along Australia's northern coast.

Upon arrival we were disappointed to find we did not have the guide nor the large bus promised, but there was naught to do but pile into a twenty-passenger van and head for Kakadu National Park, some four hours' drive away

FRIDAY, JULY 7: KAKADU NATIONAL PARK

In accordance with our guide, Peter's, instructions, everyone was in the bus at 6:30 a.m. and we were off to the nearby Yellow Waters Billabong of the South Alligator River. A billabong is an Aussie term for a pond or lagoon left behind when flood waters recede from a river's flood plain.

We boarded one of the boats and motored first to a sunrise-viewing spot where we observed and photographed the dawn of a new day. As the sun rose, we became immersed in the ornithological spectacle we were seeing—the largest concentration of bird life I have ever seen in my entire life! From the majestic White-breasted Sea Eagle to the Lotus Birds and chicks dancing their way around the lily pads, it was quite a show. We saw 27 species in all, but it was the sheer numbers that overwhelmed everyone. The Magpie Geese, herons, and egrets numbered in the thousands. Although we were told that there were more than 100 crocodiles in the billabong, we saw only one—Henry—a nine-foot specimen sunning himself on a bank, who obligingly yawned for the cameras and then he went back to sleep, to await the arrival of the next boat of camera-toting tourists!

After about a two-hour cruise, we returned to Cooinda Lodge for a buffet breakfast. Then it was back aboard the bus again for the drive to Nourlangi Rock to view indigenous art of 20,000 years ago. At Uluru, we had been fascinated to see rock art and hear about the Dreamtime stories, but the Kakadu wall paintings, portraying Aboriginal knowledge and spiritual thought, are one of the world's largest rock art sites

To view the various "galleries" as they are called, we hiked along a trail that took us from art site to art site. Peter gave good explanations of what we were viewing. Moreover, everyone enjoyed the opportunity to get out of the bus and hike a bit.

Next it was on to the Anabangbang Billabong for a picnic lunch while Black Kites soared overhead hoping for food morsels, and an immature Pied Butcherbird sat in a tree overhead and plaintively called for a parental handout!

We next made a short stop at Jim Jim Billabong camp where Peter demonstrated the art of blowing a five-foot-long horn known as a didgeridoo. "Would anyone care to try it?" Peter asked. Charlie stepped up and practically gave us a concert!Peter was amazed! The didgeridoo is not an easy instrument to play. But Charlie, it seems, once played trumpet and apparently, the technique is similar.

We took the "Old Darwin Road" back to Darwin, a gravel road that Peter warned us would be dusty and bumpy, but which proved to be far better than many roads we had traveled in Kenya

SATURDAY, JULY 8: DARWIN, NORTHERN TERRITORY

The alarm went off at 5:45 a.m. "What the heck kind of a vacation is this?" I thought, as I wearily stretched in bed.

For Alfred, the day began at 6:30 a.m. when nine of our hardy group started singing "Happy Birthday" to him in the hotel lobby! Only 10 of our 22 managed to respond to the early wake-up call for the birding trip to Fogg Dam.Peter led a walk along the levee where water lilies adorned one side and rice paddies the other.It is a spectacular waterfowl sanctuary.

At Fogg Dam, a bush breakfast was prepared by the Terra Safari Tours staff with Tom Winter, our previously promised guide, assuming some of the cooking chores. Afterwards, Tom led an hour and a half bird-walk along the forest edge, which resulted in the sighting of 29 species of birds and a few Agile Wallabies.

That evening we were invited to dine at the Winters' home. This was special as Tom was a prototype for the Mick Dundee character in the movie *In Search of the Real Crocodile Dundee*! While we enjoyed steaks and sausages (mystery bags as they are locally dubbed) cooked over an open grill, Tom and Patti Winter told of their plans to come to Canada in the fall to promote the *Crocodile Dundee* film.

SUNDAY, JULY 9: DARWIN TOCAIRNS TO ATHERTON TABLELANDS

There's no hope of getting any rest on this trip! We had another early start in order to catch the 8:15 flight to Cairns for our visit to the Atherton Tablelands and the Great Barrier Reef.

Another Deluxe bus and we headed south and then west with a twelve-mile climb to 3,000-foot elevation, through the Gillies Range and on to Lake Barrine. The Tablelands were formed two million years ago by volcanic upheavals. Today, the region contains a rain forest with 500 species of trees, 300 bird species as well as platypus, possum, and wallaby. Much of the area has been cleared for agricultural purposes. In fact, the rolling hills reminded me of part of Vermont. Those pockets of native forests that remain are now, for the most part, protected within the boundaries of several national parks.

JULY 10 – 12: ATHERTON TABLELANDS

We spent three days exploring the tablelands, looking for birds, and observing unusual plants and trees—all the while fighting off leeches during our hikes. More than once I had to deal with a leech and a blood-soaked sock. This was not my favorite locale. We did, however, manage a rare sighting of a Duck-billed Platypus in the wild. This creature, which appears to be half bird and half mammal, spends 22 hours of each day in its burrow and only comes out to feed at dawn and at dusk. Kookaburras sang on an overhead limb, Rock Wallabies scampered around the rocks, and Brush-tailed Possum, quite accustomed to tourists, begged for bits of bread. It was an interesting terrain, but I would rather have had more time in the Outback.

We made a last-minute change to our itinerary in order to visit the Kuranda Butterfly Sanctuary where we learned about the management of the sanctuary and their breeding program. Then it was on to the Kuranda Railroad Station and a 20-mile scenic train route to Cairns encompassing 20 tunnels, 98 curves, and dozens of bridges spanning deep ravines.

WEDNESDAY, JULY 12: THE GREAT BARRIER REEF

After a day at leisure exploring the seaside city of Cairns, we drove an hour north to Port Douglas, where we boarded the 300-passenger catamaran, the Quicksilver headed for the renowned Great Barrier Reef. Once on board the three-decker vessel, we were treated to tea and bickies. I went to the stern to watch how quickly the catamaran slipped out of her moorings, out into the harbor, and out to sea. The Quicksilver cruises at 30 knots, and she moves smoothly through the water.After about one and a half hours we reached the Outer Reef—Agincourt Reef—where 1,000 species of tropical fish and 200 species of coral abound.

The Quicksilver Company maintains a permanent platform at sea, of a width and depth comparable to the size of the catamaran itself. It is used as a staging and dressing area for snorkelers.

Alfred and I took the non-swimmer's approach to the appreciation of the Reef—a visit to the permanent underwater observatory attached to the platform. We walked down a flight of stairs into an enclosed underwater walkway. There, we watched the hundreds of fish that passed by the glass windows.

A second viewing opportunity was afforded us through a trip on the so-called "submersible". The semi-submarine carried about 30 passengers. Seated in rows of two, each of us with our own private window, we cruised through the reef, past the coral gardens, past the Giant Clams with their rhythmically moving blue and purple "lips", past blue Staghorn coral and fluorescent indigo blue-tipped corals as well. It was a spectacular conclusion to our trip.

THURSDAY, JULY 13:THE BIRTH OF THE PENGUIN SOCIETY

While on our flight back home, The Penguin Society was established. With two lawyers in our group, and input from everyone, The Penguin Society Articles of Incorporation were drawn up, the purpose of the Society being "to travel to exotic lands while eating gourmet food." It was a purpose the Society members subsequently followed on trips to Belize, to Kenya, to Alaska, to Indonesia, and then to Antarctica!

I hope to return to Australia someday as we had only a taste of the magic of the Outback and I'd like the opportunity to explore it further. But the next time I think it should be done camping in the manner described in Australia's unofficial National Anthem "Waltzing Matilda."

(And for those who don't know, "Waltzing Matilda" is Aussie for traveling on foot with one's belongings in a Matilda, which is a swag hung over one's back.)

> *Once a jolly swagman camped by a Billabong*
> *Under the shade of a Coolibah tree*
> *And he sang as he watched*
> *And waited 'till his Billy boiled,*
> *You'll come a waltzing Matilda with me.*
> —Banjo Patterson, 1895 Australian poet

CHAPTER 9

The Penguins Never Read the Treaty!

IT WAS ONCE KNOWN AS *Terra Australis Incognito. Antarctica. A land mass of ice, snow, glaciers, and mountains, uninhabited but for a few scientific research stations—and several million penguins, sea birds, seals, and off-shore whales. It is stark. It is beautiful. It is luminescent. And it can be dangerous and even frightening. It is the world's last great wilderness—the one place mankind has not yet managed to muck up! At least that's what I had thought. Now glaciers are melting and calving in the wake of mankind-induced climate change. I am so grateful we journeyed there when we did, in 1995.*

We boarded the World Discoverer at Port Stanley in the Falkland Islands. Having traveled on this ship previously, it felt like coming home. We were even welcomed by the same captain with whom we had sailed through Alaska's Aleutian Islands and Bering Sea. We got unpacked, settled into our cabin, and went off to collect our red Antarctic jackets. They, together with our snow pants and knee-high boots, would shelter us through wind, rain, snow, and ice.

A double rainbow appeared as we sailed out of the harbor, each end of which disappeared into the gently rolling sea. We assembled in the lounge where Captain Rolf Zander and the ship's naturalists welcomed us. This was followed by an afternoon lecture on "Plate Tectonics" by John Splettstoesser, a geologist and polar scientist, addressing continental drift. In this lecture he traced the earth's movements and illustrated how the Falklands were once a part of South Africa while Antarctica and Australia were joined. Twice the size of Australia, 98% of the Antarctic continent is covered by an ice sheet that averages one mile deep.

The continent was not even discovered until 1820, and the first landing did not occur until 1895. Exploration of the continent began in earnest soon after, and Roald Amundson, a Norwegian, was the first to reach the South Pole on December 14, 1911. Ronald Scott, a British explorer, led a team of five arriving less than five weeks later, but all perished on the return voyage. They did, however, collect the first fossils from the Antarctic plateau proving the continent was once forested.

The World Discoverer accommodates 138 passengers. In addition to about one hundred individuals, there are three groups making the voyage, a German birding group, a group under the guidance of the noted photographer Franz Lanting, and fourteen members of our Penguin Society. That night half of our group, including Alfred and I as the Penguin Society leaders, dined at the captain's table, and the rest of our group dined with him the following night. Our conversation ranged from the wherewithal of the Antarctic Convergence, the dictates of the Antarctic Treaty, the policies of cruise ships in the Antarctic, and the fact that this would be his fifty-eighth trip to the continent. Nice to have an experienced captain at the helm! The evening lecture was on "Ocean Nomads: Albatrosses of the Southern Ocean."

FRIDAY, FEBRUARY 9 THE SOUTH SCOTIA SEA

I decided to skip breakfast and lie in bed listening to a lecture over the public address system in our room. The topic was "Blubberslugs and Aquatic Pit Bulls: Seals of the South." The eight-thousand-pound Elephant Seals with their prominent proboscis are the so-called blubberslugs as they move about so slowly, and the Fur Seals, with their sharp teeth and nasty disposition, are the Aquatic Pit Bulls.

We had moderately heavy seas last night, which kept some of our group from the breakfast table for reasons other than lying in bed getting an education!

After a bit of birding on the ship's stern, we attended another lecture. But this one was quite different. For nearly two hours, Kim Heacox held a room full of people totally spell bound as he read excerpts from various books and did his own unique narration of the journey of the famous Antarctic explorer, Sir Ernest Shackleton. Kim had a way of stroking his words like a painter on a fresh canvas. Subsequent to this journey, he became an award-winning author of numerous books about the north country especially, Antarctica and Alaska.

As I listened to Kim, I was reminded of our first visit to Anchorage when we went to a small dinner theater and listened to recitations of the writings of Robert Service—*The Cremation of Sam McGee* and *The Shooting of DanMcGrew*. Kim is an excellent storyteller.As he and his wife and fellow naturalist, Melanie, are Alaskans, perhaps this is a talent cultivated during the long dark Alaskan winters!

After lunch we had the mandatory zodiac safety briefing and-discussion of the Antarctic Visitor Guidelines. There are rules for tourists down here, as well there should be, and we were instructed on how to behave in the presence of the wildlife.

SATURDAY, FEBRUARY 4: GRYTVIKEN, SOUTH GEORGIA

The weather this morning looked much like it did yesterday afternoon, murky gray skies, fog, and seas rolling off into the horizon.

The snowy mountains and shoreline of South Georgia were beginning to appear through the fog. Scores of Gentoo Penguins were diving in and out of the waves alongside the ship.It had been raining all morning. Nonetheless, it was exciting to be approaching South Georgia and Grytviken with its rich history of whaling and

Antarctic exploration.This morning's lecture on whales and whaling did much to increase our awareness of all we were about to see.

We arrived at Cumberland Bay, sailed into King Edward's Bay, and docked alongside a badly deteriorated floating dock with metal plates set down for us to walk upon. As we started to disembark, the skies began to clear and the sun bounced off the surrounding mountains. How did Shackleton ever cross them to reach this whaling station, I marveled. But more about Sir Ernest later.

Two King Penguins, four feet tall, stood near the dock as though they considered themselves the official welcoming committee. Pintado Petrels with their beautiful black and white wing plumage flew alongside the ship, and Antarctic Terns with bright red bills and red legs screamed overhead.

The Grytviken scene was more than abandoned buildings and machinery.It was a reminder of grizzly death. When I looked inside the remains of this huge processing plant, I was reminded of the Nazis death camp at Auschwitz.Massive slaughter was the name of the game. The whaling station processed twenty-five 60-foot Fin Whales every 24 hours.You could look at the structural remnants, close your eyes, and just imagine what this place must have been like when 300 men worked here and whales came in for processing daily.

We began walking along the shore and soon came upon a large number of five to seven-year-old Elephant Seals.They don't develop their big proboscis until about eight years of age, but what a massive pile of blubber!One big male reminded me of Jabba the Hutt in the movie *Star Wars*. What girth! A young Fur Seal female was charging everyone in sight, and seal pups were staging mock battles. I was reminded of the admonitions the naturalists had given us about these "Aquatic Pit Bulls". By the way, the term is an affront to pit bulls who can be very sweet if raised correctly.

There was activity everywhere you looked. In addition to the seal show, South Georgia Pintail Ducks were feeding in the little pools and rivulets fed by melting snow. Nestled in the grasses along a stream, we came upon a group of about 20 molting King Penguins who were diligently pulling feathers from their ragged bodies.Elephant Seals roared and snorted nearby, and silently on a knoll overlooking this entire scene, we saw the grave of Sir Ernest Shackleton. How wonderful a setting for his final place of rest.

People scattered—each seeking to enjoy this very special place in his or her own way. Alfred hiked up a very steep cliff, which I would not even begin to attempt, but he was on his way to photographic pursuits. I stayed along the shore photographing the Elephant Seals, Fur Seals, King Penguins, and ducks.

At four o'clock we assembled at Shackleton's gravesite. Champagne was passed around. Captain Zander came off the ship and solemnly read a tribute and presented a toast to Sir Ernest Shackleton, clearly a larger-than-life hero in this part of the world.And well he should be.

The story of Shackleton's journey is an Antarctic epic of the first order. In brief, Sir Ernest's ship, the Endurance, became trapped in ice as winter set in on the continent. Eventually, he and his 28 men and 69 huskies had to abandon ship, set up camp on the pack ice, and watch their ship be crushed by the ice. It sank before their eyes on November 21, 1915. The nearest civilization lay 1,000 miles away. For the next 16 months, the men traversed the ice, pulling their supplies and small boats behind them, and eventually rowing their small boats to Elephant Island. Shackleton and five men then left Elephant Island and traveled in a small open boat for 16 days covering 800 miles in what are known as the worst seas in the world. When, at last, they reached the island of South Georgia, they had to cross these high, snow-covered mountains and glaciers to reach a whaling station and help for the men they had left behind. Twenty-two men left on Elephant Island waited four months for the return of "The Boss". And return he did, bringing all of his men home safely. Sir Edmund Hillary once said, "For scientific leadership give me Scott, for swift and efficient travel, Amundsen, but when you are in a hopeless situation, when there seems no way out, get down on your knees and pray for Shackleton."

A small contingent of British soldiers are stationed at Grytviken, and after showing us around the whaling museum, we returned to the ship and journeyed a short distance to the Nordenskjold Glacier, named for a Swedish explorer. We anchored in front of the glacier enjoying the view. The sky was a brilliant blue, the glacier a deep indigo, and the Snow Petrels and Pintado Petrels were performing a beautiful aerial ballet overhead.

SUNDAY, FEBRUARY 5: SALISBURY PLAIN AND PRION ISLAND, SOUTH GEORGIA

At 4:15 a.m. the telephone rang! Time to rise and shine for the landing at Salisbury Plain. Coffee and sweet rolls were provided in the lounge to tide us over until late breakfast, and at 5 a.m.we boarded the zodiacs for Salisbury Plain. Once ashore we gazed upon the likes of a Super Bowl stadium filled with King Penguins! An estimated 100,000 pair of King Penguins breed here, and they were all at home when we came calling. The chicks call constantly, and somehow the parents know the sound of their own, regardless of how far up the hillsides they may be! Adults forge their way through the masses, encountering territorial pecking as they pass, until they find their own young.

The penguin welcoming committee carefully looked us over as if to ascertain what manner of red-jacketed critters we be! We had nearly three hours on Salisbury Plain, giving us ample time to work our way around the penguin colony and photograph at will. Some of the adults were incubating an egg carefully tucked atop their feet and under a fold of abdominal skin. Males and females share the egg care responsibility, carefully passing the egg from one another's feet. Other adults had young chicks tucked under their pouch. Still others had "oakum boys" begging to be fed.The oakum boys, chicks in brown fuzzy down, were about 11 months old and are, therefore, being weaned from their parents. One oakum boy thought that I would make a good surrogate mother, and it followed me as I walked, chirping continually for food.

Gradually I worked my way over to the far side of the colony, propped myself up against a wall of tussock grass, and sat down to quietly observe.Several penguins came over to give me a close inspection and a few pecked at my rubber boots. They had obviously not read the Antarctic Treaty which clearly states humans and penguins are to stay fifteen feet apart! Two rolls of film got shot as these magnificent creatures paraded past me—or simply sat quietly incubating their egg or warming their chick.There are some experiences in life one never forgets.The sights and sounds of Salisbury Plain will certainly be among them.

We returned to the ship for breakfast, after which we boarded the zodiacs again for a ride to Prion Island.Our objective here was to see Albatross on the nest. Unfortunately, we had to hike up a long, arduous, muddy trail to reach them. En route, however, several of us were slipping, sliding, and falling down on the muddy trail. But once on the top, we had breathtaking views in all directions.

The view of the nesting Albatross was also spectacular. We even caught one pair involved in a courtship display of raised heads and clacking bills. Some sought to flee, and they required a running start to get airborne. Their four-foot wingspan, however, soon had them gliding off the cliffs and out over the sea.I stumbled around in the tussock grass for a couple of hours taking photos before retreating back down the hill through the mud, and rivulets of water and rocks.

MONDAY, FEBRUARY 6: GOLD HARBOR & COOPER BAY, SOUTH GEORGIA

How can each day exceed the sights of the day before! When I awoke at six o'clock, the cabin was flooded in light. I looked out the porthole and was blinded by the brilliant sunlight shining on the mountains and glaciers of Gold Harbor.

Alfred and I got up and dressed quickly so as to be on the first zodiac going to shore at 7 a.m.The cloudless sky was brilliantly blue, the glistening seas calm, there was no wind, and although the temperature was 40 degrees F, people began peeling off jackets once on shore.So here we were, sunning ourselves in shirts and sweaters on South Georgia's beaches, while back home the northeast was getting its first major twenty-inch snowstorm! And people thought we were crazy going to Antarctica in February.

Once on the beaches we were met by King Penguins, Gentoo Penguins, Giant Petrels, South Polar Skuas, Snowy Sheathbills, Fur Seals, and Elephant Seals.We all set off to do our own thing. Alfred climbed up the mountainside to photograph the nesting Light-Mantled Sooty Albatross—a handsomely colored bird with velvet-like soft brown plumage. I started down the beach, gently breaking a path along the water's edge so as not to disturb the penguins or annoy the feisty Fur Seals.At the far end of the beach, adult King Penguins were sitting on eggs with their skin folds nicely covering their treasure. Others had days' old chicks devoid of any feathers sitting on their feet.Some were regurgitating food to feed young chicks. Predatory Skuas and Sheathbills were wandering through the colony looking for eggs or chicks they might steal.

I found a somewhat quiet nook and sat down to enjoy the penguins' antics, trying to ignore the pink penguin guano covering the ground. It was a small price to pay for the scene before me.

Once back aboard, we had to scrub our boots with brushes and pails of sea water, wash off our rubber pants, and divest ourselves of our life vest, parka, hat, gloves, and heavy socks.It was a process we would endure with each shore visit! But once accomplished, we eagerly headed for brunch!

After brunch, we had to reverse the entire dressing process for our zodiac landing at Cooper Bay, but by now I had gotten very good at quickly getting in and out of Antarctic gear. And each time we went ashore, we had to line up while a member of the crew checked to be sure that we had our life vests properly in place. One would not survive five minutes in these cold waters.

Cooper Bay has four species of penguins: King, Chinstrap, Macaroni, and Gentoo. Seeing them all together gives you an opportunity to study not only their different plumage but also their individualities.The Chinstrap does indeed have a black chinstrap, like a British Bobby, across his white face. They are a rowdy, feisty, noisy bunch. The Macaroni Penguin has striking bright orange feathers bursting from the top of his black head, and the Macaronis have a loud, brassy call.The Gentoos have a white eye patch and tend to stay apart from the others like quiet observers. As for the Kings—well, they are simply regal, and their brassy trumpeting calls are the loudest of all.

We also saw a great many of the Sheathbills, pretty, but not nice! They are scavengers who eat anything and everything—and I do mean everything—including live chicks! There also were hundreds of Fur Seals, some of which gave us chase. The Elephant Seals paid us no mind, lazily lying on the shore.

We spent three hours on the beach trying to photograph courting, mating, chick feeding, territorial fighting, pruning, and all other manner of behavior.Eastman Kodak is going to love us, as we shot ten rolls of film today.

Back to the ship at 5 p.m. had our usual debriefing and outline of plans for the 'morrow. We then had dinner and retired, happy but exhausted.

We are now in the open waters of the South Scotia Sea and the swells are huge! The best place to be is safely lying down in bed!

TUESDAY, FEBRUARY 7: SOUTH SCOTIA SEA

We have a full day at sea today as we travel to the Orkney Islands.The naturalists, therefore, are bombarding us with lectures to fill the time—"Long Distance Migration", "Sailing Around South Georgia", "Adelie Penguins", and "Ice is Nice". There are very few birds following the ship today so we are on the lookout for whales and icebergs.

The seas are rough again tonight, and the ship is listing slightly to the starboard side—due to stiff winds, according to one of the ship's officers. This being the case, we turned in early, eagerly anticipating the morning's adventure in the Orkney Isles.

WEDNESDAY, FEBRUARY 8: SOUTH SCOTIA SEA

We just had quite a night—an Elvis Presley "shake, rattle and roll" experience. Alfred and I were already in bed when crew members came in to close off our portholes. Now I understand why. At breakfast this morning they announced that we are in a Class I Antarctic storm with winds of 50 knots (57mph) and 20-foot seas. We had been sailing at the rate of 12 knots, but the storm is so bad it has slowed us down and we are running badly behind schedule. We were to reach Signy Island in the South Orkneys at 10 a.m., and now it seems we won't get there until midnight—14 hours late.

At 2:30 p.m. we had 35-foot seas. The wind was steady at 55 knots (63mph), and the storm was a Force 10 on the Beaufort Scale. But we had brilliant skies and blinding sunlight! What a strange environment!

The Orkney Islands have had to be scratched from the itinerary as we have been sailing at only 1 knot for the last several hours and are just too far behind. Moreover, with these monumental seas, there would be no place safe enough to launch the zodiacs. And so we continued sailing directly into the wind headed for Elephant Island where Shackleton's men had their long, arduous wait for "the Boss".

I feel sorry for the British research scientists whom we were to have visited at the Orkney Islands Research Station. They get so little company, and I'm sure they were looking forward to coming aboard ship, having some fresh fruit and other good food while conversing with the passengers. We, in turn, were disappointed not to have an opportunity to visit their station and learn about their research.

4:30 p.m. The storm is now only an 8 on the Beaufort scale and yet we are still riding very heavy swells.

At 5:30 p.m. we went to the Discovery Lounge to hear Kim Heacox tell us the story of Scott's and Amundsen's race to the South Pole. Unfortunately, after about 20 minutes in the Discovery Lounge I had to leave. There is something about that room that gets people sea sick at times,and I succumbed around 6 p.m. and went to bed for the night.Somewhere along the way we hit 11 on the Beaufort Scale with 35-foot swells. A hurricane is a 12 on the Beaufort Scale and 70 mph winds, so we weren't far from being in a hurricane.

THURSDAY, FEBRUARY 9: SCOTIA SEA

Miraculously, I slept well. Somehow the rocking and pitching of the ship seemed less. Moreover, we didn't hit any more "bergy bits"— yes, they are called that—so there were no loud ice-grinding noises to alarm us. Now this morning at a special announcement we learned why. They had slowed the ship to 6 knots so that they would not hit bergy bits they couldn't see. We had previously been hitting small bergy bits, and although not really dangerous, the noise is very frightening. Bergy bits, by the way, are about the size of a small cottage—which means they are not so small after all!

We also learned that at the height of the storm we were going 1 knot backwards as we pointed our bow into the wind! A glance at the map and weather charts posted in the Observation Room showed us going from moderate swells to rough seas to heavy seas to extremely heavy seas over the past 48 hours.

A special meeting was called at 9 a.m. to tell us that the storm had so impeded our progress that not only would we miss Signy Island, we would also miss Elephant Island, and we would be turning southwest to a new landing spot, Paulet Island, off the east coast of the Antarctic Peninsula.We were very disappointed to miss Elephant Island, but Paulet Island, we're told, has a great deal of resident/breeding wildlife. After three days and three nights at sea in moderate to extremely heavy seas, we are now seeing icebergs everywhere.

The day passed uneventfully. The staff did their best with lectures, videos, quiz games, etc., but three days at sea is taking its toll. There was one announced sighting of Humpback Whales, and the captain turned the ship around to take a better look, but the whales dove and vanished.

FRIDAY, FEBRUARY 10: THE CONTINENT!

Today began at 4:15 a.m. when we got a wake-up call as the ship approached Paulet Island. I hurriedly dressed and went up on deck only to find we were running nearly an hour behind schedule. It was cloudy and we had no golden sunrise on the icebergs. But did we have icebergs! They were everywhere.

We dropped anchor, and at 7 a.m. Alfred and I were off in the first zodiac to go ashore. We were also in the last zodiac to return to the ship. But in spite of having nearly three hours ashore, I felt that I was racing against time endeavoring to switch lens and cameras (a battery died in one), seek out penguins doing something interesting, watch out for aggressive Fur Seals, check my light readings, and photograph our first Weddell Seals with their big brown eyes and angelic faces!

I have not mentioned my fear of the water, the fact that I can't swim, and my need to stare at the floor when on zodiac rides, but I have learned it is the only way I'm going to get ashore, so I have gamely crawled into zodiac after zodiac, held my fear in check, and carried on! Frankly, I've been rather proud of myself these past few days.

At yesterday's photo workshop, much was said about getting down and shooting at the penguins' level. When we arrived on Paulet Island, I scanned the beach for rocks I could sit on, but often ended up sitting on gravel and rocks covered in penguin guano. Even worse was kneeling or lying down on the rocky pebbles trying to get photos of the penguins at the best possible angles. At least the beach was free of Fur Seals so I didn't have to worry about being attacked while I was down and vulnerable!

The Adelie Penguin rookery on Paulet Island consists of several thousand birds. The juveniles were in creches and in varying stages of molt. The feeding chase was on everywhere you looked, and we watched intently and with great amusement as the adult birds, their bellies filled with krill, were harassed by the chicks seeking to be fed. Here too each adult recognizes its young by their calls, and somehow each manages to find and feed only its own. It's remarkable. Once found, the little ones peck at the beaks of the adult until the adult opens its bill and regurgitates food.At this point, a chick thrusts its entire head into the adult's beak—and halfway down its neck it seemed—to feed.

Once again, I was mindful of the admonition to keep a distance of 15 feet from the penguins. But that is often impossible as they crowd around you totally unafraid of whatever manner of species we humans may be. Often the chicks came up to me to beg for food, but I unfortunately could not oblige them. They were comical little creatures given the state of their molt. Some were still dirty, fluffy little brown fuzz balls, while others had shed their down, but for "Mohawk" hairdos. Virtually all of the breasts of the adults were covered with regurgitated krill, but back they would go into the sea and emerge with more krill, clean as could be, their feathers once again pristine.

Back on ship I had a good deal of cleaning up to do—my boots, pants, jacket, gloves, and camera bag all bore regurgitated krill. Everything stunk.

About 1 p.m. we came alongside the Antarctic Peninsula and everyone raced out onto the deck. There it was—a snow and glacier covered fortress of land glistening in the sunlight. I thought of all the great explorers who had come here to conquer this land, but one look told me this continent will never be conquered. It is wild and it is free.

Seeing Antarctica for the first time leaves one with an indescribable feeling. This vast forbidding wilderness makes one feel very small and insignificant. As I stood solemnly, almost reverently, gazing upon the cliffs of ice, I thought what a privilege it was to lay eyes on this remote behemoth of a continent!

As we sailed into Hope Bay, the red buildings of the Argentine research station, Esperanza, stood in stark contrast to the landscape. What an outpost and we were scheduled to visit the research station here! Seven families, including thirteen children, live here. What isolation these little families are living in! We were all eager to set foot on the continent, but alas, it was not to be. Although the sun was shining brightly, we were once again bucking 40 knot winds and even stronger Katabatic gusts coming off the glaciers. It was a 10 on the Beaufort Scale again! Bergy bits were everywhere, and we all soon realized it would be far too dangerous to attempt zodiac landings. So close—and yet so far.Nature is in control here and she never lets you forget it!

We cruised to the end of the bay, marveling at the gigantic glaciers that surrounded us. What beauty! What unequivocal beauty! And then, when it became evident that we had no hope that the winds would decrease, the captain turned the ship around and slowly we headed back out of the bay and continued south along the Antarctic Peninsula in the Bransfield Strait.

I had to go to our cabin as I felt exhausted. It wasn't that I had done any physical labor, but there is so much to take in and to try to comprehend. There is so much that remains unknown about this continent that it remains—as it was described one hundred years ago—Terra Australis Incognito. I needed time to absorb it all.

But naps don't last long on this ship. Kim Heacox was hosting another story hour, this time about the Nordenskjold Expedition of 1901-1904. And his lecturers were not to be missed, if at all possible.

After his lecture we had a briefing about our tour of the Antarctic Peninsula. We will hope for a landing on the continent tomorrow.

During the recap of our visit to Paulet Island we questioned why we had seen so many, many dead chicks. Paulet has an estimated 60,000 to 70,000 breeding pairs of Adelie Penguins, but why were there so many dead chicks? Some of the naturalists think it is a food shortage. Krill are known to fluctuate, and our naturalists thought that even those chicks still living looked thin. Others thought the chicks could have been killed by an early spat of cold weather. No one really knew the answer.

Shortly before dinnertime, an announcement came over the PA system saying the captain had spotted an iceberg covered with penguins. Dinner would be delayed to permit us to come out on deck for the view.

What fun we had watching these little Adelies make a flying leap out of the water onto the steep side of the berg, often failing to get a toe hold and sliding backwards into the sea. Over and over, they tried. You could even see highways of their toeholds on the surface of the ice. Eventually, it seemed, most of them were making it.The captain took the ship all the way around the iceberg so everyone could get photos, and no one minded having a late dinner with a diversion like this.

SATURDAY, FEBRUARY 11:
PORTAL POINT, CONTINENT OF ANTARCTICA

Antarctica greets you on its own terms. We awoke this morning to light snow followed by sleet and then driving rain.While it would be wonderful to have bright sunshine and blue skies, I somehow feel the weather we are experiencing is more typical of the area.

We dropped anchor in Mikkelsen Harbor, and by 8:30 we were into zodiacs and on our way to Trinity Island.What a sight we were with layer upon layer of clothing and rain slickers over our jackets. We looked as plump as the oakum boys! The air temperature was 37 degrees and the water temperature 34 degrees.It was a wet landing. We waded ashore with the wind and sleet blowing in our faces.

Slowly we made our way up the rocks and across a snow field to the abandoned Argentine research hut.

The snow was pink with regurgitated krill and penguin guano.There were Gentoo Penguins breeding on this island, and some of the chicks looked cold, wet, and miserable.Many of the young chicks, still in down, buried their heads in the adults' skin flaps, leaving their little back sides to the wind.

At last, we reached the hut, and with the aid of a candle and flashlight, we were able to have a look around inside.It was a sturdy hut with a common room, kitchen, bathroom, bedroom, and storage room.Lest this sound like cozy accommodations, let me assure you it was a picture of stark functionality.Most things had been stripped from the hut, but there were a few pots, pans, and dishes around and mattresses were still on the beds. There was a table in the common room, but no chairs. There was no sink, no toilet, in short, no functioning facilities. There was but one window and it was boarded up, so the interior of the hut was in total darkness.How bleak it would be to live here in pursuit of one's research interests. The rain was relentless, and I was having a problem keeping my camera dry.One lone Fur Seal kept his sentry along the path, and we all kept our distance. These were not conditions in which one could make a quick getaway. After about two hours photographing Gentoo Penguins, I slowly made my way back to the landing site across the rocks, through the at times ankle-deep mud, and back across the snow.

Once everyone was back on board, the ship started for our next destination, Portal Point in Charlotte Bay.Here we hoped to find a landing site that would enable us to set foot on the Antarctic mainland.The sheer ice walls along the shore make landings difficult and seem to reinforce the isolated aura of the continent.It is as though Antarctica does not really want visitors and only tolerates them as they come by very seldom and rarely stay for more than a brief visit.

En route to Portal Point we came upon a Humpback Whale and calf who seemed very sociable. We "played" with them more than an hour and they gave us a spectacular show. They stayed close to the bow of the ship, and the calf frequently rolled over on its back and waved its flippers as if calling us to play.

About 4 p.m. we dropped anchor near Portal Point, and everyone prepared to go ashore.This would most likely be our one and only landing on the Continent of Antarctica.Unfortunately, the weather was awful.Skies were dark, the wind was blowing, and it was raining.We dressed accordingly and boarded the zodiacs.We could not see our landing point from the ship as the zodiacs had to go around a point of land and carefully make their way through a maze of bergy bits.And then, at last, Portal Point came into view.It was a small rocky spit of land on which stood a tiny hut built in 1956 by the Falkland Island Dependencies Survey as a base for dog sledding expeditions along the Antarctic Peninsula.It was named Portal Point because it provides a rare gateway onto the ice cap plateau.Stepping foot on the continent was an emotional experience that defies description.Everyone began taking pictures of everyone else so that the majesty of the moment would be recorded.Some threw snowballs; some climbed the glacier.We were like children who knew this was a special event but weren't quite sure how to act or what to do.

The skies were gloomy, and the rain fell at a steady pace. Those who had brought cameras ashore were trying their best to keep them dry, but without much success. While it would have been nice to have had better weather, it was weather typical and appropriate to Antarctica. After all, this ain't Miami Beach!

Suddenly it struck me as I looked at the abandoned hut on this tiny rocky outcropping how very isolated we were, how very far from all we know as so called "civilization."The immensity of the continent, the power of the ice, and the desolate nature of our environs gave me cause to stop and reflect on just where at that very moment I was standing.

As usual, it seems Alfred and I were on the last zodiac back to the ship.

SUNDAY, FEBRUARY 12 : LEMAIRE AND NEUMEYER CHANNELS/CULVERVILLE ISLAND

The day began at 5:30 a.m. for those of us who had signed up for an early wake-up call.We were scheduled to pass through the much-publicized Lemaire Channel at 6 a.m., and many early birds were out on deck for the occasion.Once again, the weather left much to be desired. There was snow on the deck initially, and later we encountered sleet and rain. Fog and low clouds obscured the peaks of most of the rocky spires. Nonetheless, it was an imposing sight. I have never passed through such an array of cathedral-like granite spires draped in a never-ending parade of glaciers.We were fortunate to be able to sail through the channel because several cruise ships had been blocked recently due to the presence of a large iceberg in the channel opening.

After we passed through the channel and entered the bay, we found that the water was choppy and there was a 30-knot wind— much too much wind to safely launch zodiacs. This meant that our planned morning at Pleneau Island had to be canceled. But an announcement from the bridge informed us that we would have a landing at Port Lockroy.

After waiting around for 30 minutes or so, it became obvious that the winds were not going to change so we sailed back through the Lemaire Channel and on to the Neumeyer Channel.

Port Lockroy was the site of a large Gentoo Penguin rookery, but we all had to turn into Rockhoppers to make our way around the area! Close views of a new phenomenon greeted us at Port Lockroy—pink and green snow algae, mosses, and lichen.I've been going through film so quickly that I decided at this landing, I would concentrate my photo efforts at the shoreline where Gentoos were hopping into and out of the water. I worked my way slowly down the rocks along the side of the rookery to the water's edge and sat down on a boulder with my back against a granite wall.There I stayed for over an hour, watching and waiting for specific shots.Soon after I settled in, a food chase scene took place about 10 feet in front of me.The adult Gentoo had just returned from the sea, and its chick was chasing it loudly calling to be fed. How wonderful it was to quietly sit there and watch the penguins going about their normal routines. I seemed not to be disturbing them at all by my presence, and I felt enormously privileged to be a quiet observer of their behaviorisms.

All too soon it was time to head back to the zodiac landing area. As usual, Alfred and I were among the last to leave.

After lunch we began our cruise through the Neumeyer Channel, and to our delight, the sun appeared!It was a beautiful passage made all the more enjoyable by the appearance of two Humpback Whales. These whales were not as curious as the two we encountered yesterday. Nonetheless, the captain stopped our journey, and we followed the whales for about a half-hour. The scenery was spectacular—more gothic cathedral-like spires draped with glaciers, but this time in sunlight.

We entered the Gerlauch Strait and proceeded to Culverville Island for a zodiac ride through the ice!At the outset, the waves were rather intimidating, and I found myself feeling less than comfortable about my decision to take the ice tour. But I managed to keep my fear in check, and eventually we turned into a sheltered area behind a wall of grounded icebergs.The scene was magical. Hundreds of icebergs had drifted into this one spot, and our zodiac wove its way among them.A host of ice sculptures now surrounded us. Some were no more than 8-10 feet high, but others rose to the height of multi-story buildings. Their colors ranged from powder blue to sapphire, and others bore hues of green and violet.Slowly, we meandered through this enchanting ice forest.

After nearly an hour of touring this incredible site, we rounded a berg and saw the ship awaiting us.The captain had moved the ship to quieter waters and we would not have to face a wild ride home. Then the Leopard Seal appeared!For more than 10 minutes he stayed at the rear of our zodiac, surfacing often, diving, then spy hopping to look us over. Closer and closer he came until he was no more than five feet behind us. Our zodiac driver was getting nervous, as Leopard Seals have been known to clamp their vicious teeth onto the cone ends of zodiacs, puncturing the air chamber and causing them to deflate. The seal followed us right up to the ship's landing platform. "Look what followed us home," I called out to the first mate, but I did not follow up with the line, "Can we keep him?" No one wanted this vicious fellow.

It was 6:45 p.m. when I retired to our cabin with a cup of coffee and one of the Clipper ship's famous chocolate chip cookies. It's always a treat to return from a zodiac tour and find the entire ship filled with the aroma of cookies right out of the oven. Many of us asked for, but were denied, the recipe. Then it appeared in a popular cooking magazine, so I'm pleased to include it at the end of this chapter. The combination of milk chocolate, macadamia nuts, walnuts, pecans, and hazelnut and coffee liqueur is a combination to be shared!

At this point I felt the need for some quiet time alone to try to come to terms with all that I had just seen.This continent is mind-boggling.Each day it seems to reveal new things about itself, and at times I feel my circuits are getting overloaded in my efforts to take it all in.

We had a late dinner, and as we dined, I looked out on the snow and ice-covered continent that was just off our starboard bow, realizing tonight we would gaze on the Antarctic continent for the last time. Our furthest southern point at Pleneau Island was 65 degree 08 minutes and 32 seconds south. Now we will turn and head back north. Overnight we will be traveling northwest toward the South Shetland Islands arriving at Deception Island early tomorrow morning. A very full day of landings on Deception and Livingston Islands is planned for tomorrow—our last day in Antarctic waters. After that, we shall sail north across the Drake Passage back to the Falklands.

Antarctica! I still don't think I quite believe I am here. But the 35 rolls of film that Alfred and I have shot will, I'm sure, help us to come to terms with this wild, untamed, and wickedly enticing continent. But now to bed. It has been a long 19-hour day!

MONDAY, FEBRUARY 13:
DECEPTION AND LIVINGSTON ISLANDS

It is 11 a.m. and we have just returned from a wonderful landing at Bailey's Head on Deception Island. The sunshine and the early morning light on the black volcanic sand beach was exquisite. Ashore we found thousands of Chinstrap Penguins and a large group of bull Fur Seals.I concentrated my photographic efforts at the shoreline, trying to capture the tentative moves of young Chinstraps entering the water for their first swim. They were such neophytes at this game as they cautiously approached the water's edge and then scurried back as the waves crashed around their feet.Finally, one brave soul would start out and then a group would follow him or her into the sea.

After an early lunch, we headed through Neptune's Bellows—a narrow gap in the crater wall—before entering the volcanic caldera of Deception Island.Our first stop inside the caldera was Pendulum Cove, where some people donned bathing suits to swim in the geothermal-heated springs that mingle with the cold ocean waters.

When everyone had done their Antarctic bathing, we pulled up anchor and headed to our final landing in Antarctica—Hannah Point on Livingston Island.Here we found Chinstrap, Gentoo, and a few Macaroni Penguins; nesting Southern Giant Petrels; Kelp Gulls; Sheathbills; Blue-eyed Shag; and a few Fur Seals and Elephant Seals.

Tomorrow we cross the infamous Drake Passage, and I pray the waters will be calm!

TUESDAY, FEBRUARY 14: DRAKE PASSAGE

Awoke this morning at 6.00 a.m. and saw a beautiful sunrise over the calm waters of the Drake Passage.As the day wore on, the sea got even quieter to the point of being as still as a mill pond.With the sun shining and the temperature relatively mild, several passengers stretched out in chaise lounges on the deck—bundled up in their red parkas, but sunning their upturned faces.

That afternoon there was a panel presentation on the subject of the Antarctic Treaty, which prohibits mining or military establishments and governs tourism.This was very interesting, but it raised almost as many questions as it answered. I raised a question about the so-called Guide Lines for Antarctic Visitors—and the differences between the theory and the practice as evidenced yesterday at Hannah Point. People had to walk through penguin colonies because there was no shoreline, photographers were up on the ridge where the Giant Petrels were nesting, and we had witnessed the horrible suicide leap over the cliff by a frightened Elephant Seal.I think my comments were important if only to alert the ship naturalists to the fact that passengers did not approve of how things were handled yesterday. There was no consistent implementation of the announced "policy" of staying away from the nesting petrels, naturalists failed to guide the tourists when high tide eliminated the pathway along which people were supposed to walk, and the naturalists as a group failed to get people off the island when they saw the Elephant Seal's agitation. There are obviously many issues yet to be resolved regarding the impact of tourism here, especially when a crew as conscientious as ours runs into problems. On the other hand, those of us who have seen this incredible area will, most assuredly, feel compelled to defend it from exploitation—in which case, tourism serves an important function.

We had the usual recap next with many comments about our smooth passage through the Drake. People speak of "The Drake" in the most respectful of terms—mindful of its reputation for having the worst seas in the world. But tonight, after dinner, we strolled out onto the deck to see a beautiful full moon reflected on a quiet sea with the Southern Cross shining brightly overhead.

WEDNESDAY, FEBRUARY 15: DRAKE PASSAGE

Another smooth night at sea and this morning we again have sunshine and calm seas.

After lunch we heard an informative lecture on "The Natural History of the Falklands." Later in the day there were even more lectures offered, but by now I found myself quite lectured out.

Dinner was served early to permit the staff to get ready for the World Discoverer Crew Show.

The crew put on something of a Harvard "Hasty Pudding" ninety-minute production. About twelve numbers were presented—each announced by a one of two "number girls", a Filipino baker and a Sri Lankan waiter dressed in a variety of drag costumes. The scenes ranged from four male cooks in tutus dancing to the music of Swan Lake to the captain and the boutique manager acting out "The Rain in Spain" from *My Fair Lady* with the voices of Rex Harrison and Julie Andrews dubbed in. There were pantomime skits and four male can-can girls and another with the Filipino baker in a chorus line performing "New York, New York." Four men of the senior engineering staff and one naturalist appeared for one musical number wearing balloon bosoms under short red dresses, and Valerie, one of our waitresses, performed the "Willkommen, Bienvenue" song from *Cabaret*. (All singing was actually mouthed to musical tapes.) The show was a smash hit. It was nearly midnight by the time we got to bed, and tomorrow will be an early morning—yet again!

THURSDAY, FEBRUARY 16: SEA LION AND
BLEAKER ISLANDS, THE FALKLANDS

Awoke to a peaceful Drake Passage again, but I find I am tired of preparing for shore excursions. Climbing into wool socks, boots, rubber pants, parka, hat, gloves, life preserver, and camera bag has become a real chore.

This morning we arrived at Sea Lion Island in the Falkland Islands and disembarked via zodiacs based on our sign up for a long walk (4 miles), a medium walk (2 miles), or a short walk (1 mile.)

A tough climb up a hill to the tall tussock grass proved to be too much for most of us, so we retraced our steps back down the beach and found a more gentle slope up into the tussock.Tussock grass is a strange type of vegetation.It grows in clumps and can reach ten to twelve feet in height. Walking through the tussock is like making your way through mini-valleys surrounded by grass mountains.

When, at last, we arrived at the Rockhopper Penguin colony, we found that most of the Rockhoppers had already left the rookery with the exception of a few molting adults.The Cormorant rookery was very interesting, however, as the birds had beaten down the tussock grass and built their nests on the remaining root clumps some two feet high. As a result, the rookery looked like a landscape of giant toadstools.

Just as we reached the shore, it started to rain heavily so we came back with wet gear, with boots smelling of goose, sheep, and penguin poop as well as an assortment of smelly seaweeds. Now we set about the big job of cleaning up *everything* as it must now all be packed into suitcases for the journey home. What a job our golden retriever is going to have when we get home, trying to decipher the "fascinating" odors on our boots and outer wear.

FRIDAY, FEBRUARY 17: SATURDAY FEBRUARY 18

Visiting Antarctica was undoubtedly one of our most memorable experiences. It has its equal only in our first Kenyan safari when we were overwhelmed by the vast African game herds. Antarctica is overwhelming as well, and it will take us many weeks if not months to digest all that we have seen and experienced within her icy domain. And last, but not least, Antarctica was, for Alfred and me, our "seventh continent" having at some point visited the other six.

And now the wonderful cookie recipe promised!

Clipper Chocolate Chip Cookies

  1 cup (2 sticks) unsalted butter at room temperature
  ¾ cup sugar
  ¼ cup firmly packed golden brown sugar
  1 tablespoon vanilla extract
  1 tablespoon Frangelico (hazelnut liqueur)
  2 large eggs
  2 ½ cups all-purpose flour
  1 teaspoon baking soda
  211 1/2ounce packages of milk chocolate chips
  1 cup chopped walnuts
  ½ cup chopped pecans
  ½ cup chopped macadamia nuts
  Preheat oven to 325 degrees(F). Using electric mixer, beat first 6 ingredients in large bowl until light and fluffy. Add eggs and beat well. Mix flour, baking soda and salt in small bowl. Stir in butter mixture. Mix in chocolate chips and all chopped nuts. Drop batter by ¼ cupful onto ungreased cookie sheets, spacing apart. Bake until cookies are golden brown, about 15 minutes, Transfer cookies to racks to cool. Makes about 3 dozen.

CHAPTER 10

Face to Face with a Polar Bear

WHAT IS IT THAT IS SO fascinating about the Polar Bear? They appear in commercials, toy stores sell stuffed polar bears, outdoor stores feature them in their catalogs, nature shows spotlight their vulnerability, and some environmental groups call them the canaries of global warming.

I can't attribute my own fascination with the bears to any of these circumstances, and I have no particular fascination with brown bears, black bears, or even grizzly bears. But polar bears? Ah, now that is something else! Ursus maritimus—I find you bewitching!

In 1997, Alfred and I traveled to Spitzbergen, Norway, where we boarded a 12-passenger Norwegian ice breaker and sailed north to within 500 miles of the North Pole. We did find a bear up there—one—that came right up to the ship to look us over, and later we saw two more far off in the distance. But this did not satisfy my craving. Eventually, I wore Alfred down, and he acknowledged that he'd never hear the end of it if we didn't go to Churchill, Manitoba, to see the Hudson Bay Polar Bears. In 2006, the trip became my birthday present! In the course of our travels, we saw seventy-three individual bears and photographed forty-four of them! The most magnificent of all I named Per Magnus.

NOVEMBER 17: BOSTON TO WINNIPEG, MANITOBA

When we boarded our flight to Winnipeg, it was 68 degrees in Boston and we were quite a sight in our Antarctic red jackets and heavy winter boots. In Winnipeg, no one gave our attire a second thought.

There were some people we met who looked at our gear and asked where we were going. When we said we were going to Churchill to photograph the polar bears, they said, "People really do this?" We seem to have a way of taking trips that elicit that kind of comment.

Once in Winnipeg we found our hotel conveniently located right across the street from the Winnipeg Airport terminal.

NOVEMBER 18: WINNIPEG, MANITOBA

After a long, boring day in the Winnipeg Airport and hotel environs, we attended a welcome dinner where we were given our name tags and baggage tags and met the other members of the group. There are thirty-eight people from seven countries—Germany, England, Holland, Spain, Australia, Canada, and the United States—taking this Tundra Buggy Tour.

We will be up at 5:15 tomorrow morning and on our way in a chartered plane to tiny Churchill, Manitoba. The mobile Tundra Buggy Lodge has not yet been moved to Cape Churchill as the ground has not yet frozen sufficiently, which means we are going to be going out there in pristine conditions with no vehicle tracks in the snow at all! And, reportedly, there are lots of bears!

NOVEMBER 19: WINNIPEG TO TUNDRA BUGGY LODGE, POLAR BEAR POINT.

We departed on our chartered plane at 7 a.m. for a two-hour flight to Churchill.

As we came off the plane, we were hit by an Arctic blast! The wind was cutting at our face and the snow was blowing all over the airfield. We piled into a school bus driven by Fred, a Cree

Native American. He drove us out to the polar bear jail and explained that this was where the "naughty" bears were put when they came too close into town.During the 1960s, the polar bears became so numerous in town the government established a Polar Bear Control Program, later called the Polar Bear Alert, to give warnings when bears came into town. The Polar Bear jail, or compound as it's now termed, can accommodate twenty-three bears, but they never keep them there more than 30 days before they are hauled off to the wilderness. One was transported by helicopter yesterday because they were getting full up in the jail. The bears are released about 60 miles away at a place called Diamond Lake, across from the Churchill River. They aren't fed in jail. They are only given water. But since the jail was opened in 1980, over 1,000 bears have been "in residence" here! Churchill's Polar Bear Alert Program works to assure that both bears and residents can cohabitate in peace!

Churchill, population 820, is a northern outpost located at the same latitude as Stockholm, Sweden.There are no roads to get you there. Access is by plane, railway, or boat only. Originally settled by the Cree and Chippewa people, the first European settlement came in 1717 as part of the fur trade network established by the Hudson Bay Company. Churchill almost ceased to exist in the years between the waning fur trade business and the development of Canadian agriculture. The railway from Winnipeg reached the port in Churchill in 1929. As the principal Arctic seaport in North America and the closest North American seaport to Europe, the port permitted Canadian grains to be shipped to Europe from this little wide spot in the road.

The town's next claim to fame came in the 1950s when the Churchill Rocket Research Range was established, a Canadian-American joint venture created to study the Northern Lights as part of the geophysical year. When it closed in 1984, Churchill was left with its grain and its polar bears.

The establishment of the first Tundra Buggy Tours in 1979 brought tourists. Now bear tours in late fall and Beluga Whale and birding tours in the spring help to support the local economy. The town, according to Kelsey Eliasson's *Polar Bears of Churchill,* is "built on some prime polar bear real estate," which, of course, is responsible for it becoming an international center of tourism. People have been coming here in October and November for decades now—just to see the bears—because there is certainly nothing else to do here this time of year. (Spring and summer tourists come to see whales, nesting waterfowl, and shore birds and for the fishing.)

Churchill is located in the middle of the northern migration route for the Western Hudson Bay bear migration. Not all of the 1,000 bears in the Western Hudson Bay population come through Churchill, as the migratory route extends from Cape Tatnam near Ontario all along the Hudson Bay south to Churchill. In mid-November, the ice begins to form on the Bay, and the bears begin to congregate around Churchill. Having survived on kelp roots and other plants since the ice went out the previous spring, they are mighty hungry and eager to get on the ice and once again hunt seal. By December, all is quiet. Both the bears and the tourists have left and the little town of Churchill goes into hibernation until the next season.

Our so-called "city tour" took us up and down the main street and the side residential streets, then out to the outskirts of town where we were shown the grain elevators that can hold 5 million pounds of grain. Sightseeing in our yellow school bus was difficult because you had to scrape the ice off your window! Experimentation taught us that a credit card worked best! I started out with my MasterCard, but then I switched to my Blue Cross/Blue Shield card, which was a little thicker and seemed to work better. This was a never-ending exercise in order to keep a little peephole open through which I could see outside. From the grain elevator along the Churchill River, we were driven to the open sea to see a stone cairn-like structure called an "Inuksuk". This Inuit word means "to act in the capacity of a human", and these stone figures serve as navigational aids, coordination points, or message centers.

The wind was brutal along the shore, slapping your face with stinging fingers. Alfred phrased it well. "Churchill is like Nome with an attitude," he said. Having been to Alaska, we would now know both towns well.We passed the road to Cape Merry, which I had read often hosted a lot of bears, but we were told the road was impassible. And then, as we circled back near the grain elevators, we got stuck in the snow. Fred rocked the bus back and forth but got nowhere. In frustration, he called for another bus to come pull us out. All the time, the wind was blowing and the snow was drifting. When the second bus couldn't pull us out, they brought out a third bus into which we all piled in order to continue on our way. The next stop was the state liquor store!

Then it was on to a little gift shop, which actually was the headquarters of Tundra Buggy Tours. There I bought a book entitled *Tundra Tales*, which tells what it is like to go on a Tundra Buggy adventure. It was written by the man who subsequently became my driver in Buggy #15, Glenn Hopfner. After lunch we drove fifteen miles out of Churchill to what is referred to as "The Launch", where the Tundra Buggies are parked in-between tours.

These motorized Tundra Buggies looked like large boxy white school buses built on fire engine chassis. There is a double seat next to each window and a wide aisle in-between. The Buggies ride on large, heavy, rubber tires about five feet in diameter. Like school buses, only the upper half of the windows opened. Thus, if a bear were to stand up at the side of a Buggy, the window opening would still be about 10 feet above the ground. That would be about nose height with a full-grown bear—as we would discover!

We all boarded one Tundra Buggy, and our luggage went on a second Buggy. After 45 minutes we saw our first two polar bears. So by our first night, I had managed to see and photograph two bears. Not bad, but I wanted more!

Shortly thereafter we arrived at the lodge, which was unlike any other facility we had ever known. Our friends were quite amused when they heard that at our "advanced" ages we were going to sleep in bunk beds with only a curtain for privacy and share two bathrooms and one shower with sixteen other people.

Tundra Buggy Lodge consists of about eight buggies linked together like a train. However, these vehicles have no engine and have to be towed in order to move. The touring Tundra Buggies will move the train when we travel to Hudson Bay's shores. There were two bunk houses with upper and lower bunks accommodating eighteen people each, a lounge car, a dining and kitchen car, a pantry car, generator and equipment car, and sleeping quarters for the staff. Each car was heated by a centrally located propane heater. The bunks were about seven feet long and four feet wide with a few being extra-long for tall people like Alfred. Each bunk had a window, an overhead reading light, and an electric outlet for charging camera batteries. There was space to store luggage under each bunk and space at the end of the bunks themselves. A denim curtain provided privacy.

The lounge car included a small bar from which complimentary wine was dispensed and tasty hors d'oeuvres were served each evening. A screen mounted behind the bar was pulled down for illustrated lectures, a computer was available for viewing digital photos, and there were enough chairs to accommodate everyone. The dining room had nine tables seating four each, with the kitchen, from whence the food was served, at the far end. Between each unit there were open passageways offering little shelter from the brisk temperatures of the outside world when passing from one car into the next. High-boarded walls protected everyone from the polar bears wandering about the camp! Passing through those "transit zones" could be invigorating!

We were given our bunk assignments, and Alfred and I got adjacent lower bunks due to our advanced age! I had packed similar items like underwear, sox, shirts, turtlenecks, etc. in two nylon net bags, which we hung from the ceiling of the bunk compartment. These bunks would be our sole source of privacy for the next eight days. Quite surprisingly, once you pulled the denim curtains closed, you really had your own snug little comfort zone where you could read, write, review your day's photography, talk into a tape recorder, or just reflect on the circumstances into which you had plunked yourself! I loved my private little world behind the denim curtains!

Once settled in, we moved to the lounge for hors d'oeuvres and safety instructions about travel in the Tundra Buggies. One point was made very clear. Throw anything out the window, food or otherwise, and you get "kicked off the island" back to Churchill!

NOVEMBER 20:
TUNDRA BUGGY LODGE, POLAR BEAR POINT

It's about 5:30p.m. I'm in my bunk, and there is something of a small cocktail party going on outside my bunk on the other side of my denim curtains. The chatter makes it difficult to concentrate on my diary, but I have just concluded a magnificent day and I'm beginning to think this trip is going to be on a par with Antarctica and our many African adventures.

I set my watch alarm to go off at 6:15 this morning. Coffee was available in the lounge as of 6:30 and breakfast was served at 7. We left in our four Tundra Buggies at 8 o'clock. We were all assigned to specific buggies, but Alfred and I had decided to split up and go on different Tundra Buggies so as not to duplicate each other's photos. This was especially important as there's not a lot of different wildlife species here, no wildflowers for me, and we're both shooting with a 70-300mm lens. I also have a 28-70mm for scenes inside the Tundra Buggy and other scenic shots.

I soon learned to change lenses quickly when I saw a bear striding purposefully toward our buggy. His firm stride, our guide Robert Taylor told me, meant he was going to rise up on his hind legs and give us a good looking over—all 10 feet of him! The first time that happened I had on a long lens; I couldn't focus because his face was so close to mine. With Robert Taylor, one of the two professional photographers leading the tour, and Glenn, a veteran driver of 20 years, I was in good hands.

Photography here is difficult. We are dealing with dark, overcast skies, filming white bears against white snow. Robert began by telling everyone to set their cameras at 800 ISO and +1 compensation in the blue, early morning light. He also told us to put the "white balance" dial on "cloudy."Almost immediately I got a couple of beautiful headshots of two bears who came over and put their paws up on the tundra buggy. Make no mistake, these bears are huge!

No more than ten people are put in a single Tundra Buggy so you have a double seat on each side of the buggy that is "yours" for the day. This means you have window access regardless of where the bear may walk. There is also an outdoor platform at the back of the buggy where there are no windows to obstruct your view. It was on that platform that I would have the biggest adrenaline surge of my life! As mentioned, windows open like school bus windows—halfway down—enough to stick your head and your lens out the window. Opening and closing those windows was difficult. They were cold and stiff and responded only to blunt force.

We had been advised to bring bean bags to steady our cameras against the window frame, given the fact that people are moving about, often from one side of the buggy to the other. I came up with my own invention. I had an inflatable airplane pillow which packs flat. I blew it up and put it on the edge of the window sill with a lanyard attached to it and then hung around my neck. I wasn't about to have it fall out the window and get myself shipped back to Churchill! It worked perfectly.

At the back of the Tundra Buggy there was a heater over which we frequently warmed our hands after photographing bears for an extended period. There was also a "honey pot" toilet aboard. Lunch consisted of hot soup and the means for making your own sandwiches. Cookies were plentiful and often were brought out for the 10:30 a.m. coffee break as well. A piece of plywood was laid across the top of three rows of seats, and that became the table for serving coffee and lunch.

It turned out to be an incredible day. We spotted twenty-six bears, and most were reasonably, if not very,close. Behaviorisms were fascinating to observe. A mother with a cub frequently had to chase away male bears coming over to have a look. Big males will kill a cub and eat it. Remember, these bears haven't eaten anything substantial since they came off the ice six months ago last May.

As Alfred and I went in two different Tundra Buggies, he was privy to a sparring bout between two young males that I did not see. They spar a lot this time of year in mock battle, which is really just play. Alfred got some great shots of "polar pugilists", but I didn't see any such action at all that day. So, our strategy of going in different buggies was working, and Alfred got the "shot of the day!"

On an African safari, when there is something special occurring, the drivers let one another know, but for the most part, we were on our own all day, quietly experiencing the Arctic in all its magnificence. What was amazing was how near to the lodge we were all day while we were shooting. We have been working back and forth between Polar Bear Point and Gordon Point—an area I knew was supposed to have many bears. At one time, there were seven bears surrounding our buggy!There were so many, in fact,I began naming them.I found I could tell them apart by their different facial expressions, different battle scars on their faces, different feet, different color to their hair. Some are white, and some are almost golden if they have been rolling in seal oil. Gypsy has a dark muzzle and dark feet. Thor has dark shading on his nose. Maria was a beautiful mother with her cub. Tuck had two scars across his nose.

I was astonished by the close proximity we had to the bears. Moreover, Glenn was excellent about knowing when to turn the bus so that you were not shooting into bad light or so you had a better angle for your shots. He also was mindful of the wind direction so the wind wasn't blowing into your face as you tried to steady your camera. He also moved the buggy ahead of the bear so that the bear walked into your picture. These drivers were truly skilled at positioning you for the best possible shot. I could certainly see the advantage of taking a tour for which the emphasis is on photography.

Today I learned that most of the bear cubs we are seeing are about twenty-two months old. When they get to be about two years old, they either get independent or the mother pushes them away. Some of the cubs we saw today are called COY bears, meaning "cubs of the year." As the cubs are born in late December or early January, the "COYS" we saw were about 11 months old.

From the two books I bought in Churchill, *Polar Bears of Churchill* and *Tundra Tales*, I learned about the life cycle of the White Bear.

The bears we are seeing each day are "hanging out", awaiting the freeze over of Hudson Bay. Salt water tides in Churchill come about every 12 hours. By November, the shore ice builds up and extends outward into the Bay. To ascertain if the ice is sufficiently strong to carry their weight, the bears will go out, spread their legs to distribute their weight, and test the ice with their front paws. Gradually, by November, the shore ice becomes strong enough to serve as the bears' hunting ground. By December, Hudson Bay is usually frozen over, and the bears are free to watch for the seals' breathing holes and lay there in wait for a meal. After a winter on the ice restoring their fat supply, mating occurs in the spring, but through a system of "delayed implantation", the pregnancy is not initiated until mid-September or early October.

In late September, females average between 330 and 550 pounds. Females must weigh at least 660 pounds for implantation to occur, and a pregnant female may weigh close to 900 pounds before denning. Mature males can weigh as much as 1,300 pounds. Once mating occurs, the female moves inland, prepares a new den or restores an old den, and settles in to give birth and care for her young. Cubs emerge from the den between late February and mid-March, and after about a week of acclimation, mother and cubs begin their trek to the ice some 20-30 miles away. Cub mortality during the first year is about 50% depending on the condition and skills of the mother. Ringed seals give birth on the sea ice in March and April so the timing of the seal birthing is opportune for mother bears trying to raise new cubs. Once the ice is gone from the Bay, the bears are left with naught but kelp root and mosses to sustain them until November when the cycle begins anew.

After dinner, Dan Cox, the second photo guide tour leader, gave an illustrated lecture sharing some of his fifteen years of bear photography as well as the work he has done with Polar Bear International and with National Geographic's Polarbearcam.

NOVEMBER 21, 2006: THE LONG, ARDUOUS, FASCINATING JOURNEY TO CAPE CHURCHILL

We woke early to totally clear skies and -8 degrees temperature. There were thousands of stars overhead, but no Northern Lights. After breakfast, everyone secured their belongings in their bunk space and we boarded the Tundra Buggies. At this point, the Tundra Buggies began to hitch up their loads. My buggy towed the propane tanks, and Alfred's buggy towed the pantry. Others lined up to tow the two bunk houses, the lounge car, the dining room, and the kitchen.

During the hitching up process, there were several bear guards with guns on the ground as the bears were very intrigued by all the activity. Bear guards have to be on watch any time anyone is performing maintenance work on the ground. Each of their rifles was loaded with three shots to warn off the bears. Their handguns carry two "firecracker shells" that make a flare and a loud boom. The last two shells in the gun are for real in the event a bear actually ignores all the warning shots and charges. *No one* wants that to happen, and I don't know that it ever has. But these bears are the world's largest carnivores, and they haven't had a piece of meat in six months!All precautions have to be taken.

We saw a flock of Common Eider fly by as we were breaking up camp. We also saw Red Fox tracks in the snow while waiting for the conga line of vehicles to get underway. Although we boarded our individual Tundra Buggies about 8:15, more than two hours passed before we started to head out.No complaints, as watching the whole process of breaking up camp was fascinating!

We took special notice of the fact that when the kitchen unit pulled out, the waste pipe for "gray water" was temporarily left behind. In no time at all, there were bears licking up the surrounding ice/water mix looking for any kitchen residue left behind. But there was little there. The bear I named Trouble was certain he could find something and refused to give up his pursuit of a morsel in the snow.He dug and dug until half his body was deep into a hole, but the camp staff collect and carry away everything so as not to have the bears associate the camp with food.

10:53 a.m. (At this point my diary was written in segments as the day wore on.) Less than twenty minutes into our journey, the truck ahead of us, which was hauling the generator, broke an axle and we have been here ever since. They called for the welder and they called up the armed bear watchers. In a flash, the owner was on the ground checking out the damage. The generator was tipped to the right at about a 45-degree angle. Fortunately, it fell over on its own tire when the spindle broke, so the trailer didn't go all the way over on its side. They called for a helicopter to take two men back into Churchill to get parts from their garage. About an hour after all this happened, all the Tundra Buggies were disconnected from the cars they were towing so that we tourists could be taken out to look for bears while all the repairs were going on. There's no leaving anyone in the wilderness out here so the conga line doesn't go until everyone is ready and able to move.

In the meantime, we found several bears and happily continued with our photography. With my long lens, I got a photo of a bear paw print the size of a dinner plate. A beautiful big male came alongside the buggy, whom I named Mishka, but I had on my 70-300mm lens. I saw him start to rise up right under my window, but I couldn't get the shot as he was too close for me to focus! But what a thrill to see that massive head coming straight at me! What beautiful, powerful animals they are. Moreover, although I know they would eat me for lunch, they make no noise nor show any aggression.

1:50 p.m. We just got a call on the radio to come back from our bear photography and hook up the propane tanks again. They are calling back all the buggies to reconnect their trailers and then we will be on our way. We should have been half way to Cape Churchill by now!

2:15 p.m. We are finally on our way – a caravan of eight vehicles slowly making its way across virgin snow without benefit of a road or trail. Our maximum speed is about 10 miles an hour as we pick our way around the rocks and gullies. How will they know where to go, I wondered? There are no roads out here. It's just wide-open spaces of snow and rocks. Then I learned they have mapped out the route by GPS and the lead buggy is navigating us. So that is why we are going to be able to travel in the dark! It seems the GPS is accurate within 15 feet. We constitute an incredible sight, like an old-fashioned wagon train – stretched out across the barren, white, rocky, frozen, snow-covered landscape. As the wagons are white and rather box-shaped, we've all commented that we look like something out of Star Wars – all we need are the white-costumed storm troopers and John Williams' music!

3:40 p.m. We've just had our second mishap. One of the vehicles ahead of us clipped a rock and the unit is listing at a 45-degree angle looking very much like the first accident. The GPS is good to within 15 feet, but that rock wasn't "mapped." Darkness is fast approaching as all the other vehicles pull up behind the crippled unit. It's the pantry this time. They certainly are having a hellish day on this trip. Glenn mumbled something about never before having had two breakdowns en route to the Cape.

4:30 p.m. Once again, we are on our way. They unhitched the pantry wagon and off-loaded some food as they are going to leave it here in order to get the rest of the caravan moving given the fact that we have another three hours of travel ahead of us. Some of the crew will come back tomorrow to get the pantry righted and able to continue.

We are now crossing frozen water out on some tidal pools and three vehicles are moving back and forth ahead of us packing the snow down as we traverse a frozen lake. Over the radio we heard the lead car say to the other drivers, "OK, put your dip locks down, four-wheel drive, and go slow."

7:30 p.m. We have just arrived at Cape Churchill, 21 miles from our previous camp at Polar Bear Point and 51 miles from Churchill.The caravan of headlights slowly moving across the tundra is an eerie scene. Often, we moved no more than 3-4 miles per hour and never more than 5 miles per hour in the darkness of the night so as not to get hung up on rocks buried by snow.

We are now in the Wapusk National Park and there is definitely more snow out here than we had at our first encampment. Wapusk is the Cree name for White Bear and they are in this park in abundance. In fact, the park is one of the largest polar bear denning sites in the world. A subarctic environment, the parklands stretch between boreal forest and arctic tundra. It is accessible only via commercial tours like ours.

Three Tundra Buggies are now going back and forth packing down the snow where the line of vehicles will be parked. I'm guessing we have another hour to go before we can re-enter the camp as they have to line up and assemble all the vehicles that were disassembled for the journey here. After everything is again hooked up, they have to get the generator going and the kitchen functional. But this has been an absolutely incredible experience and everyone has been in a good mood and "enjoying," if you can call it that, the whole scope of this operation. Just hope we don't have a repeat performance going back to Churchill. The novelty might wear off the second time around!

8:30 p.m. This is fascinating watching the camp get assembled. They pull the Tundra Buggy up alongside one of the lounge cars, and then haul out about a 20 ft. long tongue which they then attach to a trailer hitch via a steel cable. This gets the various "cars" lined up precisely. Once again, the bear guards are on duty with their guns in case any bears decide to come along and investigate all the commotion and lights. It must be an incredible sight for the bears. They've been alone out here in the wilderness, sitting along the shores of the Hudson Bay waiting for the ice to freeze – something like sitting around watching paint dry, I suppose, so they can go hunt seals. Then, out of nowhere, comes this "invasion of big, white, noisy vehicles with all sorts of lights! Many of the bears never have seen Tundra Buggies and I can't imagine what they must think of these behemoths. Last year the camp only made it up here for a week and this year, it will only be for five days. If the bears haven't happened to come around this area during those short visits, they have no idea what has invaded their territory.

9:30 p.m. We're inside the lodge! Spaghetti for dinner tonight. They had pre-cooked it for rapid preparation once we got the camp set up.

NOVEMBER 22, 2006: CAPE CHURCHILL.

We have just concluded our first day in the Cape Churchill wilderness. It was very cold last night. In spite of the blankets provided and the fleece throw I brought along, I had to open up my aluminum space blanket to get warm. Unfortunately, it makes a lot of noise when you try to unwrap it. I was trying to be so quiet about it as everyone had gone to bed and I was afraid I would wake up everyone in the bunk house. Surely, they would all wonder what I was doing with aluminum foil! The next morning, the man in the next bunk said he thought I was making sandwiches for everyone! But these things work! I put this thin sheet of aluminum under my blankets and around my body and instantly I was warm.

It was foggy and windy when we started out at our usual 8 a.m. departure time. With the wind chill, we figured it was about -13F. Our first bear of the day was a three-year old who probably has very recently left his mother and gone off on his own. We found him curled up by the old muk-tuk (a former party wagon for the camp, long abandoned) to get shelter from the wind.

We proceeded to the foggy shore of the Hudson Bay and soon came upon about a four-year old bear, a handsome fellow who promptly became the subject of several cameras. This little four-year-old was very curious, but also rather afraid, so he kept coming around to check us out before backing off and circling us once again. Finally, he sat down to just look at us, but when we made too much noise opening and closing the windows, he spooked. Our next discovery was a little bear that had made herself a nice bed in a snowdrift. I named her Julia in my photo log. She seemed quite comfortable and didn't seem to mind when it started to snow and her fur took on a mantle of snowflakes.

It was a real surprise and delight for the birders in the group when we came upon a flock of more than 100 Ptarmigan, an all-white grouse-like bird of the arctic.

We are actually camped on the shore of a frozen lake and about 30 yards away lies the Hudson Bay itself. Today we have been out directly on the ice, but the drivers try to drive on land spits created over the years. These are waves of gravel where waves of water once laid. Today we saw about sixteen bears including five mothers with cubs, but none would let us get close to their cubs. The bears here are much more inclined to be spooked by us than those at our first camp site where they had become more accustomed to people and the vehicles.

Today I really pressed into service the hand warmers and foot warmers I had brought with me. I had warmers in my boots and my gloves all day. There is a nice propane heater in the Tundra Buggy, but when those windows go open, the heat flies out. Moreover, time spent out on the back platform chills the fingers very quickly! I should mention that the sides of the back platform are 12 ft. off the ground. That's the height of a full-grown male bear when he is standing on his back feet! Most of the bears seem to stand about ten feet tall, but there are big boys out there – as we were soon to discover!

It's very important in this climate to keep your camera batteries warm, so I often warmed my camera under my jacket and I carried my spare battery in a small case inside my bra!

It was tough trying to photograph Arctic Fox and Ptarmigan today as white against white gives you virtually nothing upon which you can focus. Moreover, the fox is no larger than a small house cat.

Photographing these bears is a multi-faceted challenge. Today I got shots of their gait as these bears walk pigeon-toed. At other times, I've photographed their big feet. Sometimes one can catch the steam from their breath in the cold air. Still other times, we try to capture their mock battles and zestful sparring. We've had some very humorous shots too. Today we had a bear that was digging deeply for roots, and with his neck down deep in the earth, he gave us a good look at his wiggling fanny! We were all laughing as we took numerous polar bear butt photos. It was cold, cloudy and windy, the light was poor at times, it snowed and we had to spend much more time today looking for fox, hares and bears.Still we had a good day.

NOVEMBER 23, 2006: THANKSGIVING DAY IN THE ARCTIC

Today is Thanksgiving Day in the Arctic and we've just concluded another day of incredibly engrossing experiences. First a word on the weather – cold, windy, murky skies, and snowing. In the midst of this, we're trying to photograph white bears against white snow while battling gale-force winds and blowing snow. But as the saying goes "it is what it is" and we are simply having to cope!

We started out in the fog, unable to see beyond the end of our buggy, in an effort to find our first photographic subject of the day. That subject turned out to be a female, about five-years-old, who emerged out of the fog, white as the land around her. I decided to name her Tundra. She came forward and leaned up against the buggy, she banged her feet against the buggy and she chewed on the tires. I heard one of the guides say later that she was probably the most aggressive of all the bears we've seen because she was determined to try to get something from the buggy. In short, she was probably very hungry and she wanted to see if she could find something to eat inside this big white tin can object.

Eventually, we moved on and found a bear sleeping in the willows that was totally uninterested in us. When we returned to the camp, the same little bear we'd seen in the morning was still curled up in the lee of the muk-tuk, appearing not to have left all day.

The bears were laying low today because the weather was horrible. Since they can't yet go out on the ice, they can't hunt seals, they have only kelp roots to chew on, and their bellies are empty. Why not sleep away the day in a snow drift or a willow grove sheltered from the wind?

Later this afternoon, we saw the biggest bear we have seen thus far. He was a colossal male! I named him Brownie as his feet and legs were, indeed, brown. When he stood on his hind legs, he was probably twelve feet tall. The guides thought him to be around 20 years old. Polar Bears have a life span of about twenty-five years. The bottom of the tundra buggy windows are 10 feet off the ground.

Brownie's head was above that. He put his paws up on the edge of the back-observation platform and, thus far, no bear has come anywhere near being able to reach up so high. He probably weighed about 1000 pounds. These bears are the world's largest predators and we were warned to be mindful of their height and the reach of their paws! He was one magnificent big guy and it was positively electrifying seeing him so close. But I was still to have my own personal moment with a bear.

We had another bear today that was just beautiful – snow white, no scars, no stains on her coat – just a lovely girl. I named her Smilla in honor of the Danish book, *Smilla's Sense of Snow.*

Once again, we had a nice lunch of hot soup and a hamburger hot dish (heated on the propane stove) that was a cross between Chinese chow mien and lasagna! But there was also meat, cheese, lettuce, tomatoes and cucumbers for anyone who wanted to make a sandwich. Cookies, coffee and hot chocolate completed the menu. Tonight, as it is American Thanksgiving, they are going to serve us turkey and pumpkin pie, which is really nice as not everyone on this trip is American.

Once back at camp, we followed the usual routine. Everyone sits down and starts looking at their photos of the day. "What did I get today? Oh, shoot, that one didn't come out. Well tomorrow I'll have to try again." Most all of us took pictures of the camp in the snow because we all thought it looked like Ice Station Zebra!

We have two more days of filming out here and I must say everyone has settled into the routine very well including our bunk house lifestyle. In spite of being packed into a sardine can, we are all doing very well and people are getting along well. And no one snores loudly!

Initially, everyone was very discrete and we all squirmed around in our bunks pulling our clothes on and off before "exposing ourselves" in the aisle in order to put on our boots. But after a couple of days, people got into their long johns and then pulled on pants, shirts and sweaters out in the hall. Formality seemed a little foolish under the circumstances.After determining that my rolling around on the aluminum foil doesn't wake people up, I used my space blanket again last night. As the old song goes, "Baby, it's cold outside!" There's no getting around it. As I lay here in my bunk recording my diary, I see thick ice on my window.

There isn't a great amount of bird life here this time of year other than the Ptarmigan, but people in one buggy saw a Snowy Owl today. It must be very hard to see a Snowy Owl in the fog and blowing snow, but they found him perched on an observation tower.

Thanksgiving dinner was served and it was very enjoyable – turkey, ham, mashed potatoes and gravy, corn and pumpkin pie. The evening lecture on the Artic Fox was given by the owner's son, and it was a very nicely presented program.

NOVEMBER 24: CAPE CHURCHILL

I woke this morning to find three bears right outside our dining room windows. One was a very big male, lying there watching all the activity inside and smelling the bacon cooking. I'm sure he was wishing there was some way he could get inside.

When we boarded the Tundra Buggies at 8 a.m., the weather was still overcast. We soon found a mother and cub out on the ice, but she wasn't about to bring her cub onto the shore. Next, we came upon two sleeping bears in a willow thicket that had obviously dug in for the storm last night. We had eight bears for the morning. The photography got bad because the weather got bad and we soon found ourselves in a howling blizzard with strong winds and fog obscuring our view. In this weather, all the animals were hunkered down. Only crazy tourists like us were out and about moving around.

We found a pair of Arctic Hare, but what a photographic challenge! You've got nothing to focus on but two black eyes, a black nose and small black tips on the ears – which don't show if they have their ears lying flat.

We had a nice, hot vegetable soup for lunch, together with make-your-own-tacos. You lay a piece of aluminum foil over the propane stove, then place the taco shell and cheese atop it so it can all get nice and warm. You then add your own ham, lettuce, tomatoes and cucumbers. While enjoying our lunch, we were parked opposite the two sleeping bears, as were two of the other buggies. As the wind was so strong, there didn't seem to be much point trying to go elsewhere.One bear woke up, rolled over, played with a willow twig and then went back to sleep. The other one raised his head only once in the entire two hours we were there.

Then the storm went from bad to worse.The buggies can't get too far from camp in weather conditions like this. We had white-out conditions at times and there are no landmarks to find the way back to camp. We were driving on a frozen lake and that doesn't leave any tire marks - especially when the snow is blowing across the ice.

Today we learned that when we first arrived at Cape Churchill, the ice had been 6-8 inches thick but by now they reckoned it was 10-12 inches thick. We even have driven on Hudson Bay at times. When the wind blows the waves toward shore, the waves turn to ice, leaving very rough modules of ice. It is just too dangerous to drive over the shores of the Bay. Finally, at 2:45 we determined that the howling blizzard conditions we were experiencing left no point in staying out.

Dinner tonight was steak and baked potato and tomorrow night, we're told, it will be prime rib. Food has been very good!This trip meets our Penguin Society standards – "travel to exotic lands while eating gourmet food!" After dinner we had a very informative lecture on the Polar Bears of the Western Hudson Bay.

Outside, however, we are having a very severe snow storm. The winds are 50 mph and according to the kitchen staff, the forecast for tomorrow suggests the weather is going to be even worse! Will we be able to get out tomorrow or not! We'll just have to wait and see. After all, this is the Arctic!

It's going to feel like we're back in Antarctica on the ship again tonight. The bunk house is really rocking.

NOVEMBER 25: CAPE CHURCHILL

This was to be our last day at Cape Churchill and it turned out to be one of the most exhilarating days of my life!

The first three hours of the day were cloudy and blowy, but the wind eventually died down a bit.There were two bears at camp this morning. Soon after we headed out, we came upon three males and for the better part of two hours we watched them play in mock battles, rolling around on the snow, picking ice out of their paws, rubbing their noses into the snow and rubbing their bellies in the snow in a seal-like slither. They came over to the side of the Tundra Buggy, particularly when we started to heat up the soup. I know they could smell the food as everyone had windows open taking pictures. All three of these bears were gigantic and Glenn said they were all close to 15 years old. They were just magnificent, huge, monarchs of the north!

Then one of the bears ambled to the side of the Tundra Buggy. I decided to go out to the back, devoid of windows and meet him on the back platform. This time I had changed my camera lens and I was ready. "OK bear," I told him, "are you ready for your close-up?" I established eye contact with him. He slowly sauntered over and then began to rise up on his back legs. Leaning over the edge of the platform, looking directly at his face, I shot frame after frame. He rose up closer. Then he was so close I could no longer focus. I pulled the camera away and I had a polar bear's nose twelve inches from mine.I could feel his breath on my face! I gazed reverently into his eyes. Neither of us uttered a sound. And then I whispered to him," You are magnificent and I will remember this moment for the rest of my life!"

Slowly he backed down and ambled away. I stood there overwhelmed. My God, what just happened! I just had a private moment with a very large polar bear. There was no one else around. Just the two of us. For several minutes I leaned back against the Tundra Buggy wall - stunned. I named him Per Magnus.

Only after this incredible experience did I become aware of the roar of the surf on Hudson Bay.The waves were now pounding the shoreline ice and the sound was the voice of raw nature. Then we got a call over the radio saying, "The wind is changing. You'd better come in." In less than ten seconds, we had gale-force winds and white-out conditions. It was time to get the buggies home as it was starting to get dangerous. We traveled in tandem, waiting when two of the buggies got stuck in snow. It was essential that everyone stay together now. In weather like this, no one could be left behind.

Suddenly, we were being whipped by 70 mile per hour winds, and the snow was blowing across the ground like a raging river in high flood. The snow was compacting on the windshield of the buggies as the drivers strained to see and avoid the rocks. We were following the lead car with the GPS system and over the radio we heard someone say, "Keep your eyes sharp. We have to be some-where near the camp." But no one could see a thing! Everyone was looking out the windows trying to catch a glimpse of the camp. The wind was blowing tsunami waves of snow obscuring all view. Then, all of a sudden, Glenn almost ran into the old muk-tuk party buggy sitting on the fringe of the camp! And the little bear was just barely visible in his hide-away.

We had a full-scale Arctic blizzard going on.

When we came here, I came to see polar bears, and I'm not ashamed to say that that I cried after meeting Per Magnus. To be in this environment with these animals, to be sheltered as we were by the Tundra Buggies, and to be out on the platform having the snow falling and my face twelve inches from the face of a polar bear! There are no words. Well maybe there's one—it's supercalifragilis-ticexpialidocious!

NOVEMBER 25, 2006: RETURN TO CHURCHILL

When we went to bed last night, the storm was so severe and no one knew how long it was going to last, so there was an announced Plan A, Plan B, and Plan C depending on the circumstances we found in the morning. This morning the winds had certainly died down, but there were a lot of deep snowdrifts and we knew there would be heavy drifts across part of the track going back to town. Last night during the blizzard, I looked out the lounge window and saw the snow moving horizontally like a raging river.

The decision was to go with Plan A this morning—meaning all the people would be sent 51 miles back to Churchill in one Tundra Buggy and all the luggage in a second buggy. The rest of the crew would stay back to disassemble the camp, hitch up the buggies, and bring the camp back to town. We will go out as a trio with the little Polarbearcam in between the two tundra buggies as it has only two-wheel drive.

We loaded onto the Tundra buggy at 8:15 but didn't depart until 9:45. Kevin was leading with the luggage and breaking the trail as he went, so we moved very slowly. The Polarbearcam was in the middle and all we tourists were at the end.

We hadn't been gone very far before I heard Kevin say on the radio, "Keep your eyes on your gauges, guys; we're going to be work-ing these machines." We did have to plow through drifts, but slowly but steadily we moved along. At Wilson's Point we came upon a significant drift that was going to require a running start. Each buggy was going to take it at its own pace. As the people mover had to wait for the other two buggies to go ahead of us, everyone started to line up for the one bathroom on the buggy. With 38 people there, it ended up being a 45-minute pit stop! Robert said, "Next time, no beverages for breakfast, and we'll feed everyone sponge cake."

We saw no wildlife on our way, but the wind patterns on the snow were fascinating. The wind directions were reflected in the various patterns in the snow.The snow patterns would have made beautiful photos, but we weren't stopping for photography this time. We were trying to keep a slow steady pace in case we had a major breakdown again. The drivers really wanted to get back to Churchill in daylight. Looking at the snow configurations, I was reminded once again of the book *Smilla's Sense of Snow*, in which the Inuits speak of 17 different types of snow, depending on the snow's characteristics. You could see the direction of the winds laid out on the snow, and in some places the snow swirled around rocks leaving rivulet patterns lying there.

The clouds began to dissipate, some blue sky appeared overhead, and finally the sun appeared. We were doing very well, but about half an hour before we reached the launch site, both the front and back left tires of our buggy broke through the ice of a fast-flowing stream and down we went into the water. The first Tundra Buggy had had a bad time getting through and had radioed a warning to stay left, and Glenn did as told, but not left enough. "Hold tight," Glenn yelled, and he gunned the engine. With snow, water, and ice flying, we made it. A good piece of driving there! We reached the launch site, refueled, and continued another 45 minutes into Churchill. When we reached Churchill, it was only 3:45 p.m. but the sun was already setting.

We were divided between two hotels, the Tundra Inn and the Aurora Inn. As Glenn was about to turn down the street to the Aurora Inn, he noticed a low-lying power line, which he said the Tundra Buggy would not fit under. We had to disembark, get our baggage, and schlep our bags up the snowy street to the hotel. Getting down off the tundra buggy to ground level made us realize how high up those Tundra Buggies really are—emphasizing how tall some of those bears had been! Alfred noted that we had always entered the Tundra Buggies from the platform at the rear of the Lodge vehicles. This was our first view from ground level and the first time we had set foot on the ground in days.

As we walked the streets of Churchill, it was -13 F and the wind made it feel even colder. Once at the hotel, we were welcomed by a little husky puppy who ran around excitedly greeting everyone and licking every hand extended toward him. Except for the puppy, Churchill was a ghost town. I guess the locals have enough sense to stay inside on a bitterly cold Sunday night.

When we walked the four blocks to the restaurant, I noticed not everyone had decided to stay inside tonight. There before us were very large polar bear paw prints in the virgin snow. We later learned that the owner of a gift shop had reported two bears in town today! Most of them have now left Churchill and are heading out to the ice some 50 miles away—at Cape Churchill from which we had just come, but I guess I know where at least one of those two bears was walking today!

During dinner, we saw both an Arctic Hare and an Arctic Fox right outside the restaurant window.That, plus the presence of the bears in town tells you Churchill is just a small island in a vast wilderness.

NOVEMBER 26: CHURCHILL TO WINNIPEG

It was -14 this morning, and you knew it when you stepped outside! A bus shuttled us to Gypsy's Bakery for breakfast, which, it seemed, was the social center of town. After a very substantial breakfast, we had about an hour's free time to visit a couple of shops. We are the last of the tourist groups to come to Churchill this season, so the shopkeepers are happy to open up on a Sunday morning for possible last-minute sales. When we leave, the town will go to sleep for the winter.

I made it worthwhile for one shop owner to open by buying an Inuit soapstone carving of a polar bear. She agreed to ship it for me as it was quite heavy. It was probably the most expensive of any of our global collection of carved animals, but Eskimo art is always expensive. Some Eskimo artists do very abstract work in their portrayal of people and animals, but the artist whose work I purchased, Paul Padluq of Lake Harbor in Nunavit, carved nice detail into the bear's face, feet, and hind end!

At the Churchill airport, we saw the same local artist, Mark Reynolds, whom we had seen on arrival, and, once again, he had his small kiosk open with a beautiful array of sterling silver jewelry. Alfred bought me a necklace with a pendant featuring the face of a polar bear and a matching pair of polar bear earrings. We then discovered that he took Visa and American Express, but not MasterCard. Having misplaced our traveler's checks, we didn't have adequate cash. "That's okay," he said, "take the jewelry and mail me a check when you get home!" My word! "That's the way we operate here in the North," he explained! How remarkable!

And so ended our arctic adventure.

NOVEMBER 27: WINNIPEG TO BOSTON

We awakened to find that Winnipeg was having a snowstorm with 15 inches forecasted. Fortunately, we had a morning flight and we were able to depart, but not until we spent considerable time at the deicing station out on the tarmac. When we were adequately sprayed with lime green and orange liquid, we taxied and took off.

What a journey this has been. We saw seventy-three polar bears and photographed forty-four of them. The photos can only hint at the adrenalin-pumping moments we were privileged to experience. On the tape recorder, into which I recorded my diary, I hear the sound of the arctic blizzard our last night at Cape Churchill. The singing wind and the breath of a polar bear on my face are archived memories that will live with me forever.

CHAPTER 11

Cuba, Hemingway, and a '49 Plymouth

IT WAS A BEAUTIFUL spring New England day in 2012 when I walked down to the mailbox and found a letter from Steve Cox, Executive Director of International Expeditions, inviting us to go on a natural history-oriented People-to-People trip to Cuba. Alfred and I had long wanted to go birding in Cuba, and this seemed like a perfect opportunity to combine some excellent birding with a chance to see Cuba itself. We immediately called Steve and said, "Count us in."

The People-to-People Program was established by Dwight Eisenhower in 1956. President Eisenhower proposed the program to give everyday citizens of different countries the opportunity to meet and get to know each other in order to foster understanding, friendship, and lasting peace.

It didn't quite work out that way. Here's what really happened.

FRIDAY, JUNE 15

We were in the Miami Airport Marriott Hotel where we were given a pile of travel documents which were required by both the US and Cuban governments. We were told to be downstairs with our baggage at 5:30 the next morning to board the hotel shuttle to the charter plane section of Miami International Airport. Given the US embargo against trade with Cuba, we were told to expect lots of paper work and flak from US officials as we pass through passport and immigration control, but after that, we were free to go have breakfast for which International Expeditions provided $15 per person.

8:20 A.M. WHEELS UP! WE ARE BOUND FOR CUBA!

The group dutifully assembled in the hotel lobby at 5:30 a.m., boarded the shuttle, and headed to the airport. We didn't have time to spend $15 on breakfast. Once we were all checked in and had our boarding passes, we had about a half-hour before having to go through security, so we "dined" at "Chez Dunkin Donuts."

Our charter plane was a modern 120-seat jet. Alfred and I were not seated together, and my travel companions were Cubans. They spoke no English and I spoke no Spanish, so I spent the 50-minute flight filling out Cuban customs forms and reading an airline magazine article about Chinese immigration to Cuba in the 1800s. It seems Castro took over all of their small businesses in 1960, so the 75,000 who had been brought to work the sugar cane fields, and later set up small businesses, returned to China with nothing to show for their contributions to Cuba's development.

Our first views of Cuba from the air were of green fields, narrow dirt roads, no traffic—a paved road with only five cars—and horse-drawn carts everywhere.

WHEELS DOWN, WE ARE LANDING IN CAMAGUEY, CUBA!

We made our way out of the airport and found the Executive Director of International Expeditions, Steve Cox, a friend for more than 25 years. Steve was joining us on this "maiden voyage" into Cuba. We met Gustavo, our guide, and Frank, our driver, and boarded a beautiful, big, Chinese made, forty-four-passenger bus.

Camaguey was founded in 1514 along the northern coast, but was moved inland in 1528 due to pirate attacks, including attacks by the infamous pirate Henry Morgan. The city was laid out in a labyrinthine design to confuse unwanted visitors, unlike other

Cuban cities usually laid out around a central square. It is Cuba's third largest city with a population of about 300,000.

We had been told to expect changes to the itinerary, and the saga of the "don't believe what the itinerary says" began immediately.

The itinerary read:

> *"We board our vehicle and drive a short distance west to the small town of Florida. Here begins the first of many interactions with Cuban people from all walks of life who live and work in this small town that is so typical of Central Cuba. We learn from each other and find common ground while making the first of many new Cuban friends."*

This didn't happen, and Gustavo, our guide, appeared to never have heard of the idea.

> *"Later we will drive further east to the lake and marshes of Embalse Zaza. The marshland edges are great places for water birds during the winter..."*

Well, that didn't happen either! Gustavo said we didn't have time.

Our first stop of the day was the Camaquey Ballet where we stood for a rather lengthy introduction, during which I snuck outside to get my first wildlife shot—a beautiful blue and green Anole Lizard with a pink pouch. I had seen this little guy on the outside wall as we entered the Ballet headquarters, and fortunately he was still in the vicinity. The building was a house built in 1937 by a wealthy Cuban who left the country in 1959 when Fidel Castro began his revolution. The government took over the property, as they did most such properties, and in 1975, the Ballet moved in.

We then walked across their campus to see a rehearsal of a new production. Two men and two women put on a lovely performance.

The male star of the ballet, we were told, had won a gold medal in international competition in South Africa last year. The Camaguey Ballet has prepared a production of Tennessee Williams' *A Street Car Named Desire* in hopes of being invited to tour the US someday. Apparently, they have toured in many foreign lands. This was a nice visit, but it hadn't been what we came to see.

We then drove through the town and then walked for about a half-hour in searing heat to a restaurant where we were greeted with glasses of rum and cola (Coca-Cola being banned from sale due to the US embargo). We were offered chicken, fish, beef, or pork. I chose fish and Alfred had beef, served with French fries and cabbage salad. We would eventually learn that these would be the offerings at virtually every restaurant and, most significantly, that almost all the restaurants being state owned, are obliged to cook out of the same state-prepared cooking manual! In the course of the trip, it led to some pretty monotonous meals.

We also quickly learned that meals are a long-drawn-out process, usually requiring two hours. We Americans aren't used to dallying over our food like that, especially in the middle of the day when we always feel we have things to do and places to go!

Back on the bus, we began a four-hour drive to the city of Sancti Spiritus where we subsequently got lost wandering through narrow streets trying to find the hotel! It got quite hilarious when we began recognizing streets and said, "Ah, yes, we've been lost at this intersection before!" We had a host of locals trying to give us directions, and Frank did some amazing feats of navigation trying to turn our big bus around small corners and very narrow streets. The backstreet tour revealed very dilapidated housing, streets, and sidewalks and a haphazard mass of jerry-built electrical lines strung up across the street. After a while I think the locals were turning out just to watch the bus back up streets, turn down dead-ends, and, in short, provide their evening's entertainment.

When we finally reached the Hotel Del Rijo, they didn't have enough rooms for all of us in spite of our having confirmed reservations. Although the itinerary read:

"Our accommodations are in an 1819 neoclassical home located on a small square that is now a boutique hotel."

With no room in the inn, we twenty-five people now had to go elsewhere!

At 7:30 p.m. I wrote in my notebook, "We've been sitting here in the middle of the street for 15 minutes waiting for what, I haven't a clue."Later Gustavo told us that although the second hotel was only 200 meters away, the police wouldn't let us drive there on the narrow streets. We therefore had to drive another 15 minutes out of the city and come back into the town via another route!

We got to the Hotel Plaza, got our room keys, and, as subsequently turned out to be the nightly routine, we were told the menu and asked to make our choices. By now it was well after 8 p.m., and having already had one hot meal, Alfred and I opted for a chicken sandwich in our hotel room.

The room was actually a suite with a small sitting room, bedroom, and bath. Hot showers felt great and the sandwich was totally adequate, but late as it was, I still had the task of writing up all of my notes for the diary. So here are some general observations I made.

Many apartment buildings are Russian architecture such as I have seen before in Russia, East Berlin, and Budapest. Buildings have straight walls with simple windows, no frills, and the stucco exteriors are falling away.

We noted many organic vegetable farms along the road with small kiosks where the farmers were selling their produce.

We saw many living fences such as we saw in Indonesia—one sticks branches in the ground, strings up wire, and eventually the branches start to grow, forming small tree fences which are quite charming.

There are many Brahmin cattle with long floppy ears as well as goats, horses, and "free-ranging chickens!" (We kept wondering throughout the trip how they find where the chickens have laid their eggs.)

Occasionally we saw a well-built house, but often the humblest abode had rose gardens planted in the front yard. Cubans apparently like flowers because if it wasn't roses, it was hydrangeas and crotea. Lovely little gardens, humble little houses!

We noted many stray dogs of indeterminate breeding everywhere.

Transportation seems to be primarily by horse-drawn carts, often transporting two to four people, but with a few hauling as many as eight persons! As late as 9 p.m., the horses were still standing tethered to their carts—in case someone need a ride! I wondered how many hours these poor horses had to work each day.

The houses are colorful—lavender, blue, navy, green, peach, aqua, and yellow, but most are in very neglected condition.

Being birders, our eyes were frequently on the skies, and we did see our first Cuban endemic, a Cuban Blackbird. We also saw many Cattle Egrets, Gray Kingbirds, Black Vultures, Northern Mockingbirds, and a Cuban Emerald Hummingbird.

SATURDAY, JUNE 16

Yesterday, Gustavo had agreed to my suggestion that we leave a little early and go to the Embalse Zaza wetlands that we missed yesterday, but he "forgot" this morning so we missed our first birding site entirely.

Today's destination was the headquarters of the mountainous El Naranjal Natural Reserve where the itinerary said:

"There are several separate ecosystems represented and more than 700 flowering plants."

This visit got cancelled too!

It seems there were heavy rains two weeks ago and our big bus wouldn't be able to make it up the mountain roads.

We were offered a Russian truck sitting by the roadside, but Steve knew nothing about the truck and he didn't want to put us in an unknown vehicle. Moreover, he told us, we're going to be in two Russian trucks tomorrow in the national park and he knew those two trucks were safe. After all, the Russians pulled out decades ago and we were already seeing that the word "maintenance" didn't seem to be in the Cuban vocabulary. So we lost our second natural history site visit.

With that visit cancelled, we hit the road again, past oxen-driven carts carrying construction materials, and oxen in the fields while a farmer walked behind with a hand plow.

Our new destination was the Valley of the Sugar Mills, a UNESCO Cultural Heritage Site, which was absolutely beautiful. I had no idea Cuba was so mountainous. Sugar is no longer a major export, but during the 19th century, there were more than 40 sugar mills with elaborate estate houses, all but one of which are now in ruins. We were able to visit the one house that is being well maintained as a tribute to the past. On the grounds we had a sip of sugar cane juice while watching a Cuban Emerald Hummingbird and a large West Indian Woodpecker. Goats and chickens roamed about us. On the long walk up to the house, many women had stalls on both sides of the road selling hand-embroidered tablecloths and crocheted dresser scarves. Their hand work was so beautiful I bought two table cloths.

Then it was on to a pottery shop where the family has been making pottery for more than a century. I bought a small pottery owl for our collection.However, our itinerary said we were going to

> *"...continue our Cuba people-to-people activities with a visit to the Cienfuegos Caritas distribution center. Here we meet,"* said the itinerary, *"Caritas Cuba volunteers, learning the work they do on behalf of disadvantaged Cubans. Through this engaging dialog, we can compare and contrast the American style of volunteer service with the service of Cuban volunteers."*

Well, that never happened.

I'm beginning to suspect the Cuban government really doesn't want any dialog between American and Cuban people—the whole purpose of the People-to-People program.

The Cuban government also isn't very happy with the Catholic Church, and they probably don't want it known that Cuba has "disadvantaged people" which the church is serving. Our People-to-People program is turning into a "Cuban Show and Tell." How sad. We were all looking forward to the promised interaction.

On to the city of Trinidad which was described as "an architectural jewel proclaimed by UNESCO as a Cultural Heritage Site."A port city established in the 16th century and founded by conquistadors, it became an 18th century port of call for pirates and smugglers. Reportedly, it was the center of the homes of sugar barons, and oh what wealth they enjoyed! Unfortunately, much of it is in disrepair, but one can see where there were once palaces of great opulence.

In Trinidad, we took a walk through part of the city, stopping twice to listen to Cuban bands.Then it was on to the beautiful Hotel Las Cuevas where we were to stay two nights. The hotel is built on a steep hillside with a view of the Caribbean in the distance. The grounds are planted with yellow allamanda bushes, hibiscus in a variety of colors, and large Royal Poinciana trees ablaze with red flowers. Horses were grazing on the lawns, and stray dogs were everywhere.

I took a walk around the grounds hoping to see new birds. Using my best birder's "phishing voice" I called a Red-legged Thrush in close, but the light was bad and photographing the bird was difficult. As a storm approached, I saw a White-winged Dove and several Greater Antillean Grackles, but when the skies got black and I began hearing thunder, I raced up the hill to our cottage and arrived just as the downpour began.

At dinnertime we donned our rain ponchos and made our way to the hotel lobby where a sweet little black and white dog was making the rounds in the lobby looking for food. He got many pets, which he enjoyed, but none of us had any food. He rolled over on his back, clearly begging for a tummy rub. I obliged! You wanted to scoop him up and hug him. Instead, I had to take out the hand sanitizer before heading to dinner. You want to hug all these dogs, but we had been advised that they could be carrying diseases, so we had to be circumspect.

That evening the bus took us to a restaurant where, for a change, we were served grilled shrimp and rice, together with the usual plate of thinly sliced tomatoes and cucumbers and a bowl of boiled potatoes. Ice cream was served for dessert. Every meal comes with two free drinks—dark or light Cuban beer, an orange drink like Fanta, and a lemon drink like Sprite. And, as usual, the house specialty rum drink is offered free of charge. We didn't leave for dinner until 7:30 so it was late when we returned to the hotel. The itinerary had said:

> *"This evening, stroll Calle Simon Bolivar, visiting an art incubation studio. While there meet budding new artists, see their work and present the studio with art supplies for the new artists they serve."*

That didn't happen, but perhaps it was too late by the time dinner was over.

SUNDAY, JUNE 17

Off we went in our beautiful modern bus to a rendezvous spot along the road where we transferred to two Russian trucks with rows of very hard seats. The result we dubbed a "Russian massage" as we laughingly bounced our way up the mountain roads into the Sierra de Escambray on our way to Topes de Collantes National Park.On our way up we saw other tourists coming back down, also in Russian trucks, so this was obviously the accepted way to see the park. The scenery on our climb was breathtaking; it was so beautiful. Once again, I marveled at the magnificence of Cuba's mountains.

The paved road became a dirt road as we continued up, down, and around the mountains. Small huts indicated people were living in these mountains, but I couldn't imagine where they made their living. Perhaps they work in the city. There's a rule in Cuba that any state-owned vehicle is obligated to stop and give a person seeking transportation a ride along the route, so maybe that is how they get back and forth to work. As we neared the top, a gorgeous Cuban Trogon flew across the road in front of us giving us a nice sighting of the Cuban national bird.

After about an hour, we arrived at a nice little mountain bar and restaurant where hummingbirds and other birds were darting in and out of the trees and shrubbery. A young man introduced himself saying he would be our guide for a two-hour hike. His English was excellent and he knew his birds. Great, I thought, until we started up the trail—and I mean up!

I had suggested Alfred stay behind and try to photograph some of the birds around the restaurant. He agreed and I soldiered on up the trail—steep, rocky, muddy, and difficult. We saw some nice birds, but coming down was worse than going up. Gustavo and Steve helped any of us needing a hand or two, and I managed to complete the hike—winded, but happy.

During lunch, a little paw appeared on my leg, and I looked down to see a sweet white and gray kitty asking for a morsel of food. Of course, I obliged, as did Alfred and others. Soon a second cat joined in, and hands with food were going under the table all along our group while the kitties dined on bites of roast pork! As an animal lover, it was hard to see so many feral cats and dogs looking for food and a little love.

Then it was back to the trucks, climbing up on ladders and using a rope handle to get aboard in order to bounce back down the mountain side. On the way back, we stopped at the Gallery Topes de Collante, seeing examples of modern Cuban art. For a second time, we climbed back out of the trucks to visit a coffee house where we were told how the coffee was ground and shipped to government factories. Most of the group had small demi-tasse cups of coffee, but I found it far too strong for my taste.

Across the road a loud group of White-fronted Parrots flew into the trees and proceeded to engage in a good bit of squawking. That was another Cuban endemic bird for my Life List. Our new bird tally today consisted of the Cuban Trogan, Cuban Tody, La Sarge and Gray Flycatchers, a Streaky-headed Tanager, and a flock of noisy White-headed Parrots.

The itinerary said we would be stopping at the seaside village of La Boca where

> *"we meet our friends Joaquin and Olga Pomes, who have gathered their neighbors to meet and talk with us over pie and coffee that Olga has prepared."*

I was looking forward to this gathering, but as usual, it didn't happen. There was no pie and coffee, and Olga didn't show up either.

Dinner, we were told, would be at a "paladar," a privately owned restaurant. Raul Castro has permitted people to open small restaurants seating twelve persons, but the twelve-seat limit had been relaxed as in addition to our group, many Cubans were there to dine. This meant we would not be subject to the same state-directed food we'd been having at the state-owned restaurants. But this adventure also gave rise to an astonishing discovery. Our driver could not drive us there nor could our guide or driver eat there because they are state employees! Had they wanted to go there as private citizens, that would have been permitted, but as they were working as our tour guide and driver, they could not. This meant that Steve had to secure a fleet of private vehicles for our transportation.

At 7 p.m. a spectacular parade of vintage American cars pulled up in the middle of a thunderstorm. Everyone dashed for a car, any car, and Alfred and I found ourselves in a blue 1949 Plymouth for which the windshield wipers were nonexistent. No problem, the driver had a rag with which he periodically reached outside to wipe off his windshield in order to see through the heavy rain. These cars, which one sees everywhere, are kept running on spare parts commandeered from other old cars, and someone must have quite a business selling 1940s and 1950s spare parts. Our ride back to the hotel was in a green and white two-toned 1955 Chevy. It was all rather fun and funky, and Alfred found the leg room fantastic!

Our "paladar" was located in a tent down an alley and behind a house. The chef appeared, wearing a tall white paper chef's hat, and informed us that tonight's menu would be fish soup, a fish and vegetable crepe, his very own fish, lobster, and shrimp creation, together with boiled potatoes, fried sliced plantain, and ice cream. It was really too much food, but we all ate heartily as it was so nice to be served food that was both different and tasty.

MONDAY, JUNE 18

This was quite a day. We drove to the coastal city of Cienfuegos, population 200,000, and noticed immediately that the city was cleaner and in better condition than anywhere else we had visited. Gustavo proudly told us it was the cleanest city in Cuba. Not only was it clean, it was well maintained. Beautifully painted blue, red, and yellow buildings were immaculate and large white planters filled with red flowers and tall grasses lined the center islands of the streets. This means a city can be cleaned up if government officials want to make an effort or direct their citizens to make an effort to do so.

Cienfuegos was settled by French citizens from New Orleans who left Louisiana after the Louisiana Purchase. They settled here with Spain's blessings as France and Spain had excellent relations at the time. The neoclassical architecture that the settlers favored resulted in some magnificent buildings, but today they are being under used and under cared for.

We had a comfort stop at a large, very modern hotel with a very impressive glass and marble lobby. Steve had considered having us stay here, but he found that the air conditioning capacity of the place would cover only about one third of the rooms and the rooms facing west were very hot when he inspected the premises.

At the entrance to the hotel, we noted a small bare-branched bush upon which sat a tiny female Emerald Hummingbird in her nest incubating her eggs! Many photos were taken while she stoically sat there determined not to leave her nest. Why, I wondered, would she build in such a public site?But it was wonderful seeing and photographing her so close.

We headed north along the shores of the Caribbean, stopping at a pre-arranged rendezvous location to pick up a local farmer, Rolando, who was said to be a good birder. He took us to a site frequented by the Bee Hummingbird, a Cuban endemic and the world's smallest bird measuring only two and a half inches in length. After a bit of waiting, the little fellow did show up, but I had time to get off only one shot before he flew. Still, that was another Life Bird!

Rolando then took us into a forested area to bird.Here we saw two Cuban endemics, the tiny Cuban Tody and, after knocking on five different tree trunks, a Cuban Screech Owl popped up out of the top of a dead tree and sat there staring at us while I fired away photo after photo. "You knocked?" said he. That opportunity was worth the heat and the mosquitoes, both of which were plentiful!

At this time, Gustavo told me we were not going to go to Zapata Swamp and would only be able to look for a few water birds at a pond along the road. I was very upset, as the opportunity to bird Zapata Swamp, as the itinerary promised, was a prime reason for our signing onto the trip. Zapata Swamp is famous among birders and the itinerary had played it up saying,

> *"The Zapata Peninsula encompasses a national park*
> *protecting Cuba's most important wetland area. It is*
> *also a UNESCO Biosphere Reserve closely resembling*
> *the Florida Everglades. There are 900 species of flora,*
> *171 species of birds (18 endemics), 31 species of reptiles*
> *and many mammal species calling the Zapata Wetlands*
> *home. The world's smallest bird, the bee hummingbird, is*
> *here as are species such as the endemic tanager, Zapata*
> *Sparrow, Zapata rail and Zapata wren. Join Dr. Felipe*
> *Rodriguez and his staff and volunteers for a hike into the*
> *swamp, where we learn more about the battle against in-*
> *vasive species of fish and discuss environmental issues,*
> *we all face. Later, the families of the staff and volunteers*
> *join us for a picnic lunch. This afternoon, search for ma-*
> *natees and freshwater turtles during a boat excursion on*
> *the Hatiquanico River."*

This was how we were scheduled to spend the entire day, and Gustavo was cutting it out completely—cutting yet a third natural history site and another opportunity to meet Cuban people in the tradition of the People-to-People program. I was furious.

Alfred voiced our unhappiness to Steve Cox. Quite frankly, I was beginning to feel betrayed. I understood the itinerary was subject to change, but not at the exclusion of all the natural history sites. Pulling an entire day's detailed itinerary off the schedule to do cultural activities of the Cuban government's choice was simply not acceptable.

As something of a compromise, Steve arranged to get a birding guide to come to the hotel at 6 a.m. the following day, pick up the six birders in our group, and send us off with a water bottle and a ham and cheese sandwich. The rest of the group could sleep in and we would join them around 9 a.m. at Gustavo's alternate itinerary site—another local art center. That meant we were going to get less than three hours of birding as opposed to an entire day—but at least it was something.Steve told us there are not many good guides who know birds and plants, which as the "world leader in nature travel," International Expeditions would be seeking.The discovery of Rolando today, as a short-term guide, is a good find for Steve. But this trip hardly fills the bill of being nature travel.

The itinerary said we would next visit a large crocodile farm and while there

> *"learn about the fate of fish in the famous Treasure Lake—once thought to be the home of world's record large-mouth bass."*

Well, that didn't happen either. Instead, we were told we were going to visit a replica of an extinct Indian tribal village. The latter was, in fact, interesting, but then a tropical downpour eliminated the visit to the crocodile farm too, so another day of "itinerary changes" went by.

Lunch came next, and once again there was a darling little puppy at the edge of the dining room begging for a bite of food. John, a travel companion from New Orleans, obliged him with chicken which John found too tough to eat. Alfred's pork steak was equally tough, and my crab dish was very salty and full of bits of shell fragments, so the pup got a meal. All this came with the usual plate of sliced tomatoes and cucumbers, rice, and potatoes. Dessert was a mango puree in a saucer that tasted like strained baby food.

It is 7:45 p.m. and we are at the Bay of Pigs in the Hotel Playa Larga. It is located in a remote area and services primarily birders visiting Zapata Swamp and fishermen wanting to ply the Bay of Pigs waters. A heavy downpour precluded a walk down to the Bay of Pigs beach, which, we were told, was the primary site for the Bay of Pigs invasion in 1961. I did see the infamous body of water as we drove along the shore and at our lunch stop, but that was it.

Having a little time to reflect on what we are seeing, I am starting to form some opinions.

1) The state runs everyone's life, even to the point of determining who may buy a car or a house.

2) Cuba is a very poor country with a very low standard of living and most streets, sidewalks, and houses are in deplorable condition. Houses sit right along the narrow sidewalks with one door and one window, the latter usually covered with grillwork for security. At night, people often leave their doors open for ventilation and you can see into their living rooms, which are usually furnished with chairs and maybe a sofa facing a TV set. I assume a bedroom and kitchen are lined up behind the living room. The houses are dark, as at best they have a street-front window and one in the back of their unit.

Gustavo gives us informative mini-lectures while we are riding some distances in the bus, but I have often noticed he refers to his notes or script, which, I'm sure, has been provided by the government. Today, he spoke about the Cuban educational system. When Fidel Castro came to power, he sent university faculty and other teachers out into the countryside to conduct a Literacy Campaign. I will give him credit for that one. Today, Cuba has a literacy rate of 99.8%. According to Gustavo, "since the triumph of the revolution" (Gustavo does seem to spout the party line at times) education and public health have been the government's two highest priorities. Gustavo is in his 50s, I would guess, so he is of the generation that has never known anything but Castro's Socialist regime. Today, he also gave us a briefing about who could and could not own a car—even an old American Chevy.

3) Cuba needs a massive spay/neuter campaign for all the strays and street dogs and cats. Every hotel has a few hanging around looking for food—and for love! They are friendly little guys who want so much to have someone give them a kind word, regardless of the language, and a soft pat on the head. Several of us have been feeding them, but we touched them very little as it is obvious they have fleas and one doesn't know what else they might be carrying. They have such sweet dispositions; it is heart breaking to see their skinny bodies and skinny females laden with milk, obviously nursing pups somewhere.

4) Much of the country runs on horsepower, and many of the horses have ribs and hip bones protruding as they pull carts around the cities. Yesterday when we went to the National Park, I saw a horse hitched to a cart and tied on a very short lead to a front yard shrub. When we came back several hours later it was still standing in the same spot. Had he been given water, much less food all day while standing there at his station? It was the horrible long hours and poor care of carriage horses and horse-drawn carts in New York City that caused Henry Bergh to establish the American Society for the Prevention of Cruelty to Animals in 1866. That is what Cuba needs. (Two days after getting back to Boston, I "Googled" Cuban animal shelters and I found The Aniplant Project in Osprey, FL which supports a roaming van in Havana to spay and neuter Cuban dogs and cats. Moreover, there appear to be several animal shelters in Havana.) Obviously, some people are making a noble effort, but so much more is needed.

TUESDAY, JUNE 19

We met our birding guide, Frank, at 6 a.m.After a short drive, he took us down a wide, dirt road, but before long he turned off and we started bush whacking through grass, coral rock, fallen trees, and mud. The mosquitoes were unbelievably fierce and we were nowhere near a swamp—just mud to the point that eventually we had to turn back.

Frank did know his birds, however, and during this walking ordeal, we saw five Cuban endemic species: the Gray-fronted Dove, the Yellow-headed Warbler, the Cuban Green Woodpecker, the Cuban Yellow Vireo, and the Cuban Pigmy Owl. We also saw the Cuban Pee Wee, the Cuban Blackbird, the Tody once again, the ever-present Cuban Blackbird, a Limpkin, Smooth-billed Ani, and the national bird, the Cuban Trogan, the latter raiding a termite nest.

Lunch was to be on an island in Treasure Lake, and given the weather, Gustavo directed us to go to the boats immediately. The rain was coming down hard, and the speed of the boat was creating wind. We got drenched. We went through the swamp out into Treasure Lake. Upon arriving at the island, we walked through the foretold Indian village, and I was reminded of Plymouth Plantation on Cape Cod where there is also a replicated Indian village. This one, however, had many graceful sculptures depicting various aspects of Indian life.

Lunch was a pleasant surprise.We were served crocodile meat, baby shrimp, and calamari! After lunch, as we were heading for the boats, the downpour came. There doesn't seem to be such a thing as a gentle shower in Cuba. We waited for a while and then voted to brave it and back we went across the lake. Some people with no ponchos, raincoats, or anything were soaked through and through, and now we had a three-hour drive to our next destination.

To reach our next hotel, we had to circumnavigate Havana on a four-lane divided highway with a planted center strip. It was 5 p.m., rush hour, but there was little motor traffic, and only a few bicycles and horse carts on the highway. We reached the Hotel La Villa Soroa at 6:15, and dinner was at a local restaurant at 7:30—an excellent buffet. When we returned from dinner, tree frogs were singing.Once again, we were told the itinerary had been changed. The itinerary we had been given read:

> *"We continue past Havana and into one of Cuba's most environmentally interesting regions. In the planned ecological community of Las Terrazas, we meet with local naturalists and farmers for discussions about life in this unique planned community. We also have an opportunity to discuss locally grown vegetarian cuisine, which they have been promoting locally."*

Well, that didn't happen either. By now, all of us are talking about the fact that the People-to-People purpose of this trip is being totally ignored. We were having no opportunities to talk to the Cubans at all.

WEDNESDAY, JUNE 20TH, 2012

It rained all night and continued this morning, so our visit to the Orchid Garden was cancelled. We drove on through the Sierra de los Organos Mountains to the Las Jazmines overlook of the Venales Valley. Here we found one of the most beautiful sights you could see anywhere. Bread-loaf shaped limestone outcroppings called mogotes create a magical scene, which I could liken only to pictures of Guilin in China.

From the mogotes we proceeded to a tobacco processing barn where eighty-six women were opening up and flattening out dried tobacco leaves. The leaves were then collected and stacked in 120-pound bags. The odor in the barn was overwhelming, and I had to step outside a couple of times for a breath of fresh air. From here the tobacco goes to plants where the famous Cuban cigars are manufactured. We were told that tobacco grows well in the Vinales Valley; however, the itinerary also said,

"We will have the opportunity to explore an operating tobacco farm, meet the entire family at this farm as well as some of their neighbors. Over coffee and tea with the farmers, learn why Cubans feel their tobacco is superior and their cigars are so famous worldwide. At the same time, we discuss the regulations tobacco farmers must abide by under the Cuban system."

Well, once again, none of that ever happened.

At our hotel, the Hotel Los Jazmines, we all had balconies looking out on the beautiful valley and the remarkable mogotes. As we actually had two unscheduled hours before dinner, Alfred and I sat out on the balcony and watched for birds while enjoying the beautiful view.

THURSDAY, JUNE 21, 2012

Another long day but an interesting one. Rain continued so we were in and out of our wet ponchos constantly. During the 70-km drive to Havana, I asked Gustavo to tell us about the Santeria religion as he had promised. Santeria has a following equal to if not surpassing Catholicism in Cuba. The religion was imported to Cuba by West African slaves brought in to work the sugar cane fields in the 16th to 19th centuries. It is a polytheistic religion combining belief in Yorba gods and Catholic saints. After telling us much about the religion, he then talked about Catholicism in Cuba and other religions too.

The long bus ride gave us the opportunity to question Gustavo about other issues too. I asked if there were any wealthy people in Cuba today, given the government's efforts to create an egalitarian socialist state. Yes, he replied, there are a few who, if not wealthy, are very comfortable. I asked who these people were and I was astonished when he said the artists—and a few top sports figures.

Cubans accept their sub-standard lifestyle (by our standards) because they have free education and free health care. Doesn't that stifle initiative and creativity we asked? Yes, he admits, that is the downside of socialism. There is no incentive to work hard to get ahead, because you won't! Maybe if you're really good, you'll get permission to buy a car or a house, but wealth is not a goal in this society.

As for the state of the Cuban economy, Gustavo told us Venezuela is their #1 trading partner (oil) and #2 is China! We found that very interesting given the aggressive nature of China's overseas operations all over the world. But what does China get from Cuba? Cobalt and nickel were the answer, Alfred said, and these are important elements in many industrial processes.

When we arrived in Havana, we immediately saw a section of better housing, although building maintenance doesn't appear to be anyone's priority—including all of the state-owned hotels in which we have been staying. When we passed through Embassy Row, there were beautiful mansions and gardens all well maintained. These dwellings are owned by the Cuban government and leased to the individual countries. There were a few private homes in the same area, but most were rented by the government for the housing of embassy staff. Havana is big with a population of 2.2 million spread out over an area of 700 square kilometers.

In Havana, we followed the day's itinerary—for the very first time! We visited the Antonio Nunez Jimenez Foundation for Nature and Humanity, an independent non-profit organization established to address Cuban environmental issues. Once inside, we found it primarily a museum of the writings, photos, and artifacts assembled by Antonio Nunez, a Cuban explorer of whom we had never heard. But his travels were astounding.

The museum held his collections from 50 years of expeditions and research. He wrote 30 books, and his journals and photo albums lined two walls from floor to ceiling. He died in 1998 at age

75, but the Foundation carries on his work in a variety of fields including some in cooperation with major US universities and foundations.

The number of endemic species in Cuba is quite impressive according to what we were told:

> Amphibians: 56 species, 96% endemic
> Reptiles: 142 species, 66% endemic
> Mollusks: 1,200 species, 66% endemic
> Flora: 6,519 species, 52% endemic

They didn't mention birds, but there are only 22 endemic species among the 354 bird species in Cuba according to the *Field Guide to the Birds of Cuba*.

Cuba has a diversity of habitats we learned—rain forests, cloud forests, limestone terraces, wetlands, coral reefs, mangroves, and sea grasses, and these enable so many species to be sustained. Within these habitats there are eight categories of protected areas and 253 individual protected areas including 91 national parks. It was a very informative visit.

In the afternoon we were scheduled to visit Caritas Cuba run by Catholic Relief Services and Caritas Switzerland. That didn't happen.

What had been scheduled and had not yet been scratched was a visit to the home of Ernest Hemingway. So, at 3 p.m. with rain clouds threatening, the bus headed south of Havana for Finca Vigia, Hemingway's home.

A local guide gave us a wonderful tour of the grounds. Visitors are not permitted inside his house, but while peeking in the windows and listening to the narration about each of the rooms I got several photos including one of Hemingway's study and writing desk. All the rooms are decorated with mounted animal heads from his American and 1930s African hunting trips. The rooms have been left exactly as they were when Hemingway went to Idaho where he then committed suicide. His widow and fourth wife, Mary, gave the house to the Cuban government, gave his six cars to the staff, and his fishing boat, El Pilar, to his captain. The captain kept the boat for many years, but when it was in need of repair, he hadn't the necessary funds. The boat was then given to the Cuban government, and the government erected a special place for it on the grounds of Hemingway's home before turning the entire property into a Hemingway museum.

The famous six-toed Hemingway cats are all gone now. Hemingway kept 13 cats and even had a special room and a caretaker for them. Four of Hemingway's dogs are buried near the swimming pool, and each has its own headstone with the dog's name inscribed. There are now six dogs in residence on the property.

FRIDAY, JUNE 22, 2012

We began the morning at a former convent that now serves as a cultural and social center for seniors administered by the City of Havana Historical Commission. To our amazement, when we were announced as an American group, 500 people, mostly women, stood and clapped as we entered, filling the room, with smiling faces for the American visitors. It was a rather disconcerting experience, but their smiles were warm and many reached out to grasp my hand.It seems there were so many there because they have a Catholic Mass every Friday presided over by an itinerate priest.A meal is served each day here; they have physical therapy class in the morning (and we noted several treadmills and stationary bikes), handcraft classes, and classrooms for children ages 6-12. As we walked back through the aisle of chairs, withered old hands reached out to greet us. I clasped several hands as I passed through, eliciting many smiles on wrinkled old faces.

Leaving the bus behind, we then took a two-hour walk through old Havana. Havana had to have been beautiful in the early 19th century and early 20th century. Many of the buildings bear a strong resemblance to the architecture of the French Quarter in New Orleans. But now most are in a sorry state of disrepair. A little stucco and paint could do much to restore this Grand Dame of a city to her former glory.

Havana is an old city having been founded in 1555 by the Spanish Conquistadors.There are large fortresses at the end of Havana Bay that were erected in the 16th century due to the attacks by privateers such as Sir Francis Drake and Jean Lafitte. But Cuba's history began long before that. About 1000 BC the country was settled by Ciboney Indians and later by more aggressive Arawak or Taino Indians from South America. Columbus arrived on October 28, 1492 and returned the following year with 17 ships. In 1511 Diego de Velázquez brought a large expeditionary force to the island, and there then followed a general massacre of all the Indians. By the mid 1500s, there were fewer than 3,000 Indians left. The Spanish conquests of Mexico and Peru drew settlers away from Cuba to seek their fortunes elsewhere. Gold was what everyone was seeking, and Cuba had failed to deliver much. It is reported that there were less than 1,000 Spanish settlers left on the island by the mid 1500s. The discovery of the American continent brought Cuba back to life, and Havana harbor became the stopping-off point for Spanish ships carrying new world treasures back to Spain.

Slaves were brought to Cuba from Africa in the mid-16th century to work in the sugar cane fields, and slavery was not abolished until 1886. A series of wars ensued—the Ten Years War of 1868-1878 against Spain, the Second War of Independence (1896-1898) followed by the Spanish-American War from 1898-1902 after which Cuba became a republic. Two successive dictators, General Gerardo Machado and Fulgencio Batista, became Cuba's presidents. Both governed with US backing as the US had strong economic interests in Cuba and Havana had developed a reputation as another Las Vegas.

In 1953 Fidel Castro launched his revolution, but it was unsuccessful and he was thrown in jail. Batista later released Castro, who went to Mexico, was joined by Che Guevara, trained his soldiers, and returned in 1955 to launch his revolution. Batista fled in 1959. The US denounced Castro when he seized some $8 billion US assets, and the trade embargo began in January 1961. The Bay of Pigs fiasco occurred in April 1961, and expecting a full-American invasion, Castro turned to Nikita Khrushchev for military aid. The Russians lost no time in responding, and thus began the Soviet influence in Cuba. In October 1962 the Cuban missile crisis occurred. Everything went downhill from there on, and here we sit, more than 50 years later with the US embargo still in place and China moving in as Cuba's #2 trading power.

During our walk through old Havana, we encountered street performers on stilts with musicians following behind. Women in Cuban costumes came up to kiss the men ($2 please) so all in all it was a colorful stroll. Time once again for lunch, this time a charming restaurant where we were served grilled shrimp and an ice cream and flan desert.

At this point our planned itinerary totally fell apart. We had passed what Gustavo referred to as the Museum of the Revolution (with a Russian tank out front) and several people were interested. The Havana Art Museum was nearby, so a group within our group got off the bus for a museum visit. Some wanted to go to the Havana bar made famous by Hemingway when he lived in the Savagre Hotel. Others wanted to just walk around on their own. Everyone went their own way on this last day in Cuba.

Back at the hotel, Alfred and I sat in the sidewalk cafe, drank coffee, ate French pastry, and watched Cuban life pass before us. I wrote in my diary, and Alfred photographed old American cars, bicycles, and horse-drawn taxis. As usual, a Cuban band was playing next door, and as usual, we got an afternoon tropical downpour. The rain turned the scene into a Monet-like painting of wet streets, colorful umbrellas, people getting soaked, cars splashing water, horses drawing carts, and it all created a cacophony of sound. But this is Cuba and this is how we will remember her.

My accounts of our past adventures have been enthusiastic narrations of our global travel activities. This trip was different. It was a trip of pluses and minuses, joys and disappointments, and many thought-provoking hours. The People-to-People program was discontinued in 2019; however people can still travel to Cuba if they go by the Trump Administration's rules. Hopefully, people will be able to make the journey in the future free of political considerations and restraints. It is a beautiful country that has much to offer anyone interested in its natural resources.

CHAPTER 12

Meanwhile, Back at the Ranch...

WE DIDN'T ALWAYS TRAVEL during our fifty-six years of marriage! And we certainly did not eat all our meals in restaurants. We both had professional careers and we usually ate at home, as I'm a very good cook. I'm especially good at Viennese pastries. I'm also a good "Dog Mother", gardener, bird feeder filler, and freelance writer. Alfred was a professor devoted to his students, meaning I never got him away from his office before 6 p.m. each night, and often over dinner I would hear stories about a student he had taken to lunch to discuss a problem that usually had nothing to do with organic chemistry. He also liked to keep our tree-filled property as neat as the Vienna woods, making brush piles for bunnies as he gathered up fallen limbs. He too spoke of himself as the "Dog Father" to our many golden retrievers. Alfred never had a dog growing up in Vienna, but he became a dog-loving convert when little Miss Diora entered our home in 1980.

Diora was not my first golden retriever, as my parents raised goldens in the 1940s when I was a young child. In 1944, our family obtained our first golden retriever who we named Sunset Lad, "Laddie". His sire was the nationally renowned Ch. Tonkahof Bang owned by Henry Norton of Tonkahof Kennels in Wayzata, Minnesota. Laddie became the stud dog for my parents' kennel, Winyon Kennels, established in Alderwood Manor, WA. I was proud that my name was on the American Kennel Club registration as well.

Laddie's partner was Tawny, Dawn O'Light, whose sire was also a national specialty winner, Ch. Highland Chief, half-brother to Bang. I can still remember the night the first litter was born. I ran screaming into my parents' bedroom saying, "Mommy, Mommy, Tawny's having puppies on my bed!" I named every one of the ten puppies after my school classmates, the bully, the sweetest one, the prettiest, the most awkward, and I did that for every litter thereafter for many years. When we moved back to Minnesota, my mother, who never seemed to stick with anything very long, lost interest in raising goldens, but we always had at least one golden in the house. When my father died in 1958, my mother and I moved to Boston where we purchased a golden we named Camelot. He took great exception when Alfred started coming around, often nudging Alfred's hand away when we were sitting on the couch. After several years of marriage and years spent establishing our professional careers, we got a phone call that changed our lives.

Friends called to invite us over to see their new puppy. She was adorable, and I suggested to Alfred that we stop by the breeder's house on the way home to see the litter. "You've never seen anything cuter than a litter of golden puppies," said I.

One look and I told Al, "I want a puppy."

"We can't have a puppy; we work," he replied.

"I want a puppy," I continued.

"What would we do with it all day?" he asked

"I want a puppy," I replied.

After three days of this on-going conversation, Alfred told me to go get my puppy. When we returned to the breeder, she said she had never seen anyone who wanted a puppy as badly as did I. She also said she was very touched when Alfred said, "But the dog has rights too." On that basis, we went home with a puppy. We named her Princess D'Or, and called her Diora.

The first night, Alfred set the alarm clock, got up out of bed, and took Diora outside every two hours. By morning, she was house-broken! We constructed a wire pen in our tiled family room, filled it with toys, and set the radio on WCRB, Boston's classical music station. We arranged to have a neighbor boy come directly from school each day to take Diora for a long walk. Seeing the puppy, every other child in the neighborhood came along, and Diora, like the Pied Piper, had an entourage on her outings. Diora adapted well to our routine, but one Friday evening, after a long, hard week at work, we came home, let her out, fed her, and went back out to eat at a neighborhood restaurant. Diora was not happy with us, and she let us know of her displeasure. When we came home, she was sitting in piles of stuffing from the family-room couch, which she had torn to shreds. She trained us well. We never went out to dinner on a work night after that!

When Diora was six years old, I took her to the veterinarian for her annual check-up and noticed a poster on the bulletin board about an organization, Yankee Golden Retriever Rescue (YGRR). Why would goldens, the beloved family dog, need a rescue organization? I made inquiries, signed up as a volunteer, began doing pre-adoption home visits, and working on the auction and dog walk committees. Alfred was at my side participating in it all. I became a member of the Board of Directors the year I retired from my full-time career and initiated a capital campaign to raise the funds for the first Golden Retriever Rescue Shelter in the nation. When Riverview, a 21-acre property on the Assabet River in Hudson, MA, was purchased and the kennel and training center built, Alfred suggested we provide the funds for the naming gift for the shelter. We did, and to this day, I consider the Alfred and Joy Viola Shelter and Adoption Center one of my happiest accomplishments. Throughout this endeavor, my mentor was a woman beloved throughout the golden retriever world, Rachel Page Elliott. I spent many a happy hour with Pagey and her husband Mark in their delightful farm house talking about golden retriever history and the campaign for a home for Yankee Rescue. When Mark died, I continued to bring bagels and cream cheese to Pagey's farm where we would continue our discussions as I moved on to volunteer as Director of Development for the Golden Retriever Foundation (GRF). Founded by the Golden Retriever Club of America, (GRCA) the GRF raises funds to support canine cancer research and other golden-related health issuesas well as golden retriever rescues across the country.Between my work for Yankee Rescue and the GRF, I raised nearly $4 million for Golden Retriever Rescue and canine cancer research. I worked with the GRF for ten years and in 2008 was surprised and humbled when I was awarded GRCA's Vern Bower Humanitarian Award "for exceptional contributions and selfless devotion to the Golden Retriever."Later I was similarly honored by the Yankee Golden Retriever Club when I received their Sandy Sonntag Service Award.

When Pagey Elliott's memorial service was held, I was honored to be asked by the family to speak on behalf of the golden retriever community. I did my best to honor her life in the short time I was allotted, but the greatest tribute that day was the honor guard of 50 golden retrievers who marched onto the church grounds led by a Scottish bagpiper and then sat along the semi-circle driveway in silent tribute, wearing tartan bandanas, alongside their owners who came from through out New England and New York to honor this gracious lady.

After my decade with the Golden Retriever Foundation, I took up another golden cause, the establishment of the Friends of Guisachan (FOG).FOG was created to educate the public and the golden community, especially about the history of the breed and the breed's founding in 1868 at Guisachan, a gentleman's estate in the Scottish Highlands. Fundraising again, we commissioned a life-sized bronze golden retriever statue which stands in the conservation village of Tomich on historic Guisachan lands. The statue was unveiled in August 2014 with appropriate pomp and circumstance. A bagpiper led a parade of local celebrities, including a clan chieftain and nearly 100 golden owners with their dogs, through the village to the statue site. Flowers had been planted around the statue base, and Scotland's famous rain showers held off until the unveiling was concluded. Proudly I read aloud the commemorative plaque:

"The Golden Retriever, beloved the world over. First bred on the Guisachan Estate by Lord Tweedmouth in 1868.This tribute statue was erected on 10th August, 2014 by the Friends of Guisachan.

I journeyed three times to Guisachan for Golden gatherings, including the 150th anniversary of the breed in 2018. On all three occasions, one had to drive from Inverness to the village of Tomich on what, for me, was the "wrong" side of the road. I managed very well, but it took some time to get used to single-lane paths that were the highland roads with pullouts periodically for one car or the other to pull aside and let the other party pass. But what a wonder it was to share these celebrations with golden lovers from around the world, hundreds of whom brought their goldens with them to these Guisachan Reunions.

Tomich is a charming little village constructed by Lord Tweedmouth in the mid-1800s to house the estate staff. The Tomich Hotel was built to house the "stalkers and keepers", i.e. the men who found the game for the hunting parties and looked after the hunting dogs. The entire village is now protected as a conservation village, and any modification (such as our statue) had to be approved by the Highland Council.

I continue to be involved with FOG, working on the partial stabilization of the mansion ruins and the commissioning of an historical stone marker to commemorate the site. And now there is another Guisachan Reunion planned in 2023!

And it all started with my plea, "I want a puppy!"

In the wake of Diora, we have shared our home with Electra, Captain, Toby, Ginger, Briscoe, Bobby, Ozzie, and Apollo—goldens all and five of them, rescue dogs. We also took on a black labrador mix, Anna, when my matron of honor died. Anna has proved to be a mischievous behavioral challenge, but an incredibly sweet charmer.

I suppose it seems strange that I should write about forty years of dog ownership before writing about our combined seventy-three years of professional careers, but both were and continue to be of utmost importance to us.

Alfred and I both spent our professional careers at Northeastern University in Boston, MA. Teaching and conducting research, he became mentor, counselor, and confident to generations of students. Alfred was known to have high academic standards but a soft-heart, who would always go the extra mile for a student struggling with the complexities of organic chemistry. He loved to tell the story of the student who once came into his office to say, "You're not really the SOB my mother said you were when she had you for organic!"

At Alfred's retirement party, a past chairman of the department said, "He was the only faculty member I ever knew who could flunk a student and have them thank him for it."

When Alfred passed away, I received more than 200 cards, notes, emails, and Facebook comments about him. One stood out above all others from a student of Alfred's fifty-two years previously. It seems the young man was injured when an explosion occurred while he was mixing chemicals the last day of his freshman year in 1958.He wrote:

"I went to see Prof. Viola in 1959 after taking a year off to recuperate. I wanted to tell him how much I enjoyed the chem class, but I would not be taking any more chem from him. Given that I lost a hand and eye, I decided to switch my major to Mathematics. He allowed since he had never heard of a Differential Equation exploding, and considering my poor experimental track record, his opinion was that it would be a lot safer for me and anyone around me if I transferred. Prof. Viola was one of the good ones."

Another student who went on to become a top executive at a major chemical firm told how proud she was of being a straight A student:

> *"Until I hit organic with A.V. I got a 62 on the first exam and a 47 on the second. I studied nothing but organic chemistry for the next six weeks and got a 98 on the final. A.V.'s response was a statement that has guided me throughout my entire career … 'Now that I have seen what you are capable of doing, I expect no less of you ever again.'"*

In 1991, Alfred received Northeastern University's Excellence in Teaching Award based on letters from past and present students.

The impact teachers can have on young people is never ending. I too had a similar student/teacher epiphany. As a graduate student, I turned in a rather haphazard book review to my research director and he returned it unmarked. "Dr. Casey," I said, "you forgot to put a grade on my book report." He gave me a look and sternly said, "Joy, you're capable of better than that. Do it." I carried that admonition with me throughout my career and on more than one occasion, passed it along to others working for me.

As is the custom in academia, Alfred had sabbatical leaves every seven years. He took his first at the Institute for Organic Chemistry in Munich, Germany in 1977. In late May of that year, Boston had a major snowstorm. Trees were budding and lilacs were in bloom, but all were bent and broken under the weight of heavy, wet snow. The power went out, and all night long I lay there in the dark listening to trees crashing down around me, terrified one would fall upon the house. In the morning light, I saw the disaster. Twelve trees lay in jagged strips around our yard and nearby woods. The house became cold. There was no hot water. I carried milk outside and parked it in a snow bank.Food in the refrigerator and freezer began to go bad. I found our sleeping bags and placed them over and under me on the floor in front of the fireplace. But the fireplace gave out little heat.

When the phone line became functional, I telephoned Alfred in Munich. "Don't you know what has been going on?" I sobbed into the phone. It seems Boston's weather hadn't made the Munich newspaper headlines and Alfred was totally unaware of his wife's misery.

This was the first time I had ever had to face a significant event totally alone. I had no family around. My neighbors had their own problems, and Alfred was thousands of miles way. At that point I didn't even have a dog to cuddle. I learned a great deal about myself in the five days of the storm and clean-up. I'd always been a well-organized person and a bit of a Type A personality, but now I'd have to shovel myself out of this dilemma.

My first agenda item was to shovel out the bird feeders! My feathered friends needed food! The front steps and sidewalk were not a major chore, but our 125-foot driveway, laden with tree branches, looked like a herculean task. Two days went by before I could drive back in to work. I bathed and changed clothes in a Northeastern Ladies Room. I stayed late in my warm university office, and I bought sandwiches in the university cafeteria and carried them home for my cold supper. I tried to read by candlelight, but the house was so cold my reading usually gave way to my crawling into my sleeping bags early each night.

When at long last, five days later, the power came back on, I cleaned out the freezer and refrigerator, contracted a tree company to haul away our downed oaks and pines, replenished my food supply, and sent Alfred a long tape detailing all my successes. We exchanged mini cassette tape recordings at least twice a week, thereby keeping one another in touch with our respective lives. That year was a growing period for both of us. I gained a greater sense of independence. And Alfred, well, Alfred learned not to hate all Germans. He had been reluctant to go to Munich, but his chairman, who happened to be a fellow member of the Kindertransport, had advised him to go. It was the right thing to do. Alfred was able to set aside some of the anger he had been feeling for decades, and he become close friends with his German chemistry colleagues.Alfred had spoken very little German since his childhood, but after spending several months in Munich, and by speaking only German, he was able to give a research lecture in German and write several scientific papers, including one in the German language.

That summer, I joined him for five weeks and we toured southern Germany, Austria, and Switzerland. It was Alfred's first return to Vienna since the Nazi invasion and the break-up of his childhood home. He didn't want to go by the house where he had lived. He wanted to enjoy Vienna's culture, so he got tickets to the Vienna Opera, the Folks Opera, the Spanish Riding School, and we dined on Vienna's fine cuisine and pastries.

"The only seats I could get for the opera," he wrote me, "are in the fourth row, so you'd best bring a nice dress." The fourth row of the Vienna State Opera House? I need a ball gown! I went into R.H. Stearns in Boston and came home with a beautiful full-length shell pink dress trimmed in silver thread with a tucked bodice, long full sleeves, and a high collar. It was a statement in quiet elegance, and it cost me $50! That was a great deal of money on our budget at the time, but the dress was perfect!

The only opera for which he had been able to obtain tickets was Moussorgsky's *Boris Godunov,* a heavy, Russian production in four acts.*The Standard Opera Guide,* to which I'd quickly turned when I got Alfred's letter, read, "Boris is the regent guardian of the children of Ivan the Terrible," it continued, "but he has caused the elder prince, Dimitri, to be murdered so that he himself can rule the land." 'Oh, what a jolly evening this is going to be,' I thought to myself.

Upon my arrival in Vienna, and our entrance into the magnificent opera house the next night, I settled into my red upholstered seat and prepared to be bored by the end of the first act. The scene opened in a monastery near Moscow, the courtyard filled with two hundred people brought there to call upon Boris Godunov to accept the throne of Russia. But then those 200 people started singing; the priests entered wearing elaborate vestments lamps of incense swinging in their hands. Then Boris entered. He was a towering baritone, and his voice filled the opera house. And I was just four rows away! I was blown away! *This* is grand opera! And this was just the prologue. I was speechless. I was numb. Alfred had to poke me twice to say, "We go down for refreshments now."

I started down the red-carpeted stairway, my R.H. Sterns dress trailing behind me, and a passing Viennese lady tugged at her friend's arm, pointed at me, and said two exquisite words "schones kleid", beautiful dress. I was no longer walking on those stairs; I was floating.

The opera was magnificent, but the best was yet to come. My husband was about to prove to me that he was the most suave, debonair, sophisticated Viennese gentleman in all of Vienna! And he would do it all in his native German language.

After the opera, we walked to the nearby Sacher Hotel, the most famous in all Vienna. We planned to have a little post-opera supper and a piece of their famous Sacher Torte. That's what one does when one goes to the opera with a handsome gentleman and you are his lady in a beautiful dress.

When we arrived at the dining room, the maître d' asked, in German of course, if we had a reservation. Alfred replied in his Austrian dialect German, "No, I didn't believe it would be necessary."

"Of course not," said the maître d' and he escorted us into a small private dining room with only a few tables, but one, I quickly noticed, was set up for a large party of twelve. Interesting, now what, I thought?

He handed us tall menus filled with multiple pages. But after perusing the pages for several minutes, Alfred leaned across the table and softly said, "We have to leave. We can't afford this. I've only got $50 on me, and the traveler's checks are back in my room." By this time the party of twelve had arrived, and it was the group of people seated in row 2 of the opera—the president of BMW, we had laughingly surmised, and the CEO of Krupp Steel Works etc.

Oh no, this little Boston lady in her "schones kleid" was not going to get up and walk out. "You'll have to find something we can afford," I pleaded. He studied the menu for a while, and when the waiter came to our table, Alfred handed him the enormous menus, and with the most savoir-faire imaginable, in German, said, "I didn't find anything I cared for here. We'll just have a small omelet, Sacher Torte, and coffee." The waiter bowed low, said, "Of course, very good," and departed. We got out of there within our $50 limit, tip included, and burst out laughing once outside the hotel door.

Alfred was always a man of wit and good humor who loved puns, sometimes to my distraction, when I'd heard the same one multiple times for over 50 years, but there was no denying his Viennese charm. He proved it again two nights later. We drove through the little wine village of Grinzing with its cobblestone streets and small houses of baroque design on to the summit of Kahlenberg, a mountain overlooking all of Vienna. There was a lovely restaurant there, a strolling violinist wandered among the tables, and the meal was superb. When we had finished with our entrees it was around 9:30 p.m.

"We'd like to see the dessert menu," Alfred informed the waiter.

"Oh, I'm sorry," he replied. "We lock up the dessert cart at 9 p.m."

"I see," said my husband. "And when did this establishment change hands?"

"Oh, it hasn't," the waiter replied. "The same Viennese family has owned it for years."

My husband gave the waiter a firm stare and replied,"No true Viennese locks up the desserts at 9 p.m.!"

The dessert cart was brought out immediately.

En route home that night, I saw Alfred turn the car and drive alongside the Danube River. This wasn't the way back to the hotel. I then I realized what was happening. He was driving to his childhood home. Miraculously, the house had not been damaged by the war. We sat in the car opposite the porch where his grandmother, a victim of one of Hitler's concentration camps, had sat and watched as he and his cousin Lucy played. Tears came to my eyes as he began telling me stories of a happy childhood here. There were more than desserts on the menu that night. Alfred was facing his past.

Our professional careers were progressing. Alfred became increasingly involved in the supervision of doctoral candidates and their research and in the continuing education programs of the American Chemical Society. While Alfred was developing his professional career, I was doing likewise.

From the Press Bureau I had moved into the University Publications Office and from there to the position of Editorial Assistant to the president. I found I loved speech writing and research so I heartily agreed to become the Senior Editor when then President Asa Knowles signed a contract to produce a ten-volume *International Encyclopedia of Higher Education*. The next six years I spent researching, writing, editing, and even ghostwriting articles for the Encyclopedia. I felt it was the greatest contribution I ever made to higher education. It was often a six to seven-day work week, and, as I was the "second in command", it meant assisting with the management of an in-house staff of 50, including a staff of editors and 2,000 authors world-wide. I loved it! And out of that project came my book, *Human Resources Development in Saudi Arabia*, the story of which became Chapter 2 in this book.

The Encyclopedia files became the Center for International Higher Education Documentation and I became the Director. I went on to become Dean of International Affairs before moving to the University Development Office as Direction of Communications. Through staff meetings in the latter role, I learned about fundraising, and when I took early retirement,I spent the next thirty years using those skills to raise funds to benefit the health and well-being of golden retrievers.

During my years at Northeastern, I spent many a June day in the old Boston Garden working at the university's commencement exercises. I was part of those caring for the honorary degree recipients. I met quite a few celebrities, but my two favorites were Barbara Bush and Erma Bombeck. Mrs. Bush was on stage when Alfred walked up to receive his Excellence in Teaching Award. She had just published her book about the family dog, Millie. I decided that Diora, our golden, should extend an invitation to Millie to come play when next she was in town—perhaps en route to Kennebunkport, Maine, the Bush family compound. A week later, Diora received a signed postcard with a photo of Mrs. Bush and Millie.

I met Erma Bombeck at Logan Airport and took her in the university car to her hotel. She was every bit as down to earth and funny as her newspaper columns and her books. I met my one other favorite celebrity, Betty White, through my goldens. While working with the Golden Retriever Foundation, I organized an event at a private home in Los Angeles and invited her to come as the Honorary Hostess. She did and she too was as charming and unpretentious and funny a woman as you could ever meet. She also had a golden, which made her even more special in my book. A year later when I had a knee replacement, she sent me the largest bouquet I ever received in my life, and like a true gardener, I kept it going down to the last blossom! It was a rewarding career. I enjoyed every step of the way because, in the words of the song master, Frank Sinatra, "I Did It My Way."

After traveling and taking natural history photographs for years, I began sharing our stories and photos with others through natural history lectures to a variety of organizations. It should come as no surprise that the very first lecture was entitled "Bananaquits in the Lemonade and a Motmot in the Bedroom!"When Alfred retired, he joined me, setting up the equipment and running the projector while I gave the lecture. We were a team again in yet a new endeavor. That seemed to be the story of our marriage. We were forever teaming up to undertake new endeavors based on shared interests.

I also became a newspaper columnist for our local newspaper. I wrote, often humorously, about a variety of topics including a major remodeling task we undertook.Anyone who has ever remodeled a kitchen may appreciate this excerpt from my column, "My Kingdom for a Kitchen Sink and a Countertop":

"And this too shall pass." The author of these immortal words never had the remodeling of a kitchen in mind, but the sentiment aptly describes my feelings as I sit, slumped amongst boxes of dishes, foodstuffs, pots, pans, plants, chairs, tables, drop cloths, carpenter tools, cartons of new appliances and four weeks' accumulation of dust and dog hair. I gave up vacuuming the latter when the exercise seemed ludicrous in the total context of our discombobulated environment.

To this display of physical chaos has been added a parade of carpenters, plasterers, painters, plumbers an electrician and two countertop men. Some days, the orchestration of manpower in and out of the house seems reminiscent of the Christmas song about a partridge in a pear tree.

Initially I tackled the entire project with a spirit of adventure. "It will be like camping," I told my husband. I covered the card table with a checkered table cloth, and artful floral arrangement and candles and then I had fun creating menus from foods I could either microwave or cook in the crockpot. We learned not to linger over breakfast, (in order to get out of the way of early-arriving workmen) and I cheerfully carried dirty dishes upstairs to the bathroom sink. A friend stopped by the day before Thanksgiving and the carpenter laughingly told her I was upstairs in the bathroom making cranberry salad.

By the second week the table flowers had died and I was gratefully accepting dinner invitations from the neighbors. We began eating out more by the third week and this week I've noticed my husband has been working longer hours at the office.

Even the dogs are starting to get cranky… and the cat began giving us looks of contempt two weeks ago.

Priorities and perspectives change when you're remodeling. At the moment I have no interest in a cruise, a fur coat or a new car. All I want is a functioning kitchen sink. (Reprinted courtesy of the Weston/Wayland *Town Crier.*)

I took up gardening when I retired as well. Living in an oak and pine forest, the challenges were many, and I developed a large card file of plantings that failed to survive. Some gave me a disdainful look and died right on the spot. I got better at it, measuring the amount of sunlight and soil composition around the garden so that I put the right plant in the right place. Of course, once a plant thrived, I often had to move it to give it adequate space. Alfred decided the definition of a gardener was one who moves plants from one locale to another. But then when 30 blossoms showed up on my prize trillium one spring, he concurred that the trillium, at least, was indeed happy in its location. I also joined the local garden club, but the first time I attempted a floral arrangement for a club meeting, an "elder statesman" of the club looked at my efforts and said, "Who made this mess." Obviously, tact wasn't her strong suite, but I didn't make another arrangement for the club for twenty years!

After decades of gardening and eventually getting a nice perennial garden in place, I've learned the significance of the saying on the garden club sweatshirt I bought years ago, "A Garden is a thing of beauty and a job forever."

My gardening efforts were exceeded only by my efforts to draw birds to our yard. Birding had been a hobby of mine since age 8. In fact, I still have my first birding checklist from the Minneapolis Audubon Society. When Alfred got interested in birding, it became a significant segment of our lives. When it snows, it is the bird feeders that get shoveled out first! In 2000, Alfred and I became charter members in the Cornell University Project FeederWatch. Each week, for two consecutive days, from November to April we monitored the number of birds and the number of species coming onto our property to dine at our seed, suet, and water buffet or to just take a look around to see what their fellow avian friends were feeding on. From tiny Ruby-throated Hummingbirds to large Great Horned Owls, we've welcomed close to 70 species.

But our birding interests extended well beyond our yard. We traveled to 46 countries, and in the course of our travels, we each developed a Birder's Life List of more than 2,300 species. Of course, we didn't always succeed in seeing the same species, but our counts were close. Unfortunately, a computer glitch wiped out our actual counts. Alfred had kept precise records of all of our sightings on a software program, and he was almost inconsolable when the database was lost and unrecoverable despite the aide and attempts of experts.

Birding isn't always easy. Shoe-leather birding can be arduous. Tromping through high tussock grass in Alaska, mud and rain in Kenya, ice and snow in Antarctica, heat and humidity in Indonesia, lava rock in Iceland, and cactus in Arizona led Alfred to ask more than once, "Are we having fun yet?" But the answer was always yes, as this was a hobby we could pursue and share anywhere on the planet with only an area field guide and a pair of binoculars. And share it we did, over and over and, sometimes, even with a bit of a competitive spirit when it came to spotting Life Birds!

In 1987 we became another type of "tour guide" .We brought my ten-year-old nephew, Shane, from Minnesota to Boston, an adventure for all three of us that continued year after year and eventually included his younger sister, Jessica. I thought I knew

Boston well until I saw it through the eyes of two youngsters for whom much in Boston was new. We visited the Newport, Rhode Island mansions, summer homes of the Vanderbilts and their peers. When, during the tour, it was explained that the children usually saw their parents only for a short visit before dinner, it was a revelation to these two youngsters for whom family life centered around the dining room table. Street performers at Boston's Quincy Market gave rise to questions about the long-term financial stability of these people, and Shane wondered if they would have Social Security in their old age. And they were both utterly shocked to learn, upon a visit to the Mayflower, that the Pilgrims never bathed for the 66 days they were en route to the new world!

We also traveled on our own and on birding tours with other birders, frequently seeking lodging in a birding hot spot. It was in this manner that we discovered Savegre Mountain Lodge in Costa Rica. There we met an 18-year-old birding guide, Raul Chacon Fernandez, who not only helped us find a myriad of new species but became a friend and an important part of our lives. Young Raul was such an asset to our birding, we decided to return the favor, and with the help of frequent flyer miles, we flew him from Costa Rica to Boston where we could introduce him to 108 North American species, most of which were new to him. Although he knew many of our warblers as they winter in his own country, the cheery little Black-capped Chickadees, Tufted Titmice, woodpeckers, wading birds, ducks, and herons were all new to him, and it was a joy to see him add to his Life List while he was under our wing, so to speak.

Raul was not the only person to become a part of our global circle of friends. Oftentimes there were those with whom we shared only a single memorable day, but with whom I still exchange Christmas cards. Others, like Kim Edmunds of Kenya, with whom we took our first safari, stayed on in Kenya and subsequently guided us on safari.We birded a trailer park in Texas with Becky and David Otwell only one day, but we remained in touch over the decades.We took our lawyer and his wife, Bob Woodburn and Janet Smith, on their first safari more than thirty years ago. Friends for life, they stood at Alfred's graveside recording the COVID-19 limited services for me so I could email them to our families and to friends.

The golden retriever community from Canada and the US to Scotland and Australia has yielded friends of longstanding too. One, Arlene Blouch, made a hand-stitched quilt and toss pillows fashioned out of Alfred's neckties which were a reflection of his life—golden retrievers, birds, polar bears, penguins, elephants, deer, special locations like Cape Cod and Caneel Bay in the Virgin Islands, and yes, even the chemical periodic tables. They are all included in the quilt hanging on the wall in our project room where I keep the originals of my 46 travel diaries. It is also the room where for ten years I sorted, cleaned, labeled with Latin names, common names and location, and developed spread sheets of information for thousands of slides. Now converted to digital images and placed online through the Bugwood Network of the University of Georgia Center for Invasive Species and Ecosystem Health,(www.Bugwood.org)they are available to anyone wishing to make use of the photographic collection we amassed on our travels. It's been wonderful learning how they are being used—a bear photo for honey farmers, a mountain lion for a newspaper article about the Upper Michigan Peninsula, a tourist feeding Yellowstone bears by a park ranger. A lifetime of photos and memories now available to others.

Alfred's past friendships with his college colleagues, the Fletcher Veitch family with whom he lived, and his past students who continue to keep in touch, are all cherished friends who now sustain me. Others like The Ryan/Kane family with whom we spent 35 Christmases, Eleanor Lambert, the first woman I met at Northeastern, my bridesmaid and dearest of all friends, and Eunice Law, the young girl from Hong Kong who we sponsored and whom we have always called our Chinese daughter have deeply enriched our lives.So many friends met along the highway of life have become a part of my family as much as my relatives in Minnesota, a thousand miles away.

When Alfred suffered a stroke and developed congestive heart failure, our global travels ceased. Someone once said to me, "It doesn't matter what cards you're dealt in life, it's how you play them that counts." There were kings and queens, jokers and deuces wild in our lives, but I think Alfred and I played our cards well. That skinny, frightened, little 9-year-old Nazi refugee from Vienna and the Minnesota girl who wanted to be a writer shared a heck of a half-century together, and this has been our story. A friend said, "This book of yours is not only a tale of adventure, it is a love story." I never thought of it in that perspective, but I suppose it is.Although I'm now alone, there's no doubt in my mind we are in many ways still together. *Mizpah; The Lord watch between me and thee, when we are absent one from another.Genesis* 31:49

ACKNOWLEDGEMENTS

The writing of a book, especially one based on experiences that span the globe and multiple years, is a work to which many people lend contributions. Some are friends who help to enable the journey, some are those with whom you travel, some are those you meet along the way. Others are the friends who read your drafts and encourage your efforts. I have a deep debt of gratitude to them all.

I begin by thanking the enablers. Steve Cox, Executive Director of International Expeditions who facilitated many of our visits and joined us on others. Ambassador Wang Bingnan, Chair of the Chinese Association for the Friendship with Foreign Countries graciously hosted my visits to China. My Saudi Arabian research visit would not have taken place were it not for the invitation of Dr. Hussein Omar Mansour, Secretary General of the Manpower Council, and Sheik Turki Khalid Al-Sudairy, President of the Civil Service Bureau. Dr. John Curry and Dr. Kenneth Ryder, past Presidents of Northeastern University, kindly enabled me to follow my dreams and travel to China and Saudi Arabia.

Alfred and I had many travel companions, but most notable were the members of The Penguin Society, a magnificently diverse group of individuals who traveled intermittently with us for 25 years. They know who they are and how many wonderful adventures we shared.

Philip Schaeffer, Secretary of the Friends of the Asa Wright Nature Centre, was most helpful in keeping me apprised of the Centre's struggles through the COVID-19 lockdown and its plans for the future. I would also like to thank the staff of the University of Georgia Center for Invasive Species and Ecosystem Health who have archived our photographic collection, converted slides to digital images, and made them available to the public and to the publication of this book, notably Joe LaForest, Karan Rawlins, Sarah Jean Swain, Chuck Bargeron, and David Moorhead.

A special note of appreciation goes to the *New York Times* bestselling author Meg Waite Clayton who kept this author on track and encouraged me to push forward.

I also wish to thank the golden retriever community, world-wide, who have honored me with their friendship, bestowed their awards upon me, and helped me to find the wonderful four-footed friends with whom I've shared so many years of my life.

A major round of applause goes to those individuals who read my drafts, offered comments, and made corrections. Most notable among them is Janet Smith, my reader/editor extraordinaire who prodded and questioned and sent me searching to be sure my facts were always correct. I also thank Margaret Fearn for her knowledgeable review of the chapter on our Australian tour, giving me cultural insights based on her many years living on this wonderful continent of remarkable people. Mary Beth Russell read my drafts and offered on-going encouragement. I thank Robert Woodborn as well for his legal expertise. And a special bouquet of thanks goes to Janette Stubelt who designed my website and led this technologically challenged senior through the long corridors of the internet, patiently waiting for me to catch up time after time.

I wish to acknowledge my parents, Edward and Lilyon Winkie, who are no longer living, but who encouraged my professional dreams. And I thank my Minnesota family who have always been there to cheer me on.

Last, but most important of all, I acknowledge by wonderful husband, Alfred, who whom I shared 56 years of marriage and many hours of birding, photography, travel, and home life. I deeply regret that he was taken by COVID-19 before he knew of the publication of this book, a tribute to the life we shared.

Joy Winkie Viola

CPSIA information can be obtained
at www.ICGtesting.com
Printed in the USA
BVHW042353050122
624075BV00010B/293/J

9 781638 671572